# *Nothing Human is Alien*

## The Life and Work of Otto Allen Will Jr., M.D.

Otto Will was the consummate psychotherapist. He could reach those people others considered beyond recovery. He wrote no books that capture the subtleties of his clinical approach but, instead, conveyed it to students through well-told stories. He was a contradiction. Trained as a psychoanalyst, he was not bound by Freudian theory or metapsychology. He worked with a broad spectrum of patients, especially those diagnosed as schizophrenic, doing so without medication. He believed fully that the relationship between therapist and patient was the key element in repairing damaged lives. In that relationship he sought to discover the person burdened with the role of "patient." He asked, "Who are you?" and recognized that to share the answer to this question, one must feel respected, valued, and emotionally safe; one must know that her therapist is a complicated and flawed, but authentic, person hiding none of their own humanity. Otto Will realized that rote technique was often a dead end and that each therapist and patient created a means of relating to one another. He was dedicated to each person who put their trust in him and, though sometimes wanting to escape from what he learned of himself, he instead used this knowledge as a point of connection. His success in enlarging the lives of those with whom he worked could be breathtaking. This is the story of how a boy from a traumatic background became able to free others from the psychological shackles that bound them. Like every life story, Otto Will's includes fear, pain, and growth — but most of all, hope.

# Advance Reviews of *Nothing Human is Alien*

"Through meticulous historical research and clear writing, Carlton Cornett has brought Otto Allen Will back to life. This book comes just in time to connect to a resurgent interest among psychiatrists to learn skills in psychotherapy, and among psychoanalysts and psychotherapists to discover a method of being with patients that is less burdened by theory. In bringing Otto to life, we also learn about Harry Stack Sullivan, Freida Fromm-Reichmann, Hilde Bruch, and other pioneers of the art of listening to patients. The book also usefully offers a number of case histories of patients treated by Otto at both Chestnut Lodge and Austen Riggs. These were patients who had failed prior psychotherapeutic treatments, plus ECT and insulin coma treatments. Otto did not prescribe medications. His treatment was *himself* and his ability to make contact with the person. Elvin Semrad, one of my teachers, called Otto 'a walking anachronism.' However, Elvin advocated precisely the same values and approach. I suppose, as they say, 'it takes one to know one.' One thing that these master-craftsmen had in common was a troubled childhood. Elvin called it 'a life of sorrow and the opportunity that some people gave me to overcome it and deal with it.' How can we understand the capacity of these clinical geniuses to do this? Carlton Cornett first quotes Emerson, 'Our strength grows out of our weakness,' and then in his own words, concludes that 'we acknowledge our humanity and respond to others in distress as fellow human beings.'"

Mark F. Poster, M.D.
Faculty, PINE Psychoanalytic Society of New England
Assistant Professor in Psychiatry, Harvard Medical School (retired)
Distinguished Life Fellow of the American Psychoanalytic Association

"Carlton Cornett's *Nothing Human is Alien* is a captivating biography chronicling the life and work of one of the most creative and clinically intuitive psychotherapists of the twentieth century. Otto Will was a key figure in the development of interpersonal psychoanalysis, and Cornett's biography offers a unique perspective on the field and many of its early pioneers. Covering Will's childhood, education, and professional career—including his work with such luminaries as Harry Stack Sullivan—Cornett offers a moving portrayal of a psychoanalyst, who, like his patients, often struggled with mental illness and addiction but also embodied great resiliency and humanity. This biography is a must-read for anyone interested in the history of American psychoanalysis and the life of one of its earliest, but often forgotten, visionaries, who taught us that it is ultimately relationships that hold the greatest potential for human transformation."

Tyger Latham, Psy.D.
Teaching Analyst, Washington Baltimore Psychoanalytic Institute
Co-Chair, Psychoanalytic Studies Program Steering Committee

"Cornett's biographical account of Otto Allen Will Jr. provides a powerful narrative of his development as a psychotherapist and how that was formed through a series of significant, at times challenging, interpersonal relationships rather than intellectual mastery. The author carefully demonstrates how his capacity to meet patients 'where they are,' without resorting to premature interpretation or judgment, was a direct result of Will's formative encounters. It illustrates the central tenet that the *therapeutic relationship*, or human connection more generally, is the primary vehicle for healing. In doing so, the author's own dedicated effort to understand Otto's life, a relationship forged through writing, further reinforces this core theme."

Ira Phillips, M.D.
Faculty, Nashville Center for Psychoanalysis and Psychodynamic Psychotherapy.

"*Nothing Human is Alien* is a gentle and nourishing journey through the life and work of Otto Allen Will, Jr., who is affectionately referred to as Otto. Carlton Cornett, MSW, guides us through the winding and intersecting paths of creativity, humanity, and subjectivity in this first, full-biography of this innovative analyst. Along the way, we have the opportunity to experience small treasures and scenic detours into history, theory, clinical cases, and personal anecdotes. Each sentence captures a bit of Carlton's extensive knowledge. Step-by-step, we take a refreshingly paced journey alongside Otto as a participant-observer—experiencing his pains and passions, watching and engaging in a life unfolding."

Vincent Pignatiello, Psy.D.
Chair, Department of Clinical Psychology
Director, Psychological Services Center
Antioch University, New England

"In his book on Otto Will, Carlton Cornett tells a wonderful story about an oft-forgotten pioneer of psychoanalytic therapy who courageously treated the most troubled patients. Sadly, long-term depth therapy of such patients is rarely discussed today, but Will adapted Sullivan's interpersonal model with great caring and humanity in a genuinely relational approach years before this perspective became fashionable. Cornett's book will certainly interest readers in exploring how Will's contributions can enhance practice today."

Joel Kanter, LCSW-C
Founding Board Member, New Washington School of Psychiatry.
Faculty, China American Psychoanalytic Alliance

"This is a wonderful book about Otto Allen Will's development as a person and therapist. Carlton Cornett leads us through the development of a skilled clinician often overlooked by today's student of psychotherapy. Cornett presents Will as a dynamic therapist and a warm caring man not bogged down in theoretical dogma, authentically himself, a traveler with his patients. *Nothing Human is Alien* is a well-deserved book for the seasoned clinician and budding therapist with an interest beyond the standard CBT and DBT of today."

Richard Hamling, D.Litt. (UK), LMHC
Diplomate, American Mental Health Counselors Association

# Other Books by Carlton Cornett

*Affirmative Dynamic Psychotherapy with Gay Men* (1993)

*Reclaiming the Authentic Self* (1995)

*The Soul of Psychotherapy* (1998)

*Being with Patients* (2017)

*The Psychotherapeutic Relationship: 40 Years of Learning to be with Patients* (2023)
Download free at: https://www.freepsychotherapybooks.org/ebook/the-psychotherapeutic-relationship-40-years-of-learning-to-be-with-patients

# Nothing Human is Alien

## The Life and Work of Otto Allen Will Jr., M.D.

Carlton Cornett, M.S.W.

Kingston Springs, Tennessee

***Psyche & Society Books***
P.O. Box 605
Kingston Springs, TN 37082


Charles Knight, Editor.


ISBN: 978-1-62880-313-6 Paperback
ISBN: 978-1-62880-314-3 Hardback
ISBN: 978-1-62880-315-0 Ebook

First edition, August 2025

Photo credits accompany individual photographs.

The author gratefully acknowledges permission to reprint quotations as listed in the reference pages.



Digitally printed worldwide on acid free paper.

For DeWayne.

Who provides balm for "the fever called life."

Courtesy of Patrick Will

Otto Allen Will Jr., M.D., 1962

Director of Psychotherapy at Chestnut Lodge in Rockville, Maryland.

# Table of Contents

Preface ........................................................................................ xv

Part One: Becoming a Person ........................................................ 1

Chapter One: A Patchwork ........................................................ 3
Chapter Two: The Gifts & Burdens of Family ........................ 9
Chapter Three: The Great White Plague ................................ 21
Chapter Four: The School that Saved Otto's Life ................... 33
Chapter Five: An Unhappy Little Kingdom ............................ 41
Chapter Six: The Strongest Ties ............................................ 47
Chapter Seven: Less Than Human .......................................... 53
Chapter Eight: You're Not Going to See Any Combat ............ 61

Part Two: Becoming a Psychotherapist ........................................ 71

Chapter Nine: An Environment of Despair ............................. 73
Chapter Ten: He Talked About People ................................... 81
Chapter Eleven: A Somewhat Witty Irishman ......................... 87
Chapter Twelve: I'm Not Here to Give Interpretations ........... 97
Chapter Thirteen: A Clinical Study from Saint Elizabeths ...... 109
Chapter Fourteen: Belief Enriched by Question & Doubt ...... 115
Chapter Fifteen: The Constructive Use of Ignorance ............ 125
Chapter Sixteen: Humane Pragmatism .................................. 133
Chapter Seventeen: Endings & Beginnings ........................... 143
Chapter Eighteen: A Natural Psychotherapist ........................ 151
Chapter Nineteen: Clinical Studies from Chestnut Lodge ...... 163
Chapter Twenty: I & You ...................................................... 179
Chapter Twenty-One: A Time of Great Pain ......................... 191
Chapter Twenty-Two: Clinical Studies from Austen Riggs ..... 209
Chapter Twenty-Three: The Psychoanalytic Outsider ............ 215

Part Three: Hard Work & Common Sense ........ 221

Chapter Twenty-Four: Becoming ........ 223
Chapter Twenty-Five: Madness ........ 237
Chapter Twenty-Six: Unending Curiosity ........ 247
Chapter Twenty-Seven: A Good Man ........ 259

Acknowledgements ........ 263

Appendix Number One: Important Terms in Otto Will's Writing ........ 265

Appendix Number Two: The Wit & Wisdom of Otto Will ........ 273

References ........ 277

Index ........ 307

"I am a human being, nothing human is alien to me."

Terence, 165 B.C.E.

# Preface

Deirdre Will Vinyard, Otto Will's daughter, once told me that writing is like giving birth. She is a writer and an accomplished teacher of writing, as well as a mother, so she is intimately familiar with both processes. In writing the pages that follow, I believe I learned what she meant. In writing a biography — whatever its quality — a human being is introduced to the world. That human being is composed of those qualities that we share as human but is also unique. The biography seeks to capture both qualities — the familiar and the distinctive.

I never met Otto Will personally. I began studying his life and work because three of my mentors believed that he was a profoundly wise psychotherapist and found him deeply inspiring; they also admired — and loved — him as a friend, teacher, and supervisor. Their experiences with him were imparted to me over time. Many of *my* impressions of him were shaped by *their* direct experiences with him. Such an introduction to a human being is not the same as direct interaction, but it can fuel a yearning to learn more, and — in my case, to learn why these mentors considered him a genius and why they respected and loved him.

In addition to these experiences with my mentors who I respected, admired, and learned from in my own way, I have studied the memories of others, also impressed by Otto. Without any disrespect, I will refer to him as "Otto" throughout the book because that is how I always heard him spoken of; "Otto" was said with affection and communicated a lack of pretension about him. Yet, calling him by his first name was imbued with honor as a sign of familiarity. Though I was not able to earn that honor in the same way my mentors had (all are now deceased) — in the way Martin Buber suggested with the phrase "*Ich und Du*" ("I and You") — I believe that my contemplation of his life over many years involves some relation. I refer to him as "Otto," though, with humility.

---

Biographers differ in what they consider the heart of their work. Andrew Delbanco (2005) related that for Henry James the focus of the biographer should be *detail.* Yet, Delbanco, a biographer of Herman Melville, maintained that a goal of detail would scuttle any biography of Melville. A biography of Otto Will that seeks to document detail climbs a very steep slope. Notably, all who were interviewed or consulted for this book shared their memories of Otto with a sense of tentativeness, suggesting that he was not an easy man to know. Facts had a place in his life, but it was subordinate to experience — the essence of *being*. I have attempted to include facts — *when* and *where* — but hope that they are subordinate to *how* and *why*. Facts are also always limited; Mark Dawidziak (2023), one of Edgar Allan Poe's biographers, asserts that "sooner or later, any biographer writing about any subject must regularly cope with murky areas by falling back on such old reliable standards as *evidently*, *seemingly*, *presumably*, and *apparently*" (p. 19, emphasis in the original).

Finally, one of Ralph Waldo Emerson's biographers, James Marcus (2024), suggests that chronicling a life amounts to capturing particular "golden hours" from all the information available; these hours represent the successes and failures of the subject and culminate in a more accurate portrait than a simple assemblage of facts. The successful biographer mines such golden hours by using her subjectivity. Biography, like psychotherapy, involves participant observation. The biographer's subjectivity helps create the story being told. I am also drawn to Marcus's (2024) assertion that what is omitted is as important as what is included.

Perhaps then biography lies on a continuum: the striving for detailed facts on one extreme and the subjective molding of the story on the other. Though I no doubt fall between those two extremes, I feel more comfortable with the latter. In short, I believe that imperfection and uncertainty are always involved in conveying the essence of another human being. As Otto (1964, 1971b, 1987a) observed, such imperfection and uncertainty are as much a part of the air that we breathe as oxygen. Every human being is complex and contradictory; or, as the poet, Carl Phillips (2022), suggests, that we are composed of several selves, some that cohere and some that do not.

---

In writing this book, I have relied on three sources of information. The first is a remarkable gift from Kim Chernin, a writer, poet, and psychotherapist. For eight years she had consulted Otto about her clinical work (Chernin, 1995, 2017). Recognizing that his life and work were unusual in the field of psychoanalysis, she spent two of those years recording conversations with Otto. There was no structure to those conversations — they simply discussed whatever topic came up. Perhaps 20 years ago, she gave me the tapes of those conversations and their transcriptions. I think that at one time she had considered writing something based on these recordings, but she symbolically passed that torch to me. These recordings form the bulk of my narrative. It is therefore largely an oral history. These conversations between Kim and Otto, which took place near the end of his life, are not unimpeachable facts; they were shaped and influenced by the relationship he had with her, his awareness that he was being recorded, the haze that age often imposes on memory, and, toward the end, some deterioration in Otto's neurological functioning. If approached carefully, which I have tried to do, they constitute a rich source of information about his world. Rather than writing, "Otto told Kim Chernin" throughout the text, I have generally written that "Otto recalled" or "Otto remembered." Unless otherwise noted, the material under discussion is from these recorded and transcribed conversations.

A second source of information upon which I have relied are anecdotes, memories and feelings of others who knew him, particularly his son, Patrick, and daughter, Deirdre. Of course, this information has been colored over time by the wishes, disappointments, and moments of intimacy which expand and contract in memory. They were very generous with their time, and, in addition to sharing memories of their father, they sent me copies of letters, photographs, and newspaper clippings, as well as copies of books that their father had annotated. Similarly, I talked with some of Otto's colleagues — an ever-diminishing group of people, most of whom are gone now. They, too, sent materials that they deemed potentially helpful. There is no study of a life that can be carried out without archival research. Some of that research I have done online and some in person.

A final source of information has been the published accounts of Otto's life and work. Over the years, I have read recollections of Otto by his colleagues and students: James Gorney (2021), Eric Plakun (2021), as well as Michael and Sharada Thompson (1998) who also interviewed him. Such recollections are valuable pieces of the story. Otto's published writings have been of great assistance. He wrote in a clear, direct way, often enumerating his points as one might in an outline. His writing became more autobiographical over time, revealing aspects of himself to the reader as if inviting an intimate, but safe, experience. He (1987a) acknowledged that he wrote in this manner to also deepen an acquaintance with himself, in some ways feeling a perpetual stranger.

---

With some of this book's sources and inherent limitations outlined, it is helpful to consider the potential value a biography of Otto Allen Will Jr. offers readers. Yale historian and philosopher, Timothy Snyder (2024), offers one answer. He suggests that understanding people from the past enriches an understanding of the present. Further, understanding their motivations and the choices they made offers us different perspectives and potentially different choices.

The field of psychotherapy seems to be in crisis. Partly, this is the result of the tendency of some to deify figures like Sigmund Freud (Kwawer, 2019; Sutherland, 1989); conversely, history seems increasingly irrelevant to others. History is often deprecated by those who desire to embrace each supposedly "new" form of therapy described as more *empirically based* than others. This desire has resulted in claims that there exist over 1,245 exclusive forms of therapy (Allen, 2018). This flies in the face of common sense and would be remedied by comparative research.

This crisis is also the result of economic pressures. The devaluation of history and the therapist's use of self is encouraged by economic players (e.g., health insurance companies) with only, at best, a modicum of interest in patient care. These are times of competition and bitter conflict in the field of psychotherapy as practitioners, researchers, and academics scramble for ever diminishing financial resources by declaring that *their* way is really the *only* way. Otto Will offered a humanistic perspective on psychotherapy that honored hard-won knowledge without uncritical reverence and valued common sense, which he (2021) emphasized as a foundation of psychotherapy. There is much for twenty-first century psychotherapists to learn from this twentieth-century man.

---

It is worth noting at the outset of this story that Otto Will worked with patients diagnosed as schizophrenic, a population that some consider "lost" to humanity (Callaway, 2007). His professional reputation reflects that fact. He was proud of his work with this population. Perhaps for some readers, this will disqualify him from further consideration. He also worked with people troubled by less catastrophic difficulties. He was a training analyst and worked with psychoanalytic candidates. Well-trained, seasoned clinicians sought him out for supervision. He (1970b) believed that the principles he applied in all his work were fundamentally the same. He proposed that the heart of psychotherapy was a relationship of respect (above all), acceptance, honesty, and clear communication. Though I spent several of my forty years as a psychotherapist working with deeply troubled people, that was not the emphasis of my practice. I found Otto's perspective, though, helpful every day.

---

To tell the story of one life entails telling stories of many other lives. From family members and friends to professional influences, and, sometimes, enemies, each character has a part. In Otto's life, in addition to his original and later created families, there are people who shaped him throughout his development. He (1973) named people who were important to him as teachers and role-models as a psychotherapist: Harry Stack Sullivan, Dexter Means Bullard, Frieda Fromm-Reichmann, and Hilde Bruch. Each of these people has a chapter. I have woven other people's stories in, as well. If I have discounted anyone, I apologize and will attempt to rectify this in a future edition.

---

It is my preference to know something about the authors of books I read and so I will offer just a few paragraphs about my background. Before retiring a few years ago, I was a psychotherapist for forty years, also teaching part-time in graduate and post-graduate educational programs. The former included introducing third-and fourth-year psychiatric residents to the interpersonal point of view, the latter teaching interpersonal theory to students of a variety of disciplines in specialty psychodynamic psychotherapy programs.

I came to the psychoanalytic point of view — and within that, the interpersonal — in an informal way. During graduate school the principal perspective taught was that of Erik Erikson. Clinical practice classes emphasized ego psychology and systems approaches. However, I learned something from the work of Hellmuth Kaiser — an existentially oriented analyst — and I developed an understanding and admiration for Carl Rogers's work and life. I was impressed that much of Rogers's clinical work was influenced by social workers trained by Otto Rank at the Rochester Child Guidance Clinic (Kirschenbaum, 2007). Rank was a devoted follower of Freud until he became aware of the centrality of the real human relationship between analyst and patient in ameliorating psychological difficulties (Kramer, 2019).

During my final clinical placement, I was immersed in systems theory; I gravitated toward the work of Carl Whitaker. Whitaker had a dynamic sensibility, developed from work with the Chief Social Worker at the Louisville Child Guidance Clinic, who again had been analyzed by Rank (Neill, 1982). My interest in the practitioners that I have listed led me to study the work of Heinz Kohut. Roughly seven years after graduation I was introduced to Harry Stack Sullivan's thought and found his humane and pragmatic approach to psychotherapy inspiring. My introduction to Sullivan also came with an introduction to Otto Will. I most identify with the interpersonal heritage.

It is common for aspiring psychotherapists to follow their professional training with specialized clinical training, most often in psychoanalysis or dynamic psychotherapy. However, an alternative approach has been the development of a personal plan of study that offers more freedom (Bruch, 1974). Such plans generally include personal analyses or experiences in intensive psychotherapy, postgraduate education programs focused on psychoanalytic thought, and supervision with experienced, respected practitioners. In my view, this approach to clinical training is a form of apprenticeship. As such, it is also a form of autodidacticism. I enjoy that word because it suggests the active pursuit of knowledge in other than prescribed ways. The word "autodidact" has been applied to the poet, Robert Frost, who rankled when told what to read (Parini, 1999). In that sense, an oppositional stance toward authority is also involved — such a stance being requisite, I believe, for an effective psychotherapist.

———

New England has been described as "the child of a superstitious mother and a philosopher father" (Applegate, 2006, p. 36). Though I spent almost sixty years of my life in the South (i.e., Alabama, Georgia, and Tennessee), I have always been drawn to New England. I am not sure of all that drew me here, but it has something to do with the ambiance that Applegate describes.

My partner of over thirty years and I live in the southwestern corner of New Hampshire, with Massachusetts only a few miles south and Vermont a few miles west. This is the area in which Stephen Vincent Benét's (1936) tale, *The Devil and Daniel Webster*, is set. Ralph Waldo Emerson and Henry David Thoreau walked this land as did Nathanial Hawthorne, Emily Dickinson, Herman Melville, and, early in his life, Edgar A. Poe. Robert Frost also spent much of his life in New Hampshire and Vermont. New England is a land steeped in history, legend, philosophy and poetry.

I look at psychotherapy as a close relative of philosophy and poetry. I often think and write about these subjects interchangeably. Otto was devoted to these subjects and more, including music and science. It seems particularly appropriate in my current setting and at this time in my life to write about Otto Will.

---

A final note: in 2017 I wrote and independently published a short book sketching the lives of both Harry Stack Sullivan and Otto Will (Cornett, 2017a). At that time, I did not have the flexibility in my schedule to do more. With my retirement from clinical work and a lessening of teaching responsibilities, I now have the time to devote myself to a fuller exploration of Otto's life. Those familiar with that earlier book will find some inevitable, but I hope minimal, overlap in these pages. I ask you for both your patience and forgiveness for those instances of repetition.

Carlton Cornett, M.S.W.
Keene, New Hampshire

# Part One:
# Becoming a Person

§

"Humans must develop ties with their fellows in order to become human, but in doing so frequently learn to fear their attachments, recognizing in them the possibilities of hurt and loss as well as support."

# Chapter One: A Patchwork

Otto Allen Will Jr. was a physically impressive man. Standing six feet, four inches in height, he towered over most people. The effect of his height was somewhat lessened by his stooped shoulders. His friend, the anthropologist Edward Hall (1992), believed that his posture was the result of having to move through ship hatches during his years in the United States Navy. However, photos predating his naval service document this characteristic well before he struggled through a ship's interior. A reporter for the *Berkshire Eagle* newspaper, Steve Moore (1982), described his build as "gangly" but sturdy and noticed that he wore both suspenders and a belt. Emily Fox Gordon (2000), a patient at the Austen Riggs Center when Will became medical director, made note of his penchant for western dress — including string ties.

Otto's appearance was arresting in other ways, as well. To Kim Chernin (1995), and Edward Hall (1992), his facial features resembled those of Boris Karloff; Gordon (2000) thought he resembled a buccaneer. Chernin (2017) also likened his appearance — including his manner — to that of "a huge rock that had weathered the full assault of crashing waves and turbulent winds" (p. xii).

Added to his appearance was a flair for the dramatic. He was a consummate storyteller who could hold students and colleagues spellbound for long periods of time (Hall, 1992). Stephen Schlein undertook a two-year post-doctoral fellowship at Austen Riggs between 1971 and 1973. He told me that listening to Otto "talk about patients was mind-boggling — he wasn't bound by any rules or any particular school of thought" (personal communication, August 19, 2007). Similarly, Gerard Fromm, who completed a four-year post-doctoral fellowship at

Austen Riggs, between 1971 and 1975, described Otto as "a showman" who inspired "many to try and be like him" (personal communication, August 22, 2007). His stories were powerful teaching tools. Chernin (2017) described their use in her clinical supervision with him: "For eight years I brought to Otto the stories of people with whom I was consulting; for eight years he answered me story for story … We never discussed theory, which didn't interest him" (p. xiii).

He was often kind and generous, though he could be volatile. Schlein related, "There was a great warmth about him. He could [also] be a very scary, intimidating person. You just learned not to cross him" (personal communication, August 19, 2007). Fromm remembered that "at times, he could seem menacing" (personal communication, August 22, 2007). His daughter, Deirdre Will Vinyard, remembers that "he didn't compromise" and at times, in addition to his height, "he used his intellect to intimidate" (personal communication, January 8, 2011). Gordon (2000) wrote that she was told by Leslie Farber, her therapist at Austen Riggs, that he wound up in a physical scuffle with Otto when they disagreed about her treatment. Farber was a saturnine, existentially oriented analyst. He and his second wife, Anne, a former patient, were close friends of Otto and Gwen Will.

Some I consulted described Otto as "sad" and "lonely." Gerard Fromm related that Will was "shy, potentially brooding, lonely. There was a core of sadness to him." Stephen Schlein asserted that Otto "was a very lonely man." Toward the end of his life, Otto (1987a) described a sense of alienation from himself and those around him, often having felt more an observer than full participant. He noted that his increasingly personal revelations in his published writings served as an introduction to himself. Similarly, for Thomas Merton, who often felt a personal incoherence, his writing was a way to bring some coherence to his life (Gordon, 2018). Perhaps, like Merton, Otto's writing aided him in making sense of the world around him and his place in it.

Otto had difficulty with separation. Due to early abandonments, he found even the most basic forms of separation challenging and painful. In his writing, he seems preoccupied with the importance of ending therapy and moving on. There is, however, evidence that, while this may have been a goal, he had difficulty effectuating it.

Otto drank heavily for much of his adult life, ultimately becoming what might currently be labeled "a functional alcoholic." Patrick Will described alcohol as "a part of his life."

> That was the way it was all my life. I certainly wished he would drink less. It affected him and it affected the family life, and it took him away from a lot of interaction, he might have had otherwise. I think that anybody who knew him more than tangentially knew that he drank too much (personal communication, January 16, 2011).

Otto's relationships with women were conflicted and tenuous. Patrick remembered that his father was very attractive to women. It was not his appearance that attracted them but his ideas and his modest way of presenting those ideas (personal communication, May 21, 2011). He treated some women as sexual objects, and, at least once during his marriage to Gwen Tudor Will, he engaged in an extramarital affair of which his children learned, and which contributed to the destruction of that marriage. Becoming aware of his own father's "contemptuous view of women" Otto (1989b) admitted, "I had to recognize that although thinking I admired, respected, and loved women, I actually held many of these same derogatory views" (p. 138).

Colleagues found his approach as a psychoanalyst unconventional and the product of a bygone era. Irwin Hirsch (1998) compared Otto to "a friendly country doctor" (p. 305). Otto (1987a) related that the Boston psychoanalyst, Elvin Semrad, a clinician of great stature, thought of him as "a walking anachronism" (p. 248). Others, however, like Gerard Fromm (2004), characterized him as a "charismatic clinical genius" (p. xi). More recently, Erich Plakun (2021) described him as "a man who could see with his heart" (p. 19). In an introduction to one of Otto's book chapters, Donald Nathanson (1987) seems to have found middle ground, describing Otto as "one of the great proponents of Sullivanian psychiatry, keeping us aware of our historical roots while himself advancing the treatment of seriously ill patients" (p. 308).

Otto was considered by other colleagues to be a visionary, "ahead of his time in understanding the crucial role played by the therapist's subjectivity," Owen Renik, the editor of *The Psychoanalytic Quarterly* for a decade, informed me (personal communication, May 14, 2007). Otto was not a hostage to any school of thought. With the occasional notable exception, he listened respectfully to those who disagreed with him.

Otto democratized what is perhaps misleadingly called "psychopathology." Like his primary mentor, Harry Stack Sullivan, he believed that we all have problems in living. Essayist and poet, Emily Ogden's (2022), experience in a hospital emergency room illustrates the tenuous nature of psychological diagnoses. While enduring the long wait for attention, she overheard a conversation occurring nearby, involving three voices — two ultimately discernible as physicians and one a patient. All three were preoccupied with their sanity and attempted to convince the others — especially the patient of it. Like Ogden, Otto questioned the criteria we use to decide if someone is sane or insane. All too often we begin with the assumption that we are sane and then consider how others' thoughts, feelings, and actions differ from our own. As the poet, Wendy Bourgeois (2018), asserts, sometimes insanity results from the constant pretense of being sane. This is particularly true of society's mental health *experts*. We all share a common humanity (Will, 1960, 1961a, 1964, 1968b, 1970b, 1970c, 1973, 1975, 1987a, 2021). Flannery O'Connor was appalled by psychological language and the attempt to explain psychological phenomena as if they applied to everyone but the one describing them (Coles, 2010). If our own sanity cannot be an *a priori* assumption, then the meaning of psychopathology as applied to others must be suspect. Otto (1960) believed that to understand others, we must understand ourselves — since we are all part of the same flawed, fragile humanity.

Otto took a deeply humane approach to psychotherapy, responding to what patients needed even if such a response was not in keeping with what other clinicians believed were sacrosanct rules. Owen Renik again captured this quality: "He was not given to theorizing and concentrated always on the importance of humanity and caring in the therapist" (personal communication, May 14, 2007). Leon Lurie, who was a faculty member at the Washington School of Psychiatry for over sixty years, remembered Otto as one of his most inspiring teachers. He described Frieda Fromm-Reichmann as frequently lecturing in the U.S. Department of Agriculture Auditorium. Otto presented case material at these lectures. "His way of talking about a patient was dramatic, humane, compassionate and for me utterly entrancing. It was superbly educational" (L. Lurie, personal communication, August 8, 2007). Before he arrived to assume the medical directorship at Austen Riggs, his reputation as an "outside the box" clinician preceded him. Gordon (2000) noted that if a patient was under the bed at the time of her session, Otto would crawl under the bed, and the session would take place there.

Otto (1971b) always strove to find the *person in the patient*. He (1974) believed that listening to the human being with whom he was working was the way of learning how to do psychotherapy. Such listening also aided him in learning about himself. A fellow student at the Washington School of Psychiatry, Bea Liebenberg, related, "What struck me most about Otto was his openness, his willingness to listen. There was no dogma in this person" (personal communication, March 30, 2011). He (1972) asked patients, "Who are you?" a difficult and often painful question to answer. In return, he attempted to respond with authenticity about who he was. He (1974) viewed patients as "troubled, shy, and needful human being[s]" (p. 27). Otto (1977a) also maintained an awareness that any process that held the potential for healing — like psychotherapy — could also cause harm if pursued without great care.

Otto (2021) examined the roles of caring and love in psychotherapy. When one of his patients attempted suicide, Otto met with her in the hospital. She asked him if he cared about her. He apparently had no difficulty in affirming that he did. However, she then asked him if he loved her. "I felt embarrassed by that question and hesitated some and didn't know quite what to say," he wrote, "but later I was able to answer and say, 'Yes, I did'" (p. 2). In a paper published thirty years before, he (1971b) recounted experiencing anxiety in response to a similar question from another patient. Yet, he also wrote, "The intensity and durability of the attachment that is developed [in psychotherapy] suggest that it contains elements of affection, friendship, and love which make it 'more than' a technical, clinical exercise in the treatment of psychiatric disorder" (p. 15).

In many ways, Otto's life story includes all the emotions, thoughts, and actions that compose any life. His story will not be completely new to any reader. Yet, the nexus of these common human attributes, combined with the relationships that formed the interpersonal matrix of his life, makes a unique story. His dedication to aiding the people most rejected, if not reviled, isolated, and lonely, in our society makes it a valuable story.

# Chapter Two: The Gifts & Burdens of Family

It is challenging to pick a beginning to the story of a particular life. Physical life begins in the womb; psychological and emotional life do, to some extent, as well. However, there are still many mysteries about the beginning aspects of psychological life — aspects about which only inference is possible. What has traditionally been considered the beginning of life occurs at birth, as we awaken to the world with a cry — the most basic form of interpersonal communication (Evans, 2024). Yet, every person is shaped by the relationships and societal forces that have touched the lives of those in previous generations. The newborn, in addition to the hereditary potentialities that will be developed or remain fallow, is already invested by parents and other family members with expectations, wishes, projections, and so on. Such family influences will be passed along to the infant in both overt and covert ways, even as the infant accrues direct experiences that will create her identity. I have chosen to begin the story of Otto Will's life with the generation that included his grandparents. Though the information available about this generation is limited, it will provide clues to some of the expectations with which he was both gifted and burdened.

## The Wills

Otto Allen Will, Jr. was a third generation German American on his father's side. His grandfather, Reinholt Will, and paternal grandmother, Amalia (neeé Schumacher), were citizens of northeastern Germany. Reinholt and Amalia were born in 1842 and 1843 respectively in the kingdom of Prussia (U.S. Census Bureau, 1880). In the states that would comprise unified Germany, Prussia being the most prominent, primary education was a cultural priority and resulted in some of the highest literacy rates in Europe (Fulbrook, 1991). Reinholt and Amalia Will were both literate and most likely well educated in basic subjects such as the German language, mathematics, and rudimentary science. Reinholt and Amalia married in 1866 (U.S. Census Bureau, 1900a). In Prussia, Reinholt was employed as a *gärtner* ("gardener") probably on a wealthy Junker estate (Staatsarchiv Hamburg, 2008; U.S. Census Bureau, 1880). On a variety of documents, Amalia Will listed her occupation as *wirtschaftend* ("keeping house").

In the German states, as in other European countries, primogeniture was the rule — first-born sons were designated to receive titles, property, and other wealth. Junkers (from *Jung Herr*, or "young lord") were men, often younger sons of the German aristocracy, who took up residence in economically underdeveloped regions of Prussia and Brandenburg to make their way (Fulbrook, 1991).

The life of a laborer in Germany was not easy. Though harsh conditions were prevalent in many countries during the Victorian era, German workers were expected to put in a seventy-five hour, six-day work week. After such weeks, workers were generally exhausted. Working life began at about the age of fifteen; the most remunerative years of a worker's life occurred at about age twenty-five when men were expected to marry and begin families. Wages were then stable until about the age of forty when they began to decline (Blackbourn, 2003).

Working class Germans were particularly vulnerable to conditions rife with the potential for the development of infectious diseases. Crowded living in damp and poorly ventilated environments was particularly conducive to infection with tuberculous (Thomas, 2020). Medical care was only sporadically available to the working classes, who were also often treated by physicians who thought of them as unworthy of their attention. Blackbourn (2003) notes that, "Bourgeois families might receive advice about the virtues of a holiday in the mountains; workers, when they saw a doctor at all, were more likely to hear a lecture about their insanitary living conditions or diet" (p. 169).

What had been a confederation of Northern German states — of which Prussia was the most powerful — went to war with Napoleon III's French Empire, in 1870, after being invaded by the French (Weidner, 2024). The war was relatively short — from July 1870 to January 1871. It was, nevertheless, brutal, with over 180,000 casualties (Krishnan, 2022). France was defeated and on January 18, 1871, after the Prussian victory at the battle of Sedan, the North German states, as well as some in the south, unified and became Germany. For two years after the unification, a period known as the *Gründerzeit* ("founders' years"), Germany prospered significantly. The German railroad system expanded from 4,000 miles in 1852 to 24,000 miles in 1873 (Blackbourn, 2003). This was a tremendous advantage to economic development but also resulted in the spread of infectious diseases more widely and quickly. Manufacturing, especially in iron, coal, and textiles, expanded as well (Fulbrook, 1991). Unfortunately, much of this expansion was based on speculation, forming an economic bubble which burst in May 1873 (Blackbourn, 2003; Fulbrook, 1991). "Industrial recession and sliding agricultural prices marked the beginning of what is commonly labelled a 'Great Depression,' lasting from 1873 to 1896" (Blackbourn, 2003, p. 144).

In addition to economic collapse, Germany was also experiencing social unrest. Reacting to this unrest, some of which involved challenges to the role of the Catholic Church in daily life, the First Vatican Council met in 1870. This convocation produced statements with both social and ecclesiastical ramifications, the most controversial of which was a formal statement confirming what had long been unpublished church tradition — that the Pope was infallible. The powerful Chancellor of Germany, Otto von Bismarck, viewed this as a potential threat to his nation's sovereignty (i.e., the Pope was free to meddle in the secular affairs of the state). Bismarck, who worked assiduously to gather governmental power for himself, found this situation intolerable. Even his purported master, the *Kaiser* ("emperor"), Wilhelm I, infringed on Bismarck's prerogatives cautiously, once lamenting "*Es ist Schwer, unter Bismarck Kaiser zu sein*" ("It is hard being emperor under Bismarck") (Clark, 2009, p. 45). Bismarck's response to the infallibility pronouncement of the first Vatican Council would come to be known as the *Kulturkampf* ("culture war") (Weidner, 2024).

First, in 1871, the German clergy was forbidden from preaching about "matters of state" in the *Kanzelparagraph* ("Pulpit Paragraph") (Weidner, 2024, p. 111). Increasingly restrictive laws and decrees followed. In 1872, the Jesuit order was banned from Germany and the Catholic Church was forbidden any involvement with German schools (previously church officials had played a significant role in the supervision of educational curricula). However, the

*Kulturkampf* was also directed at removing Polish influence from Germany (Blanke, 2014). For decades — in some cases, centuries — Prussia's eastern provinces, particularly Pomerania and Posen had changed from being part of Prussia to being part of Poland and back again with each new war and treaty. The Germans looked down on the Poles, and the "Iron Chancellor" Bismarck saw a means of expunging Polish culture from Germany through the *Kulturkampf*. In addition to the decrees and laws which deprived Catholics of certain rights, Poles living in Germany were similarly deprived. Although the Wills were German, they lived in Posen — and some evidence suggests that before Posen they lived in Pomerania (Staatsarchiv Hamburg, 2008). They may have lost aspects of their cultural heritage during the *Kulturkampf*.

One family that was deeply affected by the *Kulturkampf* was named Czolgosz (pronounced Cholgosh), a Polish family living in Posen, East Prussia. As a result of the deprivations and restrictions of the *Kulturkampf*, Paul and Mary Czolgosz emigrated with their children to the United States in 1873 (the same year the Wills left Germany for the U.S.). Their son Leon was also born that year. As an adult in the United States, Leon became an anarchist and shot the conservative Republican President, William McKinley, at the Pan-American Exposition in Buffalo, New York in 1901. Both McKinley and Czolgosz became casualties of the *Kulturkampf* (Rauchway, 2003).

Whether it was economic or cultural influences (or both), the Wills determined that the best course open to them was to leave Germany for the United States. They would join one million other Germans who emigrated between 1864 and 1873. During the latter years of this wave of emigration, the United States was the destination for 90 percent of these families (Blackbourn, 2003).

Reinholt and Amalia Will had three children between the time of their marriage in 1866 and 1873, when they left Germany (Staatsarchiv Hamburg, 2008). All were born in Krotoschin in the Posen Province of Prussia (now Krotoszyn in Poland): Emma, born in 1867, Charles (also known as Carl), born in 1869, and Gustav, born in December 1872 (U.S. Census Bureau, 1880). It was, of course, common for children to emigrate with their parents — indeed, children comprised 25 percent of all German emigrants. The long journey to the United States, though, was fraught with danger and hardship (Blackbourn, 2003). If Reinholt and Amalia understood these hardships and sacrifices, the decision to emigrate was probably not taken lightly. Travelling with the infant, Gustav, would have complicated this decision.

On January 29, 1873, they began the two-month long, 3,800 mile, journey to New York from the port of Hamburg on the *dampfschiff* ("steamer") SS *Hammonia*, a ship of the Hamburg-American Line (Staatsarchiv Hamburg, 2008). Like most immigrant passengers, the Wills traveled in "steerage," also known as *zwischendeck* ("between decks"). The quarters were small and cramped, often with 200-400 passengers allotted to one compartment (Solem, 2024). There was little light and not much supervision by the crew; theft and violence were common. The accommodation of families, as well as separation of single men and women were not considered. Toileting facilities were limited to "slop buckets" and, as Edward Steiner (1906), writing about his travel in steerage noted, "The stenches become unbearable" (p. 36). For food, passengers in steerage received "unsavoury [sic] rations [that]... are not served, but doled out, with less courtesy than one would find in a charity soup kitchen" (Steiner, 1906, p. 37). Steiner (1906) summarized the experience in this way: "Every cabin passenger who has seen and smelt the steerage from afar, knows that it is often indecent and inhuman; and I, who have lived in it, know that it is both of these and cruel besides" (p. 37). Such conditions were also conducive to the spread of infectious diseases like tuberculosis. The Wills may have been exposed to tuberculosis on this trip and transmitted the infection to Otto Will's father later — or his exposure may have occurred in some other way — but tuberculosis played an important role in the young Otto Will's life.

The *Hammonia* reached New York on March 27, 1873 (Staatsarchiv Hamburg, 2008). Once in the U.S., and cleared through Ellis Island, Otto Sr.'s parents and older siblings made their way northwest to Minnesota, a region popular with Northern European immigrants (Minnesota Digital Library, n.d.). The climate was similar to that of their countries of origin, and, Minnesota created a Board of Immigration in 1867 to encourage immigrant settlement in the state; combined with the Homestead Act of 1862, this made land cheap and plentiful (Ratsabout, 2022). Yet, there was often a darker side to such hospitality. James Marcus (2024), an Emerson biographer, explains that many German and Irish immigrants would serve as "agricultural fodder, who ... [would] themselves nourish the earth after a short period of exploitation" (p. 223).

S.S. *Hammonia* (date unknown)

The S.S. *Hammonia*, a steamship of the Hamburg American Line transported the Will family from Hamburg to New York City in 1873.

Most immigrants had been farmers and planned to continue farming in Minnesota. This was probably not the case for Reinholt Will. Once in Minnesota, the Wills took up residence in Henderson, a hamlet of about 700 (in 1870) approximately 57 miles southwest of Minneapolis (U.S. Census Bureau, 1870a). In the 1880 United States Census, Reinholt's occupation is again listed as "gardener" and Amalia Will's occupation is described as "keeping house." Between 1873 and 1882 the Wills remained in Henderson, adding five children to the family: Otto Augustus (also known as Otto Allen) in 1875, Clara in 1878, and Hugo and Albert in 1879 (U.S. Census Bureau 1880). The family relocated to Minneapolis in 1882 (Shutter 1923).

Otto A. Will Sr. was born August 2, 1875, in Henderson. He appears in documents as both Otto Allen Will and Otto Augustus Will ("Augustus" being his paternal grandfather's name). He was the first birthright American citizen in the Will family.

Once in Minneapolis, Reinholt Will founded a floral wholesale business, naming it "Will & Sons." The family continued to grow; a daughter, Pansy, was born in October 1882, a son, Henry, was born in August 1884, followed by two more daughters, Elsie, born in August 1887 and Claire, born in 1888 (U.S. Census Bureau, 1900b). This brought Otto Sr.'s siblings to ten over a twenty-year period. When Reinholt Will retired, the business was renamed "Will Brothers;" Reinholt Will died in November 1904. In 1923, one Minneapolis historian described the Will family as "one of the old and prominent families of Minneapolis" (Shutter, 1923, p. 148).

In one of his final published papers, Otto Will Jr. (1989b) described his father as "tyrannical" (p. 138). To some extent, this was, of course, a cultural artifact. Blackbourn (2003) asserts that the typical German family was focused on providing the male worker with a sphere of life separate from work. To achieve this, men and women were assigned distinct, contrasting roles. Men were expected to be the public face of the family and to provide for its material needs. Women were expected to rear the children and provide a haven for the man away from work. According to Blackbourn (2003), men were socialized to be strong while women were socialized to be sensible; women were expected to provide the *warm heart* of the family while men applied *cold reason*. Men were socialized to be both ambitious and prone to venal temptations, while women were expected to be humble and virtuous. "Women, in short, represented the 'better half' — and therefore the 'weaker sex'" (p. 162).

According to family lore, Otto Sr. left the business with his brothers, after making several successful investments, though there is little available information on when he left Minneapolis and what he did between that time and 1908, when he married Florence Keeling ("Marriage licenses," 1908). Again, according to family lore, these investments included oil and mineral rights, as well as the purchase of several Woolworth retail stores. He created a trust and lived off the income it generated until his death in 1958. According to Patrick Will (personal communication, January 16, 2011) and Deirdre Will Vinyard (personal communication, January 8, 2011), Otto Jr. received some portion of this trust from his father. Little of it, however, was passed on to their generation of the family.

## The Keelings

Florence Keeling, Otto Jr.'s mother, was born in Caldwell, Kansas on May 30, 1886. Her parents were Henry Charles Keeling, born in 1848 in New Orleans, Louisiana and Ida Keeling (neé Barlow), born in 1856 in Berrien, Michigan (U.S. Census Bureau, 1900a). According to an announcement in the *Caldwell Advance Newspaper* ("Keeling-Barlow," 1883) the couple was married in October in Amboy,

Illinois at the home of Ida's parents. Their first child, a daughter named Jennett, was born in August 1884 in Kansas (U.S. Census Bureau, 1900a).

Henry Charles Keeling was of Irish origin — his father, Henry William Keeling (born 1812), and his mother, Sarah Keeling (neeé Johnston, born 1816), were from Ireland. Henry Charles was the fifth of five children (U.S. Census Bureau, 1870b). He had an older brother named William Henry born in 1835 (probably to a different mother, Nancy Hill Keeling) (Nebraska State Historical Society, n.d.); an older sister, Mary Ann, born in 1837; a second brother, George, born about 1844; and another sister, Caroline, who went by Carrie, was born in 1846 (U.S. Census Bureau, 1870b).

Young Henry's father was often apart from his wife and children, living and working in Illinois while the rest of the family resided in New Orleans. Perhaps because of his father's absence, the boy formed a strong attachment to his older brother, William, almost twenty years his senior. In 1854, Henry William Keeling returned to New Orleans to relocate the family to Amboy, Illinois. According to the *Times-Picayune* newspaper, Henry William sold off the half-lot of land he owned in Louisiana on August 13, 1855 ("Sheriff's Sales," 1866).

William Keeling, Henry's brother, led a life of adventure and travel. In 1855 he began work as a U.S. government surveyor, based at Fort Leavenworth, Kansas. In 1861, with the outbreak of the Civil War, he enlisted in the 13th U.S. Infantry with the rank of private, seeing action at Vicksburg. He served on General William Tecumseh Sherman's staff as quartermaster during Sherman's "March to the Sea," developing a friendship with the general that would last until his death. In 1867, William left the army with the rank of first lieutenant and traveled across the country primarily earning his living as a merchant. He is referred to in some records as "Major" William Keeling, though how he attained this rank is not evident (Nebraska State Historical Society, n.d.).

In 1872, William became post trader for the army and served as quartermaster for his former regiment at Fort Leavenworth. A post trader managed what was essentially a general store for the local population. At some point before 1876, Henry, then in his twenties, joined William at Fort Leavenworth as an assistant at the trading post (Nebraska State Historical Society, n.d.).

## "The Greed of White Men"

E.A. Brininstool (1935) wrote: "The primary cause of every Indian war in the United States was the greed of the white man for the lands occupied by the red man" (p. 1). Henry Keeling and his (half) brother, William, would become involved in such a war in 1878.

On June 25-26, 1876, George Armstrong Custer's command was wiped out at the Battle of the Little Bighorn in Montana. Although this battle was the result of white miners violating a treaty with the Northern Cheyenne and Sioux people (and the subsequent refusal of the U.S. government to enforce the provisions of the treaty), it became official United States policy to relocate the Northern Cheyenne and Arapaho people from the northern plains to the Oklahoma Indian Territory, 600 miles south of their ancestral lands; it was an environment to which they were unaccustomed (Brininstool, 1935; Self, 2010). Illness and hunger were constant. Though the government supplied an (inadequate) level of rations for the multiple tribes in the territory and they were allowed to hunt buffalo to augment these rations, white men often violated the tribes' territorial integrity and slaughtered their buffalo. The situation reached a crisis after a measles outbreak in 1878; ill — and starving — several Cherokee chiefs, including Dull Knife, Little Wolf, and Wild Hog, attempted to lead their people north in what became known as Dull Knife's Raid or the Northern Cherokee Exodus. The Cherokee were defeated and the survivors returned to the Indian Territory (Self, 2010).

To prevent another attempt at escape, with its attendant bloodshed and destruction of property, the U.S. government constructed a cantonment on the North Canadian River in Oklahoma between Fort Supply (sometimes called "The grocer of the West") and Fort Reno in 1879 (Rodríguez & Rodríguez, 2017). Cantonment traditionally refers to a temporary military base or fortification (May, n.d.). Apparently, William Keeling was requested by generals William T. Sherman and Phillip Sheridan to serve as post trader. He remained in this position, however, for only a short time. Presumably, on William's recommendation, Henry replaced him as post trader at the cantonment (which was never officially named) in 1879. Constructed five miles from the present town of Canton, in Blaine County, Oklahoma, this installation was composed of temporary barracks, a trader's store, and three permanent buildings (i.e., constructed of stone) which housed a commissary, hospital, and officers' quarters (Keeling, 1925; May, n.d.).

During his time as post trader, William Keeling developed friendships with the Cherokee and Arapaho and was known as "The man who shakes hands and gives us bread and meat." (Nebraska State Historical Society, n.d.). Henry Keeling was apparently similarly disposed to the Indians around the cantonment.

In 1909, Henry spoke to the Kansas State Historical Society on the topic, "My Experience with the Cheyenne Indians" (1925). This talk is largely a collection of anecdotes about his friendships with members of the Cherokee people. His writing seems balanced in apportioning responsibility for "trouble" between tribes served by the cantonment and white people. For instance, he noted that "in 1880 we had a great deal of trouble with the Cheyennes [sic] because the Interior Department had cut down their rations, although game was very scarce" (p. 60). He also writes about white men who stole horses and game from the Cherokee. He seems particularly proud that he established a friendship with Young White Horse, a chief of the "Dog Soldiers," a secret society of warriors. He wrote: "I have been told by good authority, white men who have been among the Indians for a great many years, that I was the only white man that had ever witnessed the initiation of the Dog Soldiers" (p. 65).

In 1882, the government moved the Northern Cheyenne people from the Indian Territory to Montana, and the Department of the Interior assumed control of the cantonment. It was then leased to a group of Mennonites who created a school for the remaining native children. Somewhere around this time, Henry Keeling relocated to Caldwell, Kansas. It is perhaps worth a note about Caldwell because its nature no doubt impressed itself upon young Otto Will's grandparents and parents and, through them, touched him.

Caldwell began as a rough-hewn dugout and log general store just east of the Chisholm Trail built by a former Army scout, C.H. Stone; its chief attraction was that it sold alcohol (Alexander, 2023). Because of its location just over the Kansas border from the Indian Territory, it was ideally suited to interest those desiring to imbibe. This was illustrated by two signs, one of which faced the Kansas side of the border and read, "Last Chance;" the other, faced the Indian Territory and read "First Chance." The Territory was dry (alcohol-free), and cattle drovers were drawn to the primitive structure as if those signs were flashing neon (O'Neal, 2008).

Between 1867 and 1871 other businesses and private homes grew up around the general store. In 1871, while 23-year-old Wyatt Earp hunted buffalo for hides to sell to local merchants, Caldwell became a town with the opening of a Post Office in Stone's general store. The inhabitants named the town for then United States Senator Alexander Caldwell (Alexander, 2023; O'Neal, 2008).

Because of its proximity to the Oklahoma border and the rowdy disposition of the Chisholm Trail cattle drovers, Caldwell was given the sobriquet "The Border Queen." Gunfights were frequent, as were vigilante justice and lynchings (Alexander, 2023; O'Neal, 2008).

Attempting to keep the peace and enforce the town's laws was a hazardous occupation. Bill O'Neal (1980) described Caldwell as "a trail town of such unrestrained violence that *it proved fatal for more law officers than any other Kansas cattle community* [emphasis added]" (p. 87). This is indeed remarkable when one remembers that Dodge City, Hays City, and Abilene were also Kansas railheads. Between 1879 and 1885, 18 City Marshals were murdered in the hamlet of roughly 1,500 inhabitants (O'Neal, 1980). By 1886, the cattle business moved west of Caldwell and the little town began the transition to an agricultural economy (Alexander, 2023).

After moving to Caldwell following the Army's withdrawal from the cantonment, Henry put what he had learned as a post trader to good use as a merchant. He sold real estate and insurance, and owned a hardware store in Caldwell (U.S. Census Bureau, 1900a). As a purveyor of real estate, Henry Keeling had a great opportunity in 1893 when the United States government opened parts of the Oklahoma Territory to prospective homesteaders. Caldwell briefly reverted to its chaotic and reckless past as its population swelled tenfold to 15,000 awaiting the date for the land rush. However, after September 16, 1893, it was, again, the tiny "Border Queen" (Alexander, 2023). Apart from one period at the turn of the twentieth century, Henry and Ida remained in Caldwell until Henry's death in July 1930.

In 1901, the Keelings moved to Wichita, Kansas to complete Jennett and Florence's education. The family was welcomed there, and the October 19 *Wichita Eagle* described Henry as a businessman, "with no superior anywhere," and Ida Keeling as "a woman of rare culture and refinement" ("Bought home here," 1901).

By 1910, the year of Otto Jr.'s birth, Caldwell had completed the transition from rowdy cowtown — having seen over a million head of cattle moving north — to quiet village, with wheat as its primary crop. Yet, there is little doubt that, for those sturdy individuals who had successfully endured nearly twenty years of lawlessness, violence, and the difficult struggle to create a home on the frontier, a deep memory of that period remained (Coke, 2005; O'Neal, 2008).

# Chapter Three: The Great White Plague

In December 1908, Otto A. Will Sr. married Florence Keeling ("Marriage Licenses," 1908). He was 32, ten years her senior. Although there is no contemporary evidence about the early years of their marriage, and we are left with speculation, there is no reason to believe that the marriage was a particularly happy one. Otto Jr. (1989b) would remember his father as demeaning to his mother. Further, his family's patriarchal background may have created the expectation that Florence would behave like an accommodating *hausfrau* ("housewife"), a role to which the anxious, fragile young woman who grew up in a predominantly female home was not temperamentally suited. Additionally, Florence was a well-educated woman for the era and perhaps had more ambitious wishes for her future than domesticity. As we will discover, both were seriously damaged psychologically, struggling in their own worlds. The anthropologist and poet, Loren Eiseley (2012), who Otto often cited, wrote, "The fact is that many of us who walk to and fro upon our usual tasks are prisoners drawing mental maps of escape" (p. 30). This quality is captured in the inscription of a Roman headstone describing the deceased as having enjoyed only seven years of his life — the other years he "dismissed as being no more than merely existing" (de la Bédoyère, 2017, p. 195). This may have been true of both of Otto Jr.'s parents, but it certainly seems true of his mother, who "could be both close and warm and again distantly cold and disappearing. … I feared her closeness as I did her distance" (Will, 1979, p. 575).

Courtesy of Patrick Will

Otto Augustus (Allen) Will Sr. (1875-1958)
1910

Courtesy of Patrick Will

Florence Keeling Will (1886-1960) and Otto

1910

Otto's mother was psychiatrically ill —often suicidal — for most of his life. He wrote, "I feared her closeness as I did her distance."

Otto Allen Will Jr. was born April 26, 1910, in Caldwell, Kansas. He recalled being told that his father was diagnosed with active tuberculosis within two weeks of his birth. Obviously, this was not based on his own memories and was probably part of family lore. It is perhaps best to be skeptical of the "two weeks" figure, though Otto Sr.'s diagnosis was probably soon after his son's birth.

It is perhaps difficult in the twenty-first century to imagine the multiple emotions that accompanied a diagnosis of "consumption," or tuberculosis (TB), in centuries past; the opportunity, though, to know these emotions may again be offered with multiple drug-resistant strains of the disease becoming prevalent in India and Africa (Krishnan, 2022). Otto (1973) wrote that TB, like venereal disease or mental illness, created a sense that one was somehow unclean. It was a source of shame.

Tuberculosis has been known by many names in its 9,000-year history (Daniel, 2006; Krishnan, 2022). Over the centuries, it destroyed individuals who had no protection from, nor recourse to, its fatal embrace (Barberis, et al., 2017). It also decimated entire families like that of the English Romantic poet, John Keats.

In the nineteenth century, alone, TB ravaged other families like that of Edgar Allan Poe, who lost his biological mother (Eliza Poe), his adoptive mother (Frances Allan), older brother (Henry), and wife (Virginia) to it. Ralph Waldo Emerson similarly lost his father (William — also ill with stomach cancer), two younger brothers (Edward and Charles, respectively), and his first wife (Ellen) to "consumption;" Henry David Thoreau, as well as his father (John), and two sisters (Helen, older, and Sophia, younger), fell victim to the disease. At the time of his death from tetanus, Henry David's older brother (John Jr.) was ill with tuberculosis. Four of the five Brontë sisters (Elizabeth, Maria, Anne, and Emily) died of consumption as did, Branwell, their brother (Dawidziak, 2023; Helm, 2002; Richardson, 1995; Walls, 2017). Virtually every American knew someone who had been touched by the disease. Yet, it remained a mysterious and stigmatizing illness.

Referred to in Hebrew as *schachepheth* ("consumption" or "wasting disease") in the books of Deuteronomy and Leviticus in the Bible, in ancient Greece it was known as *phtisis* ("a dwindling or wasting away"). Clarissimus Galen, personal physician to the Roman Emperor, Marcus Aurelius, was the first to document the primary symptoms of *phtisis*: fever, coughing, and blood-stained sputum; he also offered one of the earliest ideas of a treatment regimen: sea voyages, fresh air (for which sea voyages were thought to be ideal), and a diet with milk. The latter component — fresh milk — may have simply exposed the tubercular patient to more of what would finally be identified in 1882 as the *tubercule bacillus* (Barberis, et al., 2017; Daniel, 2006).

In the eighteenth century, some progress was made toward unlocking the cause of tuberculosis when Benjamin Marten, an English physician, wrote *A New Theory of Consumption* and hypothesized that the disease was infectious in nature (Barberis, et al., 2017). Treatment, however, remained based on creating a healthy environment and diet, and "depletion therapy." The latter was based on the bleeding of the patient enhanced with the administration of purgatives (Barberis, et al., 2017; Daniel, 2006; Unger, 2018).

It was also during the eighteenth century that tuberculosis became somewhat romanticized, as often occurs when an unyielding natural phenomenon, largely inexplicable, terrorizes human beings. In this way, schizophrenia has sometimes been romanticized. TB became known as the "Great White Plague" because of the almost translucent pallor of its victims. The anemic pallor of TB was often considered beautiful (Daniel, 2006; Marcus, 2024; Skal, 2016).

The prevalence and virulence of tuberculosis intensified in the nineteenth century, due to the squalor of the poor (working and otherwise) and the opportunities for the spread of disease by the proliferation of railroads and mass transportation (Krishnan, 2022). An estimate of the number of people who died from tuberculosis varies from one-fourth of the population to one out of seven adults (though even with this smaller figure, it has been estimated that three out of four children were infected). Because of its incidence among children — and the high rate of fatality — it was also known as "The Robber of Youth" (Barberis, et al., 2017; Dawidziak, 2023; Krishnan, 2022; Silverman, 1991).

"Consumption" was a term that continued to be used until the final decade of the nineteenth century, when it was replaced by *tuberculosis*, though in the United States those ill with TB were also called "lungers" and "chasers" (Krishnan, 2022). The latter pseudonym originated in the most common of medical advice given to victims of TB; they were told to "chase the cure," meaning to break away from their usual habits of life and to create a strenuous life outdoors. Treatment received a promising nudge in 1854 from a young botany student's doctoral dissertation, *Tuberculosis is a Curable Disease.* The student was Hermann Brehmer and he was ill with the disease. He described a successful cure for himself after a period of residence in the Himalayas. This would be the spark that ignited the sanitorium care movement (Barberis, et al., 2017). Brehmer founded his own sanitorium or *Heilanstalt* ("sanitorium") in Silesia in 1859. In 1867, another sanitorium was opened by Peter Detweiler in Falkenstein, Germany. In North America, the first sanitorium for the treatment of tuberculosis was opened in 1871 in Asheville, North Carolina by Dr. Horatio Page Gatchell. A few years later, in 1875, another sanitorium was established in Asheville by Dr. Joseph William Gleitsman. Mountainous regions, from the Adirondacks to the Rockies, soon saw construction of such facilities (Thomas, 2020).

Of course, there were folk remedies, as well. One of the most gruesome is described by Jay Parini (1999) in his biography of Robert Frost. Will Frost, the poet's father, was diagnosed with consumption and resorted to a remedy promised to cure it. In 1884, he took Robbie to a slaughterhouse and then Will Frost "drank cup after cup of fresh blood from the slit throat of a steer" (Parini, 1999, p. 18). Less than a year later he died. Other crank "medical treatments" included the application of sandbags on the patient's chest to force the lungs to work more vigorously and the removal of ribs to afford more area in which the lungs could function (Skal, 2016).

A further step toward the ultimate cure of TB occurred in March 1882 when Dr. Hermann Heinrich Robert Koch presented his isolation of the *tubercule bacillus* as the pathogen responsible for the dreaded disease (Koch would also discover *vibrio cholerae*, the pathogen responsible for cholera in 1884). Yet, tuberculosis was far from conquered. Indeed, by 1900, American deaths from TB were approximately 150,000 each year with at least a million more infected (Barberis, et al., 2017; Daniel, 2006; Krishnan, 2022; Silverman, 1991; Thomas, 2020). It would not be until 1944 that streptomycin, the first antibiotic effective against tuberculosis, was discovered. Isoniazid followed in 1952 and the rifamycins in 1957 (Daniel, 2006).

When Otto Will Sr. was diagnosed with tuberculosis in 1910, physicians were still prescribing stays at TB sanitoria located in dry, mountainous climates (Weber, 1907). Given the uncertainty of outcome — and high mortality rate — infant Otto's parents may have panicked in response to the diagnosis. Certainly, Kansas did not provide the recommended climate, so Otto Sr. and Florence Will hastily arranged for travel to Roswell, New Mexico; Otto Jr. was left in the care of his maternal grandparents and a Black nanny. His parents returned infrequently for visits. This series of events had traumatic and pervasive effects on the infant.

His parents left during the period when the establishment of object constancy or permanence begins. The infant, with the proper environment, begins to develop the cognitive structures that allow a mental representation to replace the primary caregiver when she or he is not physically present. The infant's ability to soothe herself while anxious and alone begins. Games like "peek-a-boo" facilitate such development. However, attachment to a primary person also facilitates the process. Later identifications (and disidentifications) will be founded on object constancy; thus, the development of identity is dependent upon it. The intermittent visits of infant Otto's parents must have been confusing.

It is also in these first months that the infant establishes or fails to establish a secure base from which she can venture forth to explore the world. If her explorations result in anxiety, she may retreat to a secure base, regroup, and be reassured, empowering her to once again move into the world (Eagle, 2013).

Between two and three years of age, building on the cognitive growth of the earliest years, object constancy is more or less secured — provided there is a favorable environment. When Otto was two years of age, his parents returned to Kansas, summarily dismissed his nanny, and returned to Roswell, separating him from his grandparents. Within a few weeks of birth, he experienced the loss of his parents and, between two and three years of age, his primary caregivers whom he had grown to love — particularly his nanny. There is, of course, some question of what he could actually recall in this largely preverbal period, but in later life, he (1979) wrote:

> I often think that I am seeking something, lost in the now distant past of my childhood, yet persistently drawing my attention. Perhaps it is the face, the voice, and the touch of the black woman who cared for me during the first two years of my life and then left, to be seen or known by me no more (p. 575).

Patrick Will believed, "That rupture affected him for the rest of his life. He felt that his mother had been taken away from him. He never really recovered from that" (personal communication, January 16, 2011). Further, Otto had described his nanny to Kim Chernin as "very loving and caring in a way that my mother never was" Patrick described his father as:

> having terrible problems with attachment and separation himself. Even something as mundane as saying "goodbye" at the door, when I was visiting from school, could be a very wrenching experience. It was frightening to him — these simple acts of separation (personal communication, January 16, 2011).

## A Strange House

In addition to being torn away from the nanny he loved, young Otto was transplanted from the home he had known into an environment seething with resentment, hate, and barely muted violence. He spent the next three years in the southeastern part of New Mexico in the village of Roswell with a population of 6,172 (U.S. Census Bureau, 1910). The sleepy village was located approximately three miles south of the cattle baron, John Chisum's, forty-acre South Spring Ranch, the headquarters of his empire. In combination with his other ranch land, much of it in Texas, he owned 150 miles of land along the Pecos River. (Alexander, 2022; Geddie, 2020; Hinton, 2017)

Like Caldwell, Roswell had seen its share of violence, particularly during the Lincoln County War, a struggle for power between rival cattle barons in 1878-1881. Henry Antrim, also known as Henry McCarty — his paternity was not clear, and both names represented possible fathers — better known as Billy the Kid, fought on Chisum's side; after the range war was over, though, Antrim believed that Chisum owed him $500, which Chisum refused to pay. Antrim began to steal cattle from Chisum in lieu of payment. Chisum then aided Pat Garrett, a candidate sympathetic to Chisum in the 1880 Lincoln County Sheriff election. It was Garrett who killed Antrim on July 14, 1881 (Wallis, 2007).

One interesting link between Roswell and Caldwell took the form of a Caldwell City Marshal named Henry Newton Brown. Apparently without too much due diligence, Brown was hired as the Caldwell City Marshal because of his reputation as a gunfighter. If the city fathers of Caldwell had carried out some research, they would have discovered that Brown had ridden with Billy the Kid in New Mexico. The result was that Brown brought order to Caldwell, but after doing so, he and a group of confederates, robbed the bank in Medicine Lodge, Kansas, about seventy miles from Caldwell; after the robbery, Brown was killed by vigilantes on April 30, 1884 (O'Neal, 1980).

As was the case in Caldwell, those days were gone by the time the Wills settled in Roswell. Otto Jr.'s mother talked of the happy days the family enjoyed there. Otto Sr. had spent a year at a TB sanitorium. His father left this institution improved — to what extent is unclear — though he was certainly not "cured." Florence Will would tell her son that the family was close during this time.

Otto Jr. remembered these years much differently. He specifically remembered that his mother disliked Roswell; to her, it was a "hot, dusty cow town." The family lived on a small farm and owned a cow and some chickens. Young Otto was responsible for milking the cow and gathering eggs. He remembered one evening when he was about five that his mother wanted chicken for supper. His father was feeling ill, and he was tasked with slaughtering the chicken. His mother "couldn't do such a dreadful thing;" so, he took a knife, held the chicken down and sawed her head off, crying all the while he did it. No one had ever taught him how to kill a chicken, and he felt sad and guilty afterward.

He described confronting his mother with his memories of the time in Roswell later in life:

> I said to her one night, I was in my forties and I said, "You're always telling me how wonderful it was when I was a little boy in New Mexico, but what was it really like when my father was sick with tuberculosis and wasn't in the sanitorium? He might be in the other room coughing and you had to keep everything sterile, and boil the dishes and all?" She responded, "I'll tell you, son: sometimes I wanted to kill him [Otto Sr.] *and kill you* and get the hell out." He then reassuringly said, "Well, now I love you more than ever."

Another incident he described from the period in Roswell captures some of the intensity in the household. Otto's father seems to have harbored violent fantasies, as well, though these may have been projected onto his wife. Patrick Will related a story that his father told him, stating: "One time, [Otto's] father found a piece of ice in a bowl of ice cream; [he confronted Otto's mother, saying to her] 'I thought that was a piece of glass — not that I would have blamed you for trying to kill me.'" Patrick also noted that his father: "described many of the relationships in his life as having macabre elements" (personal communication, January 16, 2011).

Otto described his home as a "strange house:"

> Father would go down to the bank; he didn't have a business, but he would go down to the bank. He would go to the stock market to see what he was going to bet on in terms of stocks. He was always nicely dressed when he went. My mother would be at home. She never went out to do the shopping — never learned to drive a car. She tried to learn with him teaching her, but he was so short-tempered and unpleasant that it didn't work. So, a lot of times he would be in a rage in his room with a pistol under his pillow. She'd be sobbing in the back room. He'd rush into the room once in a while to see that she didn't drink the iodine [that she kept].

Ingesting iodine can be fatal (from 200 mgs. and higher) but seldom is. In 1938, a study was published examining fatality rates among 1195 cases of iodine ingestion between 1915 and 1936 in the Boston City Hospital (now the Boston Medical Center) (Moore, 1938). Of this number, 327 of those studied had consumed iodine in some form for the purpose of committing suicide. The study noted that iodine was popular with those attempting suicide because of its availability. However, of those 327 cases studied, only one proved fatal. "Oddly enough, although iodine is used in suicidal attempts more often than any other poison, fatal cases are very rare" (Moore, 1938, p. 383).

Otto's resentment of his father's invalidism — at least when his father was home — began during these years but would intensify when the family moved to Colorado. Neighbors would inquire: "How is your dear mother and how is your nice father?" Otto (1971a) later described one of the struggles that children have with unstable parents. There is no doubt that he could have been drawing on his own experience:

> The child must also deal with conflicts between a parent's public and private images that are not easily reconciled. A father may pay his bills, be honest and respectable in his

> dealing with his business and other associates, and yet to his child be incomprehensibly demanding, unkind, anxiety-provoking, or simply ignoring (pp. 208-209).

His parents seem to have engaged in what R.D. Laing (1969) called "mystification," which will be discussed in more detail below. For the moment, though, mystification refers to one person's attempt to impose a view of the world on another — often a parent upon a child — by undermining the child's accurate perceptions of the environment. Evidence of the dissonance of the two views "must be ignored (dissociated), or explained away" (Will, 1971a, p. 208).

Late in his life, Otto recognized that he had dissociated or denied much of his mother's behavior until he was a young man in his twenties. In a paper posthumously published in 2021 (originally written in 1979), he acknowledged:

> With the decline in mutual fantasies, my mother and I were openly disappointed with each other and readily blamed and quarreled ... But in a sense she seemed more real to me. And I think that I was more real to her. We began somehow to like each other, not blinded by love (p. 4).

# Chapter Four: The School that Saved Otto's Life

Nearing his sixth birthday, young Otto's parents recognized the need for him to begin school — as it was, he would begin a year late. Options for education in the village of Roswell were meager, and the decision was made to leave for the larger town of Colorado Springs, Colorado, just over 400 miles north. The reason that Colorado Springs was chosen is not known definitively, but Otto Jr. learned that his father had spent a year being treated for TB in Colorado and some evidence (see below) suggests that this sanitorium was near Colorado Springs.

About sixty miles south of Denver, Colorado Springs had a population of 29,078 in 1910 (U.S. Census Bureau, 1910). The area which made up Colorado Springs was originally the land of the Arapaho, Cheyenne, Comanche, Kiowa, Lakota, and Ute peoples. In a familiar story concerning all of America's native people, the United States government drove them off the land through military action and "treaties" which were not honored by the government (Mondragon, n.d.).

A key event in the development of Colorado Springs was the "Colorado Gold Rush," also known as the "Pikes Peak Gold Rush," beginning in 1859. The town of Colorado City, later annexed by Colorado Springs, began as a supply area for mining camps. The gold rush also initiated the creation of the Colorado Territory as farmers, ruined by poor crop yields and a national economic downturn, flocked to the area. Supplies for mining were relatively cheap and plentiful (Abbott, et al., 2013).

In July 1867, General William J. Palmer, a Medal of Honor recipient in the Civil War and a civil engineer, built the Denver and Rio Grande

Railroad. As he explored the area, he was captivated by the natural beauty of the Pikes Peak area. In 1870, he founded the Colorado Springs Company, with the goal of selling 2,000 square acres to newly arriving migrants; in July 1871 the town of Colorado Springs was officially founded (Abbott, et al., 2013). In addition to founding Colorado College and the Deaf & Blind School, Palmer created the Cragmor TB Sanitorium near the town (Mondragon, n.d.).

By 1910, the "City of Sunshine," as Colorado Springs was promoted, boasted six additional TB sanitoria. Between 1880 and 1910, the treatment of pulmonary diseases, particularly TB, was the city's primary "industry." It advertised a moderate climate with low precipitation and wind, as well as a high level of sunshine. During this same period, 24,000 people migrated to Colorado Springs, most of them for health reasons (Mayberry, 2020).

One of these seven sanitoria, the Modern Woodmen of America (MWA), was founded by a life insurance company of the same name. The MWA Sanitorium provided free medical care for pulmonary diseases if the prospective patient met their admissions requirements. The Sanitorium was open to Caucasian men who were American citizens, believed in "a Supreme Being," and were not employed in extraordinarily dangerous jobs (Mayberry, 2020). The medical director of the MWA was Charles O. Giese, who became the Will's family physician when they moved from Roswell to Colorado Springs. This suggests that the MWA was the sanitorium at which Otto Sr. was treated for tuberculosis.

## The Cheyenne Mountain School

Though the reason that the Wills chose Colorado Springs may not be certain, the reason for the location of their residence in that city is. The family settled at 114 East Saint Vrain Street, in what was originally known as the Near North End neighborhood of Colorado Springs (in 1923, the neighborhood became known as the Historic Uptown neighborhood). According to Otto, his parents chose this location because of its proximity to the Cheyenne Mountain School, located about ten miles away. The school, under the enthusiastic leadership of Lloyd "Pappy" Shaw was beginning to establish a reputation for educational excellence. His time there would be pivotal in the young Otto Will's life.

The Cheyenne Mountain School began in 1872 as a single twelve-by-twelve-foot room in which the children of early Colorado Springs settlers were educated. It was originally built of logs and served nine students (Marold, 2012). Like all institutions, its early years involved growing pains. In 1890, the only teacher was dismissed because of an overly enthusiastic use of corporal punishment; the official report of the group investigating the complaint described the teacher as beating the male students almost daily in front of the other students with a rawhide whip. The report also called for the new teacher to be a "lady" (Young, 2020).

The following year, 1891, saw the creation of a streetcar line connecting a wider area in Colorado Springs to the school. Otto would later ride that trolley, both to school and "into town." He remembered the area as still rural enough that coyotes would sometimes block the tracks. The log schoolhouse became brick in 1899 and by 1910, the one room expanded to six-rooms (Marold, 2012; Young, 2020).

In 1916, the year Otto started at the Cheyenne Mountain School, it began a period of both physical and reputational growth with the employment of Lloyd Shaw. Shaw had completed his education at Colorado College and had three years of experience teaching. He was only 25, yet he was charismatic and had a passion for education. Perhaps more importantly, Shaw's passion for teaching was supported by his great ability to do it (Orsborn, n.d.). Ralph Waldo Emerson (1841/1993) wrote in "Self-Reliance": "An institution is the lengthened shadow of one man" (p. 26). In the case of Lloyd Shaw, this very quickly became true.

Shaw, on his way to becoming a legend, was considered a "Renaissance man" by parents and the older students. In addition to being the principal of the school and superintendent of the district, Shaw taught biology, drama, and English. For three years he coached the football team which won state championships. After the third year, however, Shaw made a controversial decision. He concluded that competitive sports emphasized being bigger and better than others (often because of physical size) and football, particularly, did not further his philosophy for the school. Football was dropped (Orsborn, n.d.). Otto recalled Shaw saying that, "He wasn't going to be part of a school where people walk around wearing letters thinking they're bigshots because they can knock other people down. That was the end of it."

Dorothy Stott Shaw was a poet and aided her husband in his teaching, as well as serving as school librarian. Both Shaws had a gift for connecting academic subjects with extracurricular activities. They introduced students to hiking, skiing, camping, and music, as well as drama and literature. Young Otto remembered that Shaw gave an inscribed copy of his book, *Nature Notes of the Pikes Peak Region*, to the first student each year who found an anemone (a flowering plant from the buttercup family, often called a "windflower"). Another former student of the school, Dena Fresh (1985), remembered that the book was presented at a ceremony in front of the entire student body. Otto coveted this prize but never won it. (He would receive one as an adult with the following inscription: "To Otto Will for finding more than the first anemone.")

He described Shaw as often spontaneously deciding that the school's students would benefit from an experience and immediately engaging them in it. He offered the following example: "[One day] He knocked on our room door and said, 'I want all the classes to come down to the auditorium. I've got a new recording of Beethoven's Fifth [Symphony].'" Shaw had also studied oratory in both high school and college — winning a state oratorical contest — and most weeks the students would gather in the auditorium to hear him speak on a topic he believed important (Marold, 2012; Orsborn, n.d.).

Other adjuncts to the formal curriculum included a cabin (later, another was added), built near Seven Springs, which provided a base of operations for outdoor excursions, an observatory built on top of the school, creation of a nature preserve and the acquisition of a valuable art collection. Otto recalled that "Pappy" Shaw was equally gifted as a fundraiser with parents and local dignitaries. He also fondly remembered Shaw as a prolific playwright. "He built a little outdoor theater … with a stage; he wrote the plays that were performed every Friday afternoon. [One week it would be for the] kindergarten, the next week the first grade, next week the second grade, throughout the year."

Parents often attended these plays, though it is not clear whether Otto's did. Of particular interest to Otto was the annual Christmas play. "I always wanted to be one of the wisemen," he recalled. "Finally, I got to be the second wiseman, and then, in my last year, I got to be the first wiseman." Apparently, the year he was the first wiseman was very important to him: "I had to give a speech — talking to the shepherds —

saying, 'Thou Bethlehem in the land of Judah are not least among the princes of Judah, for out of thee shall come a savior who shall lead my people, Israel.'"

He noted, "I've remembered that for over sixty years!"

Shaw and his wife were American folk-dance enthusiasts. Ultimately known as one of the country's experts on the round and square dances, "Pappy" wrote books on the history and practice of both. He formed a dance group at the Cheyenne Mountain School which travelled widely and won both national and international contests. The days of such competitions, though, came after Otto graduated.

Shaw brought individuals and groups to the school who could enrich the learning environment, and, in some cases, bring it to life. His interests were broad: nature, history, sociology, art, and anthropology. Otto related: "He [Shaw] had these Hopi Indians come and spend a year with us. They spoke Hopi and built a kiva [a round ceremonial structure generally at least partially underground] on the campus. They taught traditional Hopi arts and crafts."

Otto also remembered other guests that the Shaws brought to the school. One who made a strong impression on him was the Marquis Nicolò degli Albizzi, who spent a year at the school. Albizzi was a romantic figure — a member of the Russian aristocracy, a soldier of fortune, and a sportsman. He was also a champion skier.

Born in 1891, the Marquis was of mixed Florentine and Russian aristocratic blood. He was fluent in five languages and pursued a life of adventure. At the age of 20, he took part in the Italo-Turkish war (between 1911 and 1912), prompted by Italy's desire to establish a colony in Libya, nominally Ottoman territory. He was awarded several medals for valor (Allen, 2016). With the outbreak of the First World War, he joined the Italian Savoy Cavalry. Though he loved horses, he found his time in the cavalry mundane and transferred to the *Alpini* ("ski troops"), where he was known as *Il Tenente Russo* ("The Russian Lieutenant") and again distinguished himself in combat; one of his medals was inscribed with the words: "For a superb contempt for danger" (Allen, 2016, p. 27). During the Russian revolution he sided with the "white Russians" against the Bolsheviks. When the whites were defeated in the civil war, he migrated to the United States and established himself as an expert on skiing. He was married twice — his first wife drowned on their honeymoon, and the second divorced him after he allegedly kept her a prisoner in her room and physically abused her (Allen, 2016).

Otto dabbled in skiing with Albizzi as an instructor, but his father quickly forbade him to ski. Otto remembered that his father was adamant on this point: "He was always saying, 'You get hurt, people get their legs broken.'" He described one incident in which Albizzi navigated a difficult area and jumped across a dangerous chasm. Lloyd Shaw, who was with them, asked the skier: "My God, that looks impossible, how do you do it?" Albizzi's response, as Otto remembered it, seems fitting for a reckless soul: "Nothing to it — you just ride down. You come to the edge [of the chasm and] for a little while you fly."

Though the Cheyenne Mountain School had no football program, it did have a basketball team. Young Otto played on it, and, given his height, was probably quite successful. He also became involved with the school orchestra. Another of the many charismatic personalities that Shaw recruited for the school was Lou Fink who conducted the orchestra.

Born in 1881, Lou Fink became a member of the John Philip Sousa band in 1904, leaving it in 1917 after America's entry into the First World War. He was a sought-after musician in the Colorado Springs area but also had a background in education. His brother, Fred Fink, was also involved with the school's musical program. Fred Fink was posthumously inducted into the Colorado Music Educators Association Hall of Fame in 1994-1995. ("Lou W. Fink died Wednesday in Roswell," 1970; CMEA Hall of Fame, n.d.)

Otto wanted to become involved in the music program at the school and was interested in the flute. He recalled approaching Lou Fink who referred the youngster to his brother who gave individual lessons on a variety of instruments. Fred Fink played flute with a small ensemble he organized. The group played at the school's cafeteria while the students ate. This is perhaps what initially interested Otto in the instrument. He described his first lesson: "He [Fred Fink] sat down, rolled up his sleeve, and showed me a big muscle. He said, 'Playing the flute will give you that;' I said, 'Well, it's worth it.'" In addition to the school band, he joined the Broadmoor band. He had fond memories of performing at the town bandstand (P. Will, personal communication, May 31, 2025). The flute would remain an interest of Otto's for the rest of his life.

At thirteen, Otto was given access to a horse and soon thereafter joined the polo team. Polo was fashionable in that era, and he recalled feeling proud of his polo skills. When asked about his parents' interest in his school activities, he indicated that they showed very little.

Throughout Otto's memories of the men with whom he interacted at the school, there is a quality of idealization and a longing to be accepted. Men like Shaw, Albizzi, and Fink seem to have given him an alternative to his father for emulation. Though, particularly in the case of Albizzi, it may have been more show than substance, they represented many qualities that his father did not have. Otto asserted, "The school and people like Lloyd Shaw and others, they saved my life."

Otto remembered that, when he attended the school, there were 375 students enrolled from kindergarten through high school, with 13 in his graduating class. He believed that Shaw was interested in the development of his students as human beings. Jean Vanier (1998), a Canadian philosopher and theologian who founded L'Arché, an international network of communities for people with developmental disabilities, wrote: "It is only when children are accepted as they are, with their unique gifts and limits, when they are listened to and respected, that they will be able later on to accept others" (p. 81). For Otto, Lloyd Shaw was an adult who could listen and nurture. Indeed, his stated goal for the school was "happy and interested students" (Orsborn, n.d.). He was an important adult with whom Otto could identify without destructive conflict. No doubt Otto's capacity for deep and patient listening was enhanced by this identification.

# Chapter Five: An Unhappy Little Kingdom

Time away from school — time with his family — was far different. Otto described his father's routine: "Tuberculosis had become his way of life. He'd get up in the morning, have a little breakfast, read the paper. He'd go out and look at the yard." Otto remembered their house as having "a lovely yard." He aided his father in planting trees that surrounded the house, an activity his father seemed to enjoy. After some time in the yard, his father would "maybe lie down a little while."

After a morning nap, his father would have lunch, and then lie down in the afternoon for another nap. Variations in this routine included his father going into town "to do a little shopping." He recalled that his father had no friends and that, "practically no adults came to the house."

Otto entertained a fantasy that if his father's doctor had come to the house he might say: "You're okay physically, your tuberculosis is inactive, so get off your duff and do something." That fantasy, even in memory, had gone far enough: "I think my father wouldn't have anything to do with that doctor, it would've meant a tremendous change for him. He'd built this little kingdom, not a very happy one; and mother was quietly going crazy." engaging once again in the fantasy, he added: "But supposing he had changed and had to get up and go into town, go to a job, eat lunch with some friends or something.... He never did."

Immediately after this set of memories Otto described a dream he had had some years previously: "I woke up from it with a scream. It was amazing. And the dream was *nothing*. It had no black pit or no tunnel — it had no darkness. *There was nothing, best I could see.* And I was very frightened." A dream of nothing or, perhaps, emptiness, viewed as a comment on the state of internal object viability would surely be terrifying.

Otto's memories of his family paint a bleak picture of what was available to him at home. As his mother deteriorated psychologically, she increasingly became emotionally unavailable to him. He recalled that when she began to withdraw, she would avoid walking on the household carpets and tread only on the floorboards; she would also begin singing. His father seems to have been deteriorating, as well, though in his case, he seems to have been an unavoidable bully at home. Otto related: "I had a crazy household, mother going crazier and crazier." Otto Sr. would not tolerate the expression of sadness or anger, responding to either as if facing an allegation of wrongdoing. Otto recalled an instance when he felt "pretty miserable" about the family. Whether he communicated this to his father directly or the latter intuited it is not clear. Nevertheless, his father learned of his feelings and rebuked him for them.

"There's no reason for you to feel any unhappiness," he began. "You've got everything here that money can buy and everybody's just fine." Feelings had no materiality, and, thus were of no importance. Otto, of course, drew the logical conclusion from the interaction: "And so that meant, 'Don't show what you feel around here.'" This sort of rejection of feelings would play a key part in Otto's (1971a) understanding of problems in living. Having her feelings chronically rejected leads to a child being confused about what she feels. Also, the child — attuned to parental acceptance and rejection — may decide that she is unappreciative, "bad," or otherwise inadequate — in severe situations, it may also result in the child feeling "crazy." After such interactions with his father, Otto (1980) wrote that he felt no clear definition of himself or his life and could not imagine a future.

R.D. Laing (1969) and Edgar Levenson (2018) have called interactions like these "mystification." They are typical in family situations in which denial is employed. In addition to the rejection or redefinition of a child's feelings, mystification is often used to confuse a child as to what she perceives. In Chapter Two, such a situation was described in relation to Robert Frost's family.

Otto seems to have dealt with his father's narcissism and the lack of support from his mother by accepting the warmth available from the Shaws at school. He developed a close relationship with them until their respective deaths. Indeed, among Otto's keepsakes was a poem by Dorothy Stott Shaw entitled, "Christmas 1953," later published in a collection simply called *Christmas Poems* (1973). In a note, written in a strong cursive hand, she thanked Otto for "a perfectly beautiful afternoon." She continues: "And you will find, Otto, that the ingredients of this poem were perhaps a little fortified by some of the things you said — may I thank you in particular for 'star-far!'" She refers to a stanza in the poem about troubled wisemen sharing their loneliness with the baby Jesus. Given that Otto so treasured the role of the wiseman in her husband's Christmas play and that he often felt lost and lonely, the poem and accompanying note were exquisitely empathic. The note ends with an affirmation of love for Otto: "We love you very much. Lloyd and Dorothy Shaw." Until their deaths (his in 1958 and hers in 1977) the Shaws seem to have provided Otto the affectionate affirmation and acceptance unavailable at home.

In addition to these relationships, he developed a close bond with a neighbor family. Originally from Mississippi, John T. and Allie Haney (née Heidelberg), had three sons (William, Don, and Jim), two near Otto's age, and two daughters (Helen and Mary). John Haney was an attorney who represented, among other clients, a local bank (U.S. Census Bureau, 1930). Otto spent a great deal of time at their house. He recalled wondering if they ever tired of him eating dinner with them. Equally important to the fellowship he found with the boys, was the model of adults involved in a satisfying intimate relationship. "They were, to me, a very gentle house," he related, "Mr. and Mrs. Haney were very quiet and peaceful. I could never imagine Mr. Haney raising his voice." Otto's now adult children remember him speaking of the Haneys with affection and gratitude.

Otto spent a lot of time hiking Cheyenne Mountain, often with a beloved dog. In a sense this was a form of exile from his parents, though an exile that afforded him peace. Such hikes often involved spending the night under the stars. He remembered no objections from his parents, though he did not have equipment for camping. For instance, he had no sleeping bag, instead settling for a blanket. But the mountain offered freedom — perhaps a freedom worth any inconvenience.

Courtesy of Patrick Will

Otto and Bill Haney

date unknown

The Haney family provided Otto an emotional refuge and a model of successful intimacy.

# You Gotta be Strong

The Broadmoor Hotel, built in 1918, provided another escape for Otto. The Broadmoor was one of the finest hotels in the United States — the vision of Spenser "Specs" and Julia Penrose. The hotel was designed by Warren & Wetmore — the architects that designed the Biltmore and the Ritz-Carlton Hotels in New York City ("The Broadmoor," n.d.). The Olmstead Brothers (of Brookline, Massachusetts) — the designers of Central Park in New York City — designed the grounds (U.S. National Park Service, 2024). Around the age of 16, Otto was employed to help maintain the Broadmoor's grounds. His responsibilities were focused primarily on the golf course: "mowing the tees and greens — [they] had to be mowed twice a day to get it just [so]." He recalled that in 1927, it was there that he met the boxer Jack Dempsey, who was then Heavyweight Champion of the World.

Born in 1895 in Manassa, Colorado, Dempsey had scrambled from early in his life. By the age of 11 he was working in the mines near Manassa and left school after the eighth grade to work full-time. He began his boxing career at 16, fighting for food and a place to stay in tough mining camp saloons. In 1919 Dempsey won the heavyweight championship and became a celebrity on the order of Babe Ruth. Following that fight, Dempsey was given a new pseudonym — "The Manassa Mauler" — by no less a figure than the famed sportswriter, Damon Runyon. Runyon called him "the mauler" because of his fighting style which emphasized relentless punching (Summers, 2019).

Otto recalled that he was mowing one of the greens when two figures approached him. One was Jack Dempsey, and the other was Dempsey's trainer. The two men were "playing through." Perhaps out of impatience, Dempsey commandeered Otto's mower, saying "Let me push that." A few moments later, after pushing the machine, Dempsey remarked: "Hey kid, you gotta be strong to push this." Dempsey was staying at the Broadmoor Hotel and training nearby for an upcoming championship fight with Jack Sharkey. Otto took advantage of his proximity to watch Dempsey spar. He related that "people didn't much like to spar with [Dempsey] because he didn't spar, he just hit!" Will family lore maintains that Otto once sparred with Dempsey though that story may be apocryphal. Dempsey's compliment on his strength was a deep affirmation of Otto. Along with his interactions with the Shaws, Nicolò Albizzi, and the Fink brothers, he described meeting Dempsey as one of the experiences that "saved my life."

Edward Hall (1992) remembered that Otto often visited his home when both lived in the Washington, DC area. A frequent aspect of these visits was Otto bringing accessories for the Lionel train set belonging to Hall's son, Eric. Hall, who had grown up in the west, had engineered a train whistle that reproduced the sound of a Santa Fe Railroad locomotive; he described feeling a kinship with Otto as both, in reverie, returned to a past time in their lives. He wrote that Otto once told him that he needed to know that the open spaces of his earlier life remained. He related that if those spaces ever disappeared, or that he could no longer visit them, "my anxiety level would increase intolerably" (p. 238).

There was one area in his development that both of Otto's parents resisted — though his father's opposition rose to a psychotic level. That area involved dating and sexuality. Otto remembered that his parents interfered little in his sports or musical activities; even overnight trips to the mountain brought no interference. However, when there was the possibility that he might meet a young lady, the family anxiety became palpable.

The tension with his father particularly intensified at these times. Patrick Will related an incident that captures the senior Will's behavior. "In high school dad would take a girl out for a soda and he had to walk by his house to take her home" (personal communication, January 16, 2011). On at least one occasion, Otto Sr. stepped out of the house, yelling: "What are you doing with that whore!" He fired a shotgun into the air to emphasize his condemnation. The young lady was the daughter of the local bank president and was apparently of sound reputation. There are stories of other conflictual interactions involving young women in the adolescent Will's home. As he got older, these conflicts became more intense and more dangerous — on occasion — involving firearms. His father's bullying increased, and the lengths to which he would go to maintain his dominance intensified. To his son, Patrick, Otto never talked of his father with admiration. Patrick also shared an observation: "I don't have a single picture of my grandfather" (personal communication, January 16, 2011).

# Chapter Six: The Strongest Ties

As he completed high school at the Cheyenne Mountain School in 1929, Otto considered college. He remembered considering the University of Colorado, where many of his classmates were applying. His father, however, disapproved of this plan — he was determined that *his* son attend Stanford University. Otto recalled thinking that Stanford was a "good college" and was agreeable. At this point in his life, Otto apparently had little ambition to attend medical school. Probably because of the influence of Lloyd Shaw, he was drawn to the social sciences. He applied to Stanford and was awarded a scholarship. He remembered that tuition was about $60 per quarter. According to the website, MeasuringWorth.com (2025), that is just over $6,000 in 2025 dollars. The amount not covered by the scholarship was paid by his parents.

In the summer of his eighteenth year, there was a family tragedy. A cousin, the child of his mother's sister, Jennett, was cleaning a pistol. It was loaded and fired, killing the young man. He was with a companion who swore that it was not suicide. Otto visited the family in Oklahoma. When he arrived, his aunt told him that a "Black lady" had asked to see him during the visit.

The town, like many in the South, was segregated and Otto made the short trip to the area where she lived. When he reached her address, the woman excitedly ran toward him, "threw her arms around [him] and said, 'Oh, my baby, you've come back to me!'" Otto had no idea why she had responded to him in this way, and no one was willing to clear up the mystery. He would not find out for several years that this woman had been his nanny when he was an infant. He expressed regret that, "I wasn't told that so I [couldn't] respond to her." It is uncertain when he was finally told the story of his first three years, but he was an adult.

Prior to leaving Colorado Springs for college in California, Otto recalled working for a gas station and garage. The job was basic: pumping gas, cleaning windshields, and repairing flat tires. It was also during this time that he covertly courted a young woman.

Apparently, he had not given up on the banker's daughter, whom his father had labeled "a whore." However, he found her increasingly critical, particularly regarding what she perceived as his lack of ambition. Otto wanted to marry her, though he was aware that she was probably in love with someone else. He remembered being at the garage, loading a gasoline tanker truck. He sadly described watching the train that took her away when she left for school. After her departure, and perhaps because of her criticism of his lack of ambition, he did begin to think about becoming a doctor.

Otto matriculated at Stanford that fall. He seemed to enjoy aspects of college — he joined the football team, an experience unavailable to him at the Cheyenne Mountain School. Yet, he had not really escaped home — his father was still an intrusive bully. In his first quarter history class Otto received a B; he recalled that his father travelled from Colorado Springs to Palo Alto to speak with the professor of that class. Apparently, he had just one question: was his son "bright enough" to attend Stanford — given his B performance?

Despite the new experiences and the reminder of his father's crushing narcissism, Otto recalled being dogged by what he called "homesickness" throughout his first year. It was also toward the end of his first year that he became ill. He was unsure what malady he contracted — though he thought it was "probably the flu" — but he took the need for recuperation as an opportunity to, as he put it, "run away" from Stanford. He returned to Colorado Springs and was reluctant to return to the California university. His father intervened once again, telling him that enrolling at another university would be "backing down [and] — a failure" and demanded that he return to Stanford.

Discussing these events with Kim Chernin, Otto asked rhetorically, "[Why] the hell was I homesick? Why wasn't I just happy at Stanford?" As others have stated, Otto was not particularly interested in theory. His answer to these self-queries was a simply and directly worded allusion to attachment theory: "The strongest ties seem to be with the unpleasant — that's what holds you. Seems to me … some of the tightest ties I have witnessed, including I must say … my own as a kid, were to situations which were generally unpleasant."

Though still "terribly homesick" Otto ambivalently returned to Stanford the next fall. Otto indicated that, although he had been on the football team the first year, he was not allowed to try out when he returned. He guessed that it was because he had been ill and left school. "[It] actually broke my heart," he related. "I'll never forget walking across campus … to turn in my uniform — I was crying." This was an injury to his self-esteem, and he responded by setting another goal for himself: "I said to myself: if I can't be on the football team, I'll make the best [academic] record there is at Stanford."

For the next two years, Otto excelled academically, receiving marks of A or A-plus in his classes. He joined the band, and, in 1931, his sophomore year, he was inducted into Phi Beta Kappa, the national academic honor society, and into Kappa Kappa Psi, the national honorary band fraternity. In terms of social activities, Otto joined a club called "El Capitan" (a member of the so-called "Toyon clubs," named for the hall in which they met), a Stanford "eating club" for male students who wanted more than the university supplied in its cafeterias ("Stanford Eating Clubs Records," n.d.). The El Capitan Club provided fellowship and made a social statement. At a time when racial and religious discrimination characterized many campus organizations, the El Capitan erected no such barriers to membership. Otto enjoyed relationships with students who were viewed as unacceptable to other groups. At the same time, the club restricted membership to men. There is often a fine balance to prejudice that makes aspects of it harder to recognize.

It was in college, Otto (1965) wrote, that he was first introduced to people troubled enough to be hospitalized. He described taking a class in abnormal psychology that had a component of what might be referred to as "experiential learning." Periodically, the class would meet at a nearby psychiatric institution (probably still known as an asylum). Along with his classmates, he observed patients demonstrating psychiatric pathology such as *cerea flexibilitas* (what is now termed "catatonia" or "waxen flexibility"), "command negativism" (resistance to the instructions, expectations, or expressed wishes of others) and delusions (what he also terms "false beliefs"). He described a collection of objects with which deceased patients had mutilated themselves — both externally and internally. Anxiety, bewilderment, and embarrassment interfered in his learning. "I felt a loneliness and shame and hoped that I should never have the ill fortune to succumb to the disease dementia praecox [schizophrenia], or in any way become a psychiatric patient" (p. 5).

Those patients diagnosed with dementia praecox were particularly anxiety-provoking to Otto. This diagnosis was to many a sort of "living death" and one that could not be transcended; those patients were quickly transferred to crowded "chronic wards" in state hospitals.

Besides academics and extracurricular involvement, Otto (2021) also wrote about a young woman he dated during his first two years in college. She stimulated his thinking about interpersonal dynamics. He described her as an attractive redhead who was intelligent and socially sophisticated. The couple shared some common interests and enjoyed each other's company. He described complimenting her often for the many traits he admired in her. However, he noted that, during one such instance, she stopped him with a tone that suggested something like irritation and sadness, and asserted that he did not know her, and did not *want* to *really* know her. He wrote that this conversation ended their relationship, though, he took her rebuke seriously and considered their interactions. Ultimately, he confirmed, at least to himself, that she was "a stranger" to him.

At some point, then or later, he connected this experience with his mother. He (2021) remembered that, when he was a preadolescent, "there appeared a blackness in her" (p. 4). He found instances demonstrating her withdrawal of care from him "intolerable" and did not recognize them as being part of "his mother." He recognized that she probably did not perceive him as he was either and referred to something Harry Stack Sullivan suggested about his relationship with his mother — that he was simply a receptacle for her projections.

By 1930, probably after Otto's return to Stanford, his parents left the house he grew up in for Number 6 Winfield Street. It was a one-bedroom, ranch style house in the Broadmoor Park area of Colorado Springs. Was this merely downsizing, or a closing of space available to Otto or both? Such decisions are usually complex with multiple, sometimes contradictory, motivations.

Otto continued his pursuit of the highest marks with obsessive scrupulosity until his senior year when he remembered questioning his motivation for doing so. "[During] my last quarter at Stanford, I said I didn't want any more As or A-pluses." He shared recalling a desire to be "like the other folk, so I deliberately got a C." Many years later, in October 1975, he wrote to Patrick, who was beginning his undergraduate studies at the University of Chicago, and suggested that he avoid the compulsive pursuit of what the university might deem appropriate:

> I recall that years ago I found at Stanford none of the personal, intimate qualities that I knew before I went there. There is a driving hard and often seemingly cold quality to some university work; sometimes I think they go too far in that direction.

He also encouraged his son to avoid a preoccupation with grades: "Do not concern yourself with trying to get the highest grades; you don't have to please us in that regard; simply try to take advantage of the excellent program with which you are presented" (O. Will, personal communication, October 29, 1975).

At some point during his undergraduate experience, Otto began to consider medical school. The exact time at which he decided to pursue a medical education is unclear and it was probably, like most major life decisions, a gradual process. Perhaps it was a culmination of his interactions with physicians earlier in his life. He remembered a physician from his childhood in Roswell, New Mexico named McClane. Between roughly 1912–1918, there were two physicians in Roswell named McClane — a father (Thomas) and son (Jean Edward). Both were general practitioners ("Wabash Native dies in Southwest," 1925). Either could have been the source of Otto's memories. In any event, Otto remembered making rounds with Dr. McClane in his horse and buggy. He remained in the buggy while the physician attended to the patient in her home. Otto also remembered fondly that when rounds were over and the horse was put away in the barn, he would reach into the barrel of bran (there for the horses) and eat a handful.

Otto also remembered Dr. Charles Giese in Colorado Springs. He was the Will's family practitioner and medical director at the Modern Woodmen of America Sanitorium (Obituaries, 1957). Though Otto was disappointed that Giese did not motivate his father to expand his identity beyond that of a TB "invalid," he admired him. He recalled:

> I remember he'd come in — he was kind of a portly man — … [with] a little black bag. And Mother would make coffee and get cookies or something for him. He called her Florence, and he would sit in the kitchen and talk with Florence; he'd see my father. He always said, "Aw, you'll be alright." He was quite a nice figure to model yourself after. He always seemed to be in control of everything.

He also recalled sitting with Dr. Giese in his office when Giese said, "I want you to see that [his] desk." Giese continued, "$30,000 a year passes over this desk." According to MeasuringWorth.com (2025), $30,000 in 1930, the year Otto began at Stanford, is roughly equivalent to $2,000,000 in today's dollars. As the Great Depression deepened, the aspiration for this kind of income may have motivated Otto to seriously consider medical school.

The primary motivation for his interest in medicine, however, seems to have been a mixture of a yearning for power and altruism. He (1987a) noted that doctors were "both powerful and good" (p. 242).

# Chapter Seven: Less than Human

Otto graduated from Stanford in 1933 with an *Artium Baccalaureus* degree (A.B., the traditional degree for Ivy League schools), *Magna Cum Laude* ("with Great Distinction") ("155 Pass State Test for Medical Licenses," 1940). His degree represented concentrations in both economics and sociology. After his graduation, he returned to Colorado Springs. He had decided to pursue a medical education but needed some time at "home."

During this period, he took a position in the auditing department of General Mills. Otto recalled interviewing for the position. The interviewer told him that there might be an opening in accounting. Otto told him that he knew very little about accounting — "I'd just had one course in college." He had his Phi Beta Kappa key on, and the interviewer pointed to it and said, "You can learn." A job was offered, and Otto accepted it.

He recalled feeling surprised that he was given a desk — and more surprised that "it was piled with papers." The office manager said, "Look in the left-hand side of the desk; there's a bunch of stuff from the federal government about reports we've got to make. On the right-hand side of the desk is a lot of stuff about the milling industry. Supposing you make out that report." He found the job "very challenging" and General Mills "a good place to work." His supervisor, the senior auditor, wanted Otto to be more confident. Apparently, after watching Otto move from his desk to the water fountain, he called the young man into his office. According to Otto, he said, "Look when you get up from your desk and go to get a drink, I want you to walk over there like you own this place." The senior auditor encouraged him to save money for his return to school but was taken aback by the small amount Otto tipped the server after a meal. "You should be saving up your money," he told Otto but [if] you keep leaving tips like that, you'll [find] some strange things in your soup." Otto, reflecting further on this, said: "Wisdom comes in many forms. It makes me think of the person who consulted a very wise person, and [asked] 'O Wise One, what is the secret of life?' The Wise One said, 'Tip high.' So, [I began] to tip a lot." According to his son, the habit of generous tipping stayed with Otto through the rest of his life, sometimes to the astonishment and exasperation of his family (P. Will, personal communication, May 29, 2025). Though he enjoyed this job, it required a great deal of travel which Otto did not enjoy. Medical school also beckoned, so he returned to Stanford.

As he contemplated becoming a physician, he developed an interest in psychiatry. He recalled this as primarily a result of curiosity about the nature of his family (Will, 1987a). He began reading Freud. In his hand annotated copy of Freud's 1933 *New Introductory Lectures on Psycho-Analysis* (translated by Sprott), he noted on the book's first blank page Freud's contention that, "life; it is not worth much, but it is all that we have."

Otto began at Stanford Medical School in 1936. Founded as the Medical Department of the University of the Pacific in 1858, it was, at that time located in San Francisco. In 1882, it became Cooper Medical College, named in honor of Dr. Samuel Elias Cooper, founder of the Medical Department. The first professor of surgery at the new school was Dr. Levi Cooper Lane (Elias Cooper's nephew) (Rytand, 1984).

Lane expanded the physical size of the school, as well as its educational opportunities. Between 1893 and 1894 Lane and his wife funded and oversaw construction of a new 200-bed hospital adjacent to the Cooper School of Medicine. Lane Hospital opened as a teaching hospital in 1895. The Lane family would continue to enlarge the school and hospital until Levi Cooper Lane's death in 1902. Lane had begun to realize that a medical school would have important advantages if it was part of a university; after his death the Cooper Medical College board of directors began to explore the possibility of bringing this about. In 1908, they made the decision to gift all the school's property to Stanford; the final class of the Cooper Medical School graduated in 1912. The Lane Hospital became Stanford-Lane Hospital. It remained in San Francisco as the Stanford University Medical School until 1959, long after Otto's graduation, when it was moved to Palo Alto, California (Wilson, 1999).

## Otto's Smile

Otto was very successful in medical school, but he had to overcome two obstacles to do so. The first was apparently an appetite for adventure, and the second was giving up an interest in psychiatry.

In July 1936, about the time that Otto entered medical school, the Spanish Civil War began when a group of Spanish army officers launched a coup against the democratically elected government of Spain. The rebels objected to the Republic's attempts to secularize Spanish society and break the traditional political power of the Catholic Church. Called the *alzamiento* (insurrection) by the rebels, it was led by 44-year-old Francisco Franco, the youngest general in the Spanish army (Ranzato, 1999).

A similar set of events had taken place in Mexico in 1862 when Benito Juarez, the duly elected president of the Republic of Mexico, had introduced land reforms (particularly redistribution of church lands) and measures to secularize Mexican society. Reactionaries rebelled and unsuccessfully attempted to overthrow Juarez's government.

The fascist countries of Europe — Germany and Italy — saw in Franco a potential fascist ally and supported his rebellion, first logistically and then with their own combat troops. Ultimately, the fascist dictators Adolf Hitler and Benito Mussolini sent 100,000 troops to Spain. Ironically, Mussolini's given name, Benito, was meant to honor Benito Juarez (Bosworth, 2002).

The Western democracies remained neutral in the conflict. The Soviet Union, however, did not. In addition to arms and equipment sent by the Soviet state, 2,000 soviet citizens took up arms in Spain. The Communist International Association of National Communist Parties (Comintern) was well positioned to recruit volunteers for duty in Spain. The Comintern organized seven international brigades, broadly encompassing volunteers from various regions and countries. About 4,000 American volunteers formed the Abraham Lincoln Brigade, though many of these volunteers had neither military training, nor combat experience (Hobsbawm, 2001; Ranzato, 1999).

Leftist intellectuals and students were particularly drawn to support the republic. Eric Hobsbawm (2001) remembered that, as an English college student with a commitment to leftist ideas, he experienced pressure to go to Spain and fight. Otto was becoming interested in politics, though there is no evidence that he had any involvement with the Communist Party. Indeed, he registered as a Republican in California in 1936 (California Voter Registrations, Santa Clara County, 1936). However, as reflected in the name adopted by the American brigade, an affiliation with the Republican Party did not mean then what it has come to mean in recent decades. It certainly did not mean what it means in 2025. Otto developed a deep appreciation of writers while at the Cheyenne Mountain School. He may have been influenced by the writers, particularly poets, who joined the republican forces. These included W.H. Auden, Rupert John Cornford, Miguel Hernández, Federico Garcia Lorca, Pablo Neruda, Edwin Rolfe (who came to be known as "the poet laureate of the Abraham Lincoln Battalion"), and Tristan Tsara (Cunningham, 1980). For whatever reason, Otto wanted to volunteer in Spain. He remembered planning to interrupt his medical studies and join the Spanish Republican Army. Since he had not completed his medical degree, it is doubtful that he could have been other than a combat medic, or driven an ambulance like Auden; perhaps, however, he had a romantic vision of what combat would be — many young men had such visions, only to return disillusioned (Mendelson, 2017). Although an overwhelming majority of Americans wanted to see the fascist rebels defeated, conservative members in the institutions of the United States feared the advance of communism (Hobsbawm, 2001; Payne, 2008).

Among the conservative element at Stanford was Dr. Arthur L. Bloomfield, a distinguished medical faculty member (Rytand, Cox, & Hilgard, 1962). When he learned of Otto's plans, he approached the young man with an authoritative directness. Otto remembered Bloomfield saying, "If you do … [go to Spain], I'll see that you're never able to practice in the United States." Otto remained in the United States and in medical school. Despite this interaction, Otto and Bloomfield grew to respect and hold each other in some esteem. Otto remembered that, on December 7, 1941, the day Japan attacked Pearl Harbor, he was on rounds with Bloomfield. A nurse heard news of the attack on the radio and informed the staff. Otto recalled a tender exchange: "Dr. Bloomfield said to me, 'I suppose this means I'll be losing you.' I said, 'Yes' and he said, 'What will I do without Otto and his smile?'"

## Horrified and Enthralled

The second obstacle Otto faced was an interest in treating the psychologically distressed. This resurfaced in medical school, but psychiatry was looked down on at Stanford (Will, 1987a, 1989b). In addition to a lack of collegial support for pursuing a psychiatric career, he viewed the treatments in vogue at the time with disgust and shame. Psychiatry in the United States of the 1930s was largely concerned with physiological explanations for mental illness and its treatment. Psychotic people were viewed as less than human and treated accordingly (Will, 1965, 1987a, 1989b). Yet, Otto (1965) wrote that he could see aspects of these people in himself, "and at this [he] felt horrified and enthralled" (p. 5). Treatments advocated included surgery to remove so-called "septic" parts of the body (e.g., teeth, tonsils, areas of the bowel, and colons to name a few) believed to be causing aberrant behavior.

Of the search for so-called "focal sepsis" there was a grim example in the work of Henry Cotton, superintendent of the Trenton State Hospital in New Jersey from 1907 until 1930. Cotton studied under Adolf Meyer, a Swiss immigrant named the first professor of psychiatry in the United States at the prestigious Johns Hopkins Medical School. Meyer would soon come to be known as the "Dean of American Psychiatry" and his theories, subsumed under the title of psychobiology, were considered cutting edge and pragmatic (Lamb, 2014). Psychobiology broke with the traditional emphasis of the era on categorizing psychological dysfunction in discreet "disease" entities. Instead, psychobiology approached psychiatric symptoms as failed attempts at adjustment. With the advent of Meyer's psychobiology, there was an opportunity to move beyond the popular representation of psychotics as "degenerates and defectives, tainted creatures whose blighted minds were but a reflection of their hopeless heredity" (Scull, 2005a, p. 21).

While psychobiology embraced multiple treatment approaches, including a form of psychotherapy, many psychiatrists who were searching for a "scientific" basis for their work, focused on its physiological components. In addition to his study with Meyer, Henry Cotton had studied with such notables as Emil Kraepelin and Alois Alzheimer in Germany. Influenced by their research on the biological bases of mental illness, Cotton ensconced biological intervention as the bedrock of treatment at the Trenton State Hospital (Scull, 2005a). Initially suspecting teeth and tonsils as primary culprits in the development of mental illness, Cotton later suspected ovaries, testicles, tracts of intestines, and the colon, and he would remove all, with or without consent, in the pursuit of cure (Jones, 2005; Scull, 2005a).

These surgeries had a high mortality rate — when colons were resected, more patients died than improved. As the staff became more experienced in colon resections, Cotton claimed that mortality dropped to 30 percent, but improvement also dropped to 15 percent (Scull, 2005a). Though patients who survived such surgeries were maimed for life, many of the physicians involved felt like "*real* doctors" (Scull, 2005a, p. 25, italics in the original). Cotton's results were occasionally presented to professional groups (in the best light possible) but they were more often suppressed. With the support of Meyer, Cotton continued these surgeries until 1930 when, suffering symptoms of psychiatric disorder himself, he was forced to retire from the hospital (Scull, 2005a).

Otto (1965) wrote that he felt pressure — both internal and external — in medical school to act — *to be a doctor*. When exposed to patients considered mentally disordered, he focused his actions, however, on history-taking and diagnosis. "With the completion of history and diagnosis, I often felt lost; the patient and I were then alone, in awkward silence and mutual apprehension" (p. 6). If the patient was diagnosed with dementia praecox, she was quickly transferred to a state hospital — the consensus being that nothing further could be done.

It may be difficult to believe that there was a time in the United States that Sigmund Freud's theories were rejected out of hand in psychiatry. Yet, Otto's time in medical school was such an era. Though, as noted above, Otto read Freud (with it seems only a modicum of satisfaction), many medical schools did not endorse Freudian ideas. This was perhaps a response to the deeply ambivalent stance taken by psychiatrists like

Adolf Meyer toward Freud. Meyer was attempting to institutionalize his psychobiology as psychiatry's primary theoretical foundation, and his ideas dominated psychiatric education (Will, 1946). Meyer's most promising students were quickly filling the newly developing departments of psychiatry, and many chaired these departments (Lamb, 2014, 2015). Otto (1946) expressed ambivalence about psychobiology in an early paper. He seemed to find the element of "common sense" suggested within its application refreshing but also noted a superficiality to which it was vulnerable in this regard (see Lamb, 2015 and Marx, 1993 for further discussion of this "common sense" element). Further, he criticized its lack of a comprehensive theory of personality development.

Generally, though somewhat obliquely, Otto (1946) criticized the exposure he got to psychiatry in medical school and in his residencies as "lip service" paid to individual therapy. At the same time Otto was becoming increasingly disenchanted with psychiatry in medical school, another psychiatric perspective was forming that would later resonate. During the 1930s Harry Stack Sullivan was articulating his ideas about interpersonal relations as the fundament of psychiatry and by 1940 had published *Conceptions of Modern Psychiatry*, which quickly went through several printings. Sullivan's personal idiosyncrasies and refusal to advance his ideas through professional political avenues, however, hindered the widespread dissemination and acceptance of them. Before Otto became aware of Sullivan's writings, he had given up his interest in psychiatry to pursue the field of internal medicine. This was considered "real" medicine at Stanford.

Sometime in the 1930s, Otto met and married Adeline Emma Rowe, a dark-haired beauty two years his senior. Adeline was born on February 12, 1908, in Great Falls, Montana, to James and Ida Cecelia Rowe (neé Rhein) (U.S. Census Bureau, 1920a). She was the third of four children born to the couple, with an older brother, Clarence, four years her senior and sister, Dorothy, two years her senior. She also had a younger sister, Evelyn, who was three years her junior (U.S. Census Bureau, 1920a). She was educated through high school in Great Falls.

On November 28, 1930, Adeline married Stuard (known as Samuel) Zirkle; both were 22 ("Marriage License," 1930). Samuel Zirkle worked in the construction industry in Montana. As a result of the depression, he lost his job. Very soon after their marriage, Samuel and Adeline relocated to San Francisco where he found a job. According to Rowe family lore, Adeline was pregnant and had an abortion. Abortions were illegal in both Montana and California in 1930, and in California having any part in an abortion was a felony. However, abortions were available for the right price and could be contracted secretly.

Settling near San Francisco, Adeline took a position as a secretary, and Samuel Zirkle began work driving heavy equipment on a site on Government Island, now known as Coast Guard Island. On Friday, November 6, 1931, he was driving an earthmover, which turned over, and he was killed three weeks short of the couple's first wedding anniversary ("Funeral Services for Stuard Zirkle," 1931).

I could discover nothing about how Otto and Adeline met; they were married on September 2, 1937. Otto was 27 and Adeline 29 (U.S. Census Bureau, 1940). They lived in a one-bedroom, one-bath apartment at 2339 California Street in the Pacific Heights neighborhood, one of the most desirable neighborhoods in San Franciso. The view from Pacific Heights included the bay, the Golden Gate Bridge, the Palace of Fine Arts, and Alcatraz (which at that time housed Al Capone and former Public Enemy Number One, Alvin "Creepy" Karpis). Otto was in his second year of medical school, and Adeline continued her work as a secretary. Little is known about the nature of their marriage, though family lore suggests that Samuel Zirkle had been the love of Adeline's life.

Otto graduated from medical school in 1940. According to *The San Francisco Examiner*, he sat for the California State Medical Board Examinations in June of that year. He received a score of 92, the highest of the 155 who passed that exam ("155 Pass State Test for Medical Licenses," 1940).

The next steps in Otto's medical training were residencies. He completed two at the Stanford-Lane Hospital in San Francisco — one in pediatrics and the other in internal medicine. By the time he completed these residencies, the world was aflame.

# Chapter Eight:
# You're Not Going to See Any Combat ...

## *Hakkō ichiu*

In 1941, the Nazis had been in power for eight years in Germany. Hitler had attacked Poland two years before and in September 1939 the Second World War in Europe had begun. Hitler was seeking *lebensraum* ("living space") for the German people, and, after defeating France in 1940, he was looking toward the east, preparing for "Operation Barbarossa," the invasion of the Soviet Union (Toland, 1992).

Hitler's ally, Japan, had become both highly militaristic and nationalistic and had gone to war with China in 1937. Hitler believed that the Aryan people, particularly the Germans, were the "Master Race." There were those in Japan — including Prime Minister, Hideki Tojo — who believed that the Japanese people were superior to all others (Mutsu, 1993). Japan was aggressively pursuing a political-spiritual belief that the world should be under the dominion of her empire, expressed by the slogan *Hakkō ichiu* ("All the world under one roof"). Though the war between Japan and China had been going on for three years and the Japanese had created a puppet state, Manchukuo, in Manchuria, the West had taken no real action. By 1940, however, it became increasingly obvious that Japan had designs on The Dutch East Indies, British Malaya, and French Indochina. Each of these European colonies had the raw materials needed to expand the war across the Pacific. Franklin Delano Roosevelt, president of the United States, launched embargos against Japan on aviation fuel, and scrap metal and provided China with $100 million in assistance. A collision between Japan and the United States was coming and it arrived on December 7, 1941, at the U.S. naval base at Pearl Harbor in Hawaii (Hoyt, 1993; Smith, 2007).

According to Otto, he enlisted in the navy on December 8, 1941, though he was, according to U.S. Navy records not called up until May 2, 1942 (after completion of his residency in internal medicine) (U.S. Navy and Marine Corps, 1944). His daughter, Deirdre, told me that he often talked fondly about his time in the service (personal communication, January 8, 2011), and Beulah Parker (1987) noted this, as well. Additionally, this period was prominent in his conversations with Kim Chernin. Perhaps this was a period during which he felt a sense of belonging.

Otto was 32 and, naturally enough, assigned to the Medical Corps. However, he recalled his initial months in the navy as chaotic. He recalled reporting for duty at the Norfolk Navy yard in Portsmouth, Virginia. He was told that he would be assigned to the cardiology service of the Mare Island Hospital, a center for innovation in naval medicine near San Francisco. However, before he could leave, he received a supervening order directing him to Bethesda Naval Hospital for a training course in tropical diseases. When he arrived in Bethesda, he discovered that the course he was to attend had already taken place. He then received orders to join the crew of the U.S.S. *Stringham*, a destroyer, as the medical officer. Initially, though, it was not clear where the ship was. A little bewildered, Otto asked around and was ultimately directed back to the Norfolk Naval Yard. He returned to Norfolk, but the *Stringham* was not there, so he took a room. The *Stringham* docked about a week later.

As a young man, having newly completed his residencies — neither in surgery — Otto felt anxious and apprehensive about assuming the role of medical officer on a combat vessel. He described searching out the commander of medical personnel on the base. When he found the commander, who was a captain, Otto was apparently too casual and received a dressing down for not standing at attention. Otto explained that he had no surgical training or experience and asked to be assigned to a larger vessel (e.g., a cruiser or carrier) on which he could assist a senior officer with his medical duties.

> He remembered the captain asking, "Doctor, do you have a medical degree?"
>
> Otto affirmed that he did.
>
> "You're not going to see any combat. If you do, then send your patients to a hospital. I hope you have a nice trip."

Courtesy of Patrick Will

Lieutenant Commander Otto Will
1942

The years he served in the U.S. Navy were important to Otto as a period of acceptance and the development of self-esteem.

With that, the discussion was over. Recounting this interaction later, he asserted, "It's the best thing that ever happened to me!" It apparently ended his vacillation about his qualifications, he had to go and do his best since there was no other option. Additionally, with the advantage of hindsight, he recognized that a posting to a larger ship would have increased the danger of his becoming a casualty.

His next steps were to go to a medical bookstore at the naval yard and to look up surgeons stationed there. He approached one surgeon: "I've got to go to sea, and I need some surgical books — will you sell me some of yours?" The older man obliged the young doctor. "So, I took his books, and I read them." Thus armed, Otto assumed his post as medical officer aboard the U.S.S. *Stringham*.

## Guadalcanal

The U.S.S. *Stringham* was a Wickes-class destroyer, assigned the hull number "DD 83." Hull numbers, unique to each ship, make identification easier. The *Stringham* was built during the First World War and assigned to convoy escort and antisubmarine duties in the Atlantic. With the end of that war, she had been decommissioned in 1922, though not scrapped (Clark, 2003).

In 1940, the *Stringham* was rehabilitated and recommissioned at Norfolk. She was designated an APD (Auxiliary Personnel Destroyer) and refitted with the space and equipment required to carry landing craft (and marines). Painted a mottled green for camouflage, the *Stringham* and other such refitted destroyers were called "Green Dragons." Their primary function was to convey troops to destinations for amphibious landings and supply them after landing (Clark, 2003). Like all destroyers, the *Stringham* was also known as a "tin can" to other sailors because of her light armor (Hornfischer, 2005).

The U.S.S. *Stringham* was obsolete with respect to her medical facilities. She had no designated sick bay, nor even an operating table. Otto recalled that there was no anesthesia on board because ether was flammable and chloroform could result in liver disease when administered in tropical climates. She carried no antibiotics. The ship's pharmacist's mate, who assisted Otto with surgery, bartered for antibiotics with land-based hospitals. What Otto remembered having in abundant supply was sulfa and morphine. He used them.

Initially, the *Stringham* was assigned to convoy duty, escorting ships along the Eastern Seaboard to the Panama Canal. She was quickly in the thick of battle, pursuing a submarine. Though the crew was certain that the submarine had sunk under a barrage of depth charges, this was never confirmed. During her first run, Otto recalled the captain received sealed orders and then said to Otto, "I want you to be prepared for any medical emergency." The orders were duly opened, and the *Stringham* was directed to the Solomon Islands. Along the way, the *Stringham* docked in Bora Bora, part of the French Society Islands. Otto and the pharmacist's mate took the opportunity to go ashore where an American hospital had just been built. Otto recalled getting drunk with the hospital commander who gave him the antibiotics he needed and plaster for casts, but anesthetics were not included. The *Stringham* proceeded to Guadalcanal to join "Operation Watchtower" — the first offensive operation by the American Navy against the Japanese Empire (Hornfischer, 2011). Ultimately, because both Japan and the United States had to keep their forces on Guadalcanal supplied by sea, "the struggle for Guadalcanal was to a great extent the battle of the high-speed transport" ("USS *Stringham* DD-83 Ship History," 2016).

Located in the Solomon Island chain, Guadalcanal, code-named "cactus," by the Allied forces, is 3,600 miles from Pearl Harbor. It became a combat theater after the Japanese built an airstrip there which threatened supply ships bound for Australia. On August 7, 1942, sixteen thousand marines landed on the island to dislodge the Japanese. Included among these marines was Captain James Roosevelt II, the son of President Franklin and First Lady Eleanor Roosevelt. James Roosevelt won the Navy Cross at Guadalcanal. Another marine hitting the beaches at Guadalcanal was Lieutenant Colonel Lewis "Chesty" Puller, the most decorated marine in the history of that service (Hoffman, 2002).

APD destroyers like the *Stringham* were faster than traditional landing craft; they ferried the marines onto the island and were then responsible for supplying them once a beachhead was established. Much has been written about the battles that took place ashore, but Guadalcanal was also the scene of seven naval battles between August 9 and November 30, 1942. A total of fourteen destroyers were lost, and total human losses from these battles included 5,041 sailors. James Hornfischer (2011) asserts that "almost three sailors had died in battle at sea for every infantryman who fell ashore" (p. xix).

Otto described being embroiled in combat, probably at the Battle of Savo Island, which occurred on August 9, 1942, and was a defeat for American naval forces. A few days later, he stood on the bridge with the captain when the *Stringham* came under attack by Imperial Japanese Navy cruisers. Salvos were fired back and forth for a few minutes, but the *Stringham* was no match for a cruiser (much less several). She could use her superior speed to evade the enemy but that did not keep the Japanese forces from firing upon her. Otto told his son, Patrick, that during this fight a ship in the *Stringham's* formation took a direct hit by a Japanese shell. This hit was deadly because it tore through her magazine and the vessel exploded (personal communication, May 29, 2025). With Kim Chernin, Otto vividly recalled that the captain turned to him, and said, "Doc, just like Hollywood, huh?"

The next day Otto and the rest of the crew searched for survivors and recovered bodies from the water. Such rescue efforts were not without danger. Otto and a few crew members in a skiff maneuvered between human bodies, searching first for survivors. When that search was exhausted, they pulled corpses out of the water. Otto recalled that recovering both survivors and corpses required him to lean out of the skiff, while a sailor held his ankles. More than once, he had to struggle with one of the ubiquitous sharks in those waters that had attacked the body. Patrick Will remembered that Otto would not take him to the motion picture *Jaws* because of his memories of such experiences (personal communication, May 29, 2025).

Even some who were still alive were wounded so badly that they did not survive. Otto felt intense grief when that occurred. Of the seven or so that Otto pulled from the sea, only one was alive. The captain ordered the corpses to be placed on the fantail and covered with canvas. A Japanese bomber appeared, and the captain realized that the white canvas would mark the ship as a target; he ordered the bodies thrown overboard.

On August 23, the *Stringham* was attacked by a Japanese submarine. The submarine fired a torpedo that nearly struck her, and the *Stringham* went on the attack. In classic combat between a destroyer and submarine, the *Stringham* dropped eleven depth charges and forced the submarine to the surface. However, the destroyer then lost contact, and the submarine lived to fight another day ("USS *Stringham* DD-83 Ship History," 2016).

## We Worked as Fast as We Could

Otto described the conditions under which he worked. He had no operating table, and, with the help of the pharmacist's mate, lashed two typewriter tables together and fastened them to a wall (leaving him only one side from which to operate). There was still no anesthetic, so Otto gave the wounded men large doses of morphine. This would sedate them briefly, and he would operate as quickly as he could.

Among the other equipment he lacked were surgical gloves, which rotted in the tropical heat and humidity, gowns, and masks. Often, he operated bare to the waist. The sailors who had been in the ocean and the marines who were transported to the *Stringham* were filthy, sometimes incontinent, and needed to be washed to lessen the danger of infection. Otto related: "We bathed them, put them on the goddamned table, gave them intravenous morphine, [and] worked as fast as we could."

Otto remembered his most desperate case — a marine artillery spotter who had been hit by shrapnel after making an inaccurate calculation. "The right side of his chest was opened up — not much I could do but pack it." He was transported to Espiritu Santo, approximately 630 miles southeast of Guadalcanal, the largest base in the area. Otto remembered a conversation between them that occurred when they arrived:

> "Well, you'll be going back to the States; what are you going to do when you get back there?" Otto asked.
>
> "I'm going to gunnery school," the marine replied.
>
> "I think that's a damned good idea."

Otto met the marines under other circumstances, as well. He remembered the *Stringham* being stationed off Guadalcanal. A Japanese plane was shot down by another vessel and crashed near the *Stringham*. The crew fished the pilot out of the drink. He was frightened, wet, and cold. A *Stringham* crew member dried him off and got him fresh clothes. A small boat from Guadalcanal pulled alongside with a marine captain in it. He took the pilot prisoner. As Otto recalled it, the pilot was lowered into the boat; he stumbled and bumped into the marine captain. "The captain pulled his pistol and hit the man [the Japanese pilot] on the side of the head with the pistol. I was shocked and thought it was a lousy thing." He remembered turning to his pharmacist's mate and commenting, "It's terrible!" The pharmacist's mate responded: "Well, you see, if a marine can't eat something, fuck it, or kill it he doesn't know what to do with it." He continued, "Sailors are different — sailors got to deal with the sea. [We] haven't got time to hate." Though Otto knew differently, he thought about what the young man said. "Once at sea awhile, you know it's pretty big, [and] you aren't so big. You're surely not in control of the sea — can't have any illusion there." The young man who sought control through being a doctor could give up that illusion, as well.

The majority of the wounds that Otto remembered treating were those to limbs. His guide to treating these was a book written by Josep Trueta, the chief surgeon in Barcelona for the Republican forces during the Spanish Civil War. Otto called *The Principles and Practice of War Surgery* (1943) his "little bible." He described the procedure he followed: "[We] opened the wound, debrided it, leaving only the flesh that had good circulation [and] laying the bones in line. [We would] put sulfa on and then wrap it in Vaseline [coated] gauze." He related that he followed up with as many of the men he treated as he could, and he found none had lost a treated limb.

Ultimately, the fleet command ordered destroyers to be outfitted with a sick bay. The space came from an area just behind the bridge — a previous adjunct to the mess facilities. The machinists even installed a more practical, though hardly ideal, operating table.

While serving on the *Stringham*, 32-year-old Otto displayed leadership qualities. For example, his ability to lead appeared in an incident involving the captain of the *Stringham*.

It is not clear how many captains the U.S.S. *Stringham* had during the time that Otto was assigned to her. However, one had a place in his memory primarily for his incompetence. He was involved in at least two collisions with other ships, each one serious enough that the *Stringham* had to put in to dock for repairs. According to Otto, during the second collision, the captain of the other vessel shouted at the *Stringham's* captain, "Why don't you go back to Montana and herd sheep — that's what you ought to do!"

The captain continued to make serious errors of judgement, and the crew became concerned. If his navigation skills could not be trusted in safe sea lanes, what would it be like in combat conditions? Otto recalled, "One of the petty officers came to me once, and he said he wanted to tell me that they [members of the crew] were going to kill the captain." He told Otto that the crew was planning to throw the captain overboard one night. Noting the darkness and omnipresent sharks, the petty officer said, "Nobody'll find him." Otto argued with the petty officer, but ultimately, "thought they might kill this guy." Otto, probably unsure what to do, was given a way out.

Orders came in for the *Stringham* to return to Guadalcanal, after which the captain became ill. Otto saw his opportunity. He diagnosed the captain with pneumonia and asked him to go ashore for treatment. He recalled the captain's irritated response: "I'm going [on the mission] — I'm *the* captain!" It is not clear whether Otto arranged for the battle group's commodore to inspect the ship or whether it was by chance (probably the former). The discussion arose again in the presence of the commodore who brought it to an immediate resolution. Otto recalled the commodore saying to the captain, "You *are* the captain. I want to introduce you to the medical officer — *in medical matters, he has the word.*" The *Stringham* returned to Guadalcanal with another captain. However, the former captain apparently wanted the *last* word. According to Otto, the former captain, exacting a measure of revenge, gave him a poor fitness report.

Otto's time in the navy saw him develop from an anxious and harried young man to one with confidence. "I learned I could do things that I thought I couldn't do."

## Guadalcanal Neurosis

Battle fatigue has existed since the advent of war, though it has gone by many names. During the civil war, it was called "Nostalgia" as physicians thought it was primarily caused by homesickness and the memory of better times. It was also known as "Soldier's Heart" and "Da Costa's Syndrome" for Dr. Jacob Mendes Da Costa, who first documented the syndrome (Schultz, 2025). During the First World War, the syndrome was called "Shell Shock," and "Old Sergeant's Disease" (Decuers, 2020). Soldiers suffering from symptoms of the disorder seldom received treatment.

In early 1943, it was observed that marines having seen prolonged combat on Guadalcanal were returning with "neurotic" symptoms. In *Time* magazine ("Medicine: Guadalcanal Neurosis," 1943) Lt. Commander Edwin R. Smith, stationed at the Mare Island Naval Hospital, described what he believed to be a new phenomenon. His remarks were based on his work with 500 marines who had seen combat on Guadalcanal before facing an acute psychiatric crisis and being transferred to his care. Symptoms included weight loss, tremors, generalized anxiety, insomnia, rage, and an overreaction to loud noises. After a regime of rest and emotional support, only about 30 percent could be returned to combat duty. The American Psychiatric Association (APA) responded by calling this combination of symptoms "Guadalcanal Disorder" (Schultz, 2025). Yet, nomenclature was not enough — the statistics pointed to an emergency. Over 500,000 sailors, marines, army infantrymen, and pilots faced a psychiatric collapse during combat; 40 percent of medically related discharges were based on psychiatric disorders (Decuers, 2020). The number of men discharged for such disorders was the equivalent of fifty divisions lost to the nation's war effort (Schultz, 2025). Menninger Clinic research suggested that by early 1945, one thousand service members were discharged each day for combat-related psychological trauma (Friedman, 1990).

An Army neurologist, Captain Frederick Hanson, devised a treatment protocol. During their first hospitalization for "Combat Fatigue," a diagnosis replacing "Guadalcanal Disorder," patients were given Sodium Amytal and slept for up to forty-eight hours. When they emerged from sleep, they showered, were given a hot meal, a clean uniform, and returned to the front. The success rate was between 50 and 70 percent, the other 30 to 50 percent being transferred to a psychiatric hospital for long-term care (Decuers, 2020; Schultz, 2025).

The extent of combat fatigue stirred the military and civilian leadership into action. They needed more experts — psychiatrists — quickly. Physicians in all branches of the military were offered a crash (six week) course in psychiatry. In addition to his initial interest in psychiatry, Otto had seen enough psyches damaged by the war and expressed his interest in the training. He filled out the application and was accepted for the training course at Saint Elizabeths Hospital in Washington, DC.

# Part Two: Becoming a Psychotherapist

§

"There is currently no compelling evidence that the complex ways of man's living can be reduced to simple formulae or 'explained' in terms of unitary causes."

Otto Allen Will

# Chapter Nine: An Environment of Despair

When Otto was assigned to Saint Elizabeths Hospital in 1943, it was 88 years old, having been founded in 1855 and originally named the Government Hospital for the Insane. Its mission was to provide psychiatric care for the United States Army and Navy. This mission would ultimately extend to all branches of the armed forces and citizens of the District of Columbia. During the Civil War, however, members of the armed forces treated there resented the word "Insane" in its name. They referred to it by the land's original name, Saint Elizabeths. In 1917, Congress officially changed the hospital's name to Saint Elizabeths (leaving out the apostrophe) (Moore, 1976).

Over the years, many people have been fascinated by the inner workings of psychiatric institutions. This fascination has often been stoked by intrepid investigative journalists who have arranged for their own commitment to an asylum or psychiatric hospital to report on what occurred there. One of the first such exposés was undertaken by Julius Chambers, a reporter for the *New-York Tribune*, who arranged his own commitment to the Bloomingdale Asylum in New York in 1872 (Horn, 2019). Another such episode of investigative reporting was undertaken by Elizabeth Cochrane Seaman, writing under the name Nellie Bly, for Joseph Pulitzer's *New York World* in 1887. Her experiences at the Insane Asylum on Blackwell's Island in New York became the classic book, *Ten Days in a Mad-House* (Bly, 1887/2019). In 1894, a reporter from The *New York Herald*, Adele Porter Porre, infiltrated the facilities on Ward's Island New York (though she did so as a nurse, not a patient). The title of her resulting article, "Horrors of Bedlam," described what she found (Horn, 2019, p. 247).

The 1940s and 50s saw this fascination rekindled after the Second World War ended and America's collective danger had passed. Just after the war, a journalist refocused attention on the horrors perpetrated in American state psychiatric hospitals. Albert Maisel (1946) detailed in *Life* magazine what transpired in these hospitals. Although his expose is littered with denigration of the "conscientious objectors" (referred to as "conchies") who served their country as attendants in state hospitals, his indictment of these hospitals is extensive. Maisel catalogued the regularity of physical assaults by staff that patients endured — some dying from beatings. He noted a sad inscription on the wall of one hospital ward, known as "the dungeon;" "George was kill [sic] here in 1937." Interestingly, Maisel did note that the subtly denigrated "conchies" were less likely to engage in patient abuse and more likely to report the abuse they witnessed than other staff members. In the age of antibiotics, he reported that tuberculosis was up to thirteen times more common among patients in state hospitals than in the general American population.

Some hospitals maintained their patients on diets costing as little as $.17 *a day*. Diabetic patients received the same meals as non-diabetic patients. Fraudulent menus were developed to show the few regulatory bodies and their investigators. In some hospitals physicians and other medical personnel were found to be incompetent — in some cases psychotic and/or alcoholic. Abuse and indignities were not confined to the living. One elderly patient died and was laid out in the morgue of one hospital. Before she was given a burial service, her face was eaten by rats. Maisel (1946) quotes one unidentified governor as lamenting, "our cows in the hospital barns get better care than the men and women in the wards."

In 1951, another investigative newspaper reporter went undercover to expose conditions at the Cleveland State Hospital. Alexander (Al) Ostrow, employed by the *Cleveland Press*, did not commit himself as a patient but, instead, joined the hospital staff as an attendant. In a series of articles, Ostrow documented beatings of patients by the staff, punitive restraints, and a general atmosphere of disinterest in patient welfare (Carmosino, 2013).

In 1972, Karlyn Barker of the *Washington Post*, checked into Saint Elizabeths under an assumed name complaining of depressive symptoms.

Though not uncovering the type or extent of abuse that Seaman had on Blackwell's Island — and though it was nearly 30 years after Otto was assigned there — Barker discovered what anyone who has ever been to a psychiatric hospital has experienced, including: depression and discouragement, boredom, anxiety, and fear. The ammonia-like smell of urine was pervasive; she observed the boredom and withdrawal from the patients by the staff, which Gwen Tudor (1952) described in her research on mutual withdrawal (see Chapter Seventeen). At least one patient bullied more vulnerable patients. Interactions with staff members were shallow and infrequent, and she felt such despair that after a few days she truly feared for her sanity (Barker, 1972). Psychiatric hospitals often breed despair, and into this environment Otto entered at the age of 33.

Of course, the hospital had not begun as a place of despair but was established as a haven of hope. Like many institutions of the day, including the Sheppard and Enoch Pratt Hospital in Maryland, the Trenton State Hospital in New Jersey, and the Worcester State Hospital in Massachusetts, Saint Elizabeths was a Kirkbride Hospital.

Thomas Story Kirkbride (1809-1883), a Quaker physician and Superintendent of the Pennsylvania Hospital for the Insane, developed a plan for hospitals/asylums that included architecture as a key component of recovery (Yanni, 2007; Ziff, 2012). Kirkbride studied The York Retreat in England, a revolutionary private hospital founded by English Quakers and a center for the new idea of "moral treatment." Moral treatment's first tenet was that an asylum ought to be a place of care, not punishment. Treatment focused on high quality food, rest, the maintenance of personal hygiene, and a daily schedule. Patients were treated compassionately, talked with as reasonable, and were expected to be cured — with a return to society. Superintendents of moral treatment asylums encouraged their staff and patients to view each other as members of an extended family. Moral treatment advocates believed that such an atmosphere helped to correct any traits learned in the family that interfered with effective social functioning (Yanni, 2007).

The Kirkbride plan, sometimes called the linear plan, emphasized the use of natural light, well-crafted landscaping, and homelike interior furnishings. Kirkbride encouraged the building of asylums in the country on large tracts of land, using rock and brick (Yanni, 2007).

Shortly after the turn of the century, however, the ideals of Kirkbride and other advocates of moral therapy had been replaced by the conviction that science was the way forward. Stacy Horn (2019) notes that apostles of science dismissed physicians practicing in asylums as: "a pathetic lot — old, old-fashioned and hopelessly influenced by their Christian beliefs" (p. 61). While the novel always, at least for a time, replaces the familiar, the practitioners of the new scientific psychiatry also dismissed the central tenet of moral therapy — "if we treat patients like fellow human beings they will respond with humanity" (Horn, 2019, p. 5). It was one of the great accomplishments of Otto Will's work to remind us of that truth. However, first he faced struggle with himself about this belief.

## It Was Terrible

In 1943, as Otto began the six-week course in psychiatry at Saint Elizabeths, it must have seemed like déjà vu. Rather than a new, perspective-broadening experience, he found the treatment offered at Saint Elizabeths demoralizing. "I thought it was terrible there. It was all shock, surgery — just awful!" Aside from the compilation of histories, interactions with patients were minimal and staff members wanted to be regarded as *real physicians*. As they had been when he was in medical school, patients were treated with a quality near contempt. He again found himself unsure how to be of help to patients struggling with their humanity. He (2021) remembered that schizophrenic patients were thought to have some form of biological illness, and experimentation was done with intrathecal horse serum — "15 ccs of sterilized horse serum." He recalled that some of the psychiatrists at Saint Elizabeths believed that bacteria produced schizophrenia. The horse serum created a fever that would kill the offending agent. As this produced little change in patients' psychiatric symptoms, staff interest shifted to insulin coma therapy. Otto (1965) noted: "Now we — the staff — were less uncertain, our roles being familiar to us" (p. 6). Yet, along with the tenuous comfort of a more medically defined role, Otto (2021) described losing the human being and — seeing only "a patient."

Insulin coma therapy, also known as insulin shock therapy (IST), was discovered by Manfred J. Sakel, an Austrian psychiatrist and neuropsychiatrist. "Sakel's technique," as Sakel himself referred to it, involved inducing a hypoglycemic coma by an overdose of insulin. Though he had discovered this treatment while working with a morphine addict, Sakel believed that the same treatment could be used with psychotic disorders. In 1933, while a researcher at the University of Vienna's neuropsychiatric clinic, he began to induce insulin comas in schizophrenic patients. Patients routinely received five to six induced comas per week. His results seemed remarkable, and, through his publications, he influenced American and British psychiatrists to employ his methods. Insulin coma therapy was used widely in the 1930s and 1940s, though it had deleterious side effects, including patient dread and hyper-anxiety (Wellington, 2022).

One highly publicized failure of insulin coma therapy occurred in 1949 when Secretary of Defense, James Forrestal was hospitalized at Bethesda Naval Hospital. William C. Menninger was asked to consult and diagnosed Forrestal as suffering from severe depression. Treated by the Surgeon General, Forrestal was given IST, as well as sodium amytal for prolonged sleep. While initially seeming to improve, Forrestal ultimately leapt from the sixteenth floor of the naval hospital to his death (Hoopes & Brinkley, 1992).

After IST, came training in the use of Metrazol (Will, 1965). Metrazol (pentylenetetrazol), originally developed in Germany for respiratory illnesses, was proposed as a treatment for schizophrenia by a Hungarian psychiatrist, Ladislas von Meduna. Meduna observed that epilepsy and schizophrenia seldom occurred in the same patient. He proposed that epileptic seizures could ameliorate psychotic symptoms. His advocacy of the treatment was met with guarded optimism (Finkelman, Steinberg & Liebert, 1938).

The difficulty with Metrazol was similar to that of IST. It was not well-tolerated by patients. It was introduced into the patient's system by intravenous injection, usually between 5-10 ml. in a 10-percent diluted solution. The patient would generally experience dread within a few seconds, followed by a seizure that could last for several minutes. During this seizure the patient would experience tortuous bodily movements, often screaming. A study by Charles Read (1940) showed that patients could suffer spinal compression fractures, develop pulmonary tuberculosis, and incur myocardial damage from such seizures. The improvement rate among patients with psychotic symptoms of three years or less was 43 percent. Chronically psychotic patients showed significantly less improvement, at just over 13 percent (Read, 1940).

By most measures, the real damage done by Metrazol treatment was emotional. The feelings of dread and doom that accompanied the seizures left their mark. At least some of the patients who had undergone the treatment developed symptoms of "combat fatigue" or Post-Traumatic Stress Disorder (PTSD). Otto (2021) wrote that he remembered the patients, restrained by wet sheet packs, begging not to be given the injection that resulted in such emotional pain. He (1965) wrote that he felt "engaged blindly in a traumatic procedure that promised little" (p. 6).

Between 1903 and 1937, under the enlightened eye of its superintendent, Dr. William Alanson White, Saint Elizabeths became one of the leading research facilities in the United States. White valued the potential of psychotherapy and the value of neurological research. In 1924, White created the Blackburn Laboratory at the hospital, a two-story brick Renaissance Revival structure on the East Campus ("Blackburn Laboratory," n.d.). It was named somewhat ironically for Dr. Isaac Wright Blackburn, a pathologist who specialized in brain diseases. Blackburn performed over 2,000 autopsies on deceased Saint Elizabeths patients from 1884 until his death in 1911. During one autopsy he cut his hand with a scalpel and became ill with septicemia; he died of pancreatitis as a patient in Saint Elizabeths (Swift, 2017). With the opening of the Blackburn Laboratory, White appointed a promising 29-year-old neurologist with an impeccable medical pedigree, Walter Jackson Freeman II, as the laboratory's first director. Freeman was fascinated by the potential proposed by psychosurgery and was eager to begin it at Saint Elizabeths. White, however, would not allow it. Freeman left Saint Elizabeths in 1933 for faculty positions at both Georgetown University and George Washington University, which were receptive to the idea of psychosurgery (Caruso & Sheehan, 2017; El-Hai, 2007; Scull, 2005b).

Freeman and his surgical partner, James Watts, performed the first lobotomy in the United States in September 1936. Freeman lobbied White to allow him and Watts to perform lobotomies on patients at Saint Elizabeths. White, in unmistakable terms, informed Freeman that he would never allow Freeman to operate on his patients (El-Hai, 2007). In 1937, however, White died, and his successor, Winfred Overholser, was not as adamant in his resolve to keep lobotomies out of Saint Elizabeths. Otto described Freeman as: "very handsome, very bright — and from [his] point of view as a psychiatrist, a very frightening sort of person." Otto shared some harrowing details of Freeman's work:

> I heard that Walter did fifty [trans]orbitals [lobotomies] in one afternoon at the state hospital in West Virginia. What he would do is give the person an electric shock — knock them out — and then he would run the ice pick in above their eye and cut up the frontal lobe. Then he would step back and take a picture.

Otto vowed never to practice psychosurgery.

## ECT

Finally, Otto was introduced to electroconvulsive therapy (ECT). With fewer side-effects, Otto found ECT more acceptable. Yet, he described a morning ritual involving ECT at Saint Elizabeths as something like an inhuman production line. He remembered that, just after awakening, usually 30 or more patients would be lined up, each, in turn, receiving an ECT treatment and then taken to a room full of mattresses on which each would be laid until ready to return to their rooms.

Despite his concern about its prevalence, he co-authored two journal articles on ECT and considered himself "an expert" in its use (Will & Duval, 1947; Will, Rehfeldt, & Neumann, 1948). Later in his career he was invited to give a series of lectures at the University of Iowa.

> I'd given some lectures, and I went through their psychiatry department. They showed me the psychiatric hospital, which was very nice. I walked through a section of it, and nobody yelled at me, and when I came out the director said to me, "How do you like it?" I said, "I don't know, what's your electric bill?" I was sure all [the patients] had been shocked stupid.

Otto found his experience at Saint Elizabeths largely unsatisfying, and questioned his interest in and suitability for psychiatry. He still found the role of physician more comfortable than psychotherapist, though that would begin to change after he heard a lecture by Harry Stack Sullivan.

Before exploring the effect that Sullivan had on Otto, it is necessary to describe another source of pain that Otto experienced in 1943 — the death of his child. Otto and Adeline had a daughter in 1943 who they named Kathryn. Otto remembered that she was born with a congenital heart defect and died a few days after birth. Otto was devastated and recalled: "I remember saying at that time to myself, I didn't want to care about anything anymore." The marriage to Adeline also soon ended.

Over the past century, much has been written about the effects on parents having lost a child. Christ, et al. (2003) have pointed out that, until recently, the deaths of infants have been responded to by medical professionals as "nonevents." However, they cite studies demonstrating that grief reactions to the death of a child are more intense than those associated with the loss of a parent or spouse. Parents who lose a child are prone to the symptoms of PTSD and can experience depressive symptoms up to two years after the loss of their child.

The stresses on the bereaved parents' marriage are intense. These stresses include: guilt, one or both blaming the other for the death, decreased or dysfunctional communication, gender-based differences in styles of grieving, an inability to support each other and subsequent withdrawal (Christ, et al., 2003; Schoenberg, 2020). Despite these stresses, roughly one quarter of marriages survive the death of a child, and the pre-loss health of the marriage must be considered (Christ, et al., 2003). Patrick Will told me that he had little knowledge of his father's first marriage. "That part of my dad's life has never been a very open book." Nevertheless, "family lore" held that Kathyrn's death "was one of the reasons for the dissolution of his marriage to Adeline" (personal communication, February 26, 2011). After Adeline and Otto divorced, she did not remarry; she died in 1999.

# Chapter Ten: He Talked About People

As part of the six-week psychiatry course, Otto attended a lecture by a psychiatrist of whom he had not previously been aware — Harry Stack Sullivan. Though it is impossible to know what Otto expected, given the circumstances, it would not be surprising to infer that his expectations were low. However, Sullivan made a deep impression on him.

The lecture took place in the auditorium of the Blackburn Building. Otto remembered his first impression of Sullivan as frail. He was thin and sat in a chair behind a desk. But what he said was so different from what other instructors described: "Boy he made sense — the first real sense I had heard about psychiatry. ... he didn't talk about cases — dementia praecox and so forth — [he] talked about people." Sullivan challenged the efficacy of shock and other physiologically based treatments, emphasizing instead a form of deep, empathic listening which required patience and respect. Sullivan maintained that it was the relationship between physician and patient that produced improvement. As Sullivan (1954) often said, psychotherapy with patients was "plain hard work" (pp. 9-10).

After hearing Sullivan, Otto became increasingly conflicted about shock therapies as the primary treatment for hospitalized patients. He became acquainted with Frieda Fromm-Reichmann in a similar way, first hearing her present a lecture on "Assets of the Mentally Handicapped." Later he (1989b) noted that, like Sullivan, she "made sense to me, giving me both relief and encouragement to look at my work in a different way" (p. 131).

Though I am once again speculating, there is some evidence to suggest that Otto approached Sullivan after his lecture. Otto recalled that Sullivan told him, "I think you'd better go on with this." Sullivan, though intuitively gifted, was not clairvoyant. Sullivan's encouragement seems more like what might be said to an ambivalent young man attempting to discern a path forward in his career. Otto did go on.

On December 21, 1945, the poet, Ezra Pound, was admitted to Howard Hall, which housed Saint Elizabeths criminally insane patients. There is no record that Otto and Pound ever communicated. However, Otto would likely have taken an interest in Pound, given Otto's affinity for poetry. Otto had developed a keen appreciation of poetry in his days at the Cheyenne Mountain School through his relationship with Dorothy Stott Shaw. According to Deirdre Vinyard, her father "loved poetry, art, and music." She related that *A Child's Christmas in Wales* (1952/2022) by the Welsh poet, Dylan Thomas, was a Christmas tradition during her childhood (personal communication, January 8, 2011).

Always controversial, Pound was confined to Saint Elizabeths after being found incompetent to stand trial under an indictment for treason. Throughout the Second World War, Pound — an antisemite and admirer of Benito Mussolini — made propaganda broadcasts for the Italian dictator. At Saint Elizabeths the 60-year-old Pound became Patient 58,102 (Swift, 2017).

Of the 4,109 men in treatment at the federal hospital, Pound was viewed as special. He was one of the most famous or infamous inmates at the hospital, rivaled only by Charles Guiteau — the assassin of President James Garfield. Pound spent 13 months in Howard Hall (a high security unit) before being transferred to Cedar Ward, a minimum-security unit in the hospital's Center Building. There acolytes came to visit, and he was even allowed to give lectures to small groups of aspiring poets on the grounds (Swift, 2017).

Pound's poetry, particularly his early work, contained psychological hypotheses. He asserted that "the self" or "the personality" is not a stable structure that determines who and how we are. It is, rather, spoken words that create our being. He labeled much of psychological theory "bullshit." Speaking was the consummate creative act. He told the poet, Donald Hall (2021), that madness worked in much the same way: "If you get used to the company of nuts ... you get out of the habit of making sense" (p. 212).

Pound's cantos also dealt with abstract economic theory, a subject in which Otto majored at Stanford (LaZebnik, 1957). Though LaZebnik predicted that Pound would remain in Saint Elizabeths for the rest of his life, he was discharged in 1958; his discharge owed much to the lobbying efforts of other poets like Robert Frost and T.S. Eliot who pressed the U.S. government to dismiss the treason indictment against him (Hall, 2021; LaZebnik, 1957; Swift, 2017). Although again, there is no evidence of Otto meeting Pound, the idea of it almost demands fantasy.

## Awfully Sick

Otto's six-week training period ended in 1943. During that period, he demonstrated administrative and management skills. In addition to patient care, his responsibilities involved communication with the families of patients and members of congress concerned about constituents. He brought his personal charisma and charm to these duties and Otto recalled Sullivan later telling him that he "knew how to get things done." His effectiveness was recognized by the Navy, and, after he graduated from the training program, Otto was appointed director of the naval unit at Saint Elizabeths.

In 1944-1945 Otto began to experience recurrent abdominal pain. He recalled consulting his internist who found nothing during two separate exams. During a third, he found what he believed to be a tumor in Otto's stomach. His internist immediately suggested a surgical consultation. As he was still an active-duty naval officer, the navy wanted him to consult a navy surgeon. However, after completing his residencies at the Stanford Lane Hospital, he had been offered a fellowship in internal medicine at the Mayo Clinic in Rochester, Minnesota. Because of the war, he was not able to pursue it. Yet, that offer still represented goodwill at Mayo, and Otto decided to meet with a surgeon there.

Diagnosed with cancer of the stomach, Otto was urged by the surgeon he consulted to immediately undergo a partial gastrectomy. This would involve a partial removal of the stomach, including lymph nodes and fatty tissue. After removal, the stomach would be reattached to the esophagus or small intestine. The navy again objected, and Otto was informed that the only way that he could receive surgery performed by a civilian was in the event of an emergency. While the consults were taking place, a Mayo internist suggested that Otto undergo a vagotomy — a severing of the vagus nerve that regulates gastric acid. Research in Sweden on vagotomies was promising (Woodward, 1987). However, the chief of abdominal surgery emphasized to Otto that the situation was an emergency and pressed for the gastric resection — the best chance of removing all the cancer. He then called Washington and informed Otto's commanding officer that the situation was emergent. The procedure was performed in Minnesota.

Otto remembered that, prior to the surgery he weighed 248 pounds, and over the next year his weight dropped by about 95 pounds, to around 153 pounds. "I was awfully sick," he recalled; "I could hardly eat anything. They tried me on diets and this, that, and the other thing." He once more consulted the internist who had referred him for surgery. According to Otto, his internist told him: "Doctor, with your trouble, there's nobody in the world who could blame you for being a gastric cripple — nobody could criticize you. You just have to decide whether you're going to be or not." I wonder if his father crossed Otto's mind. Otto remembered, "I walked out of that office, went up the street and had two big martinis. They didn't kill me."

It was a victory to have his choice affirmed. "That was one of the best things [anyone] ever said to me!" Yet the emotional crisis had not passed. He was still ill and did not feel like working; he turned his responsibilities for the naval unit over to his deputy. He was depressed and the future looked desolate. This was a harrowing time for Otto, though it would introduce him to intensive psychotherapy as a patient.

It is unclear how many noticed his struggle to regain some equilibrium in his life, but one who certainly did was David MacKenzie Rioch, a neuropsychiatrist, director of research at the Chestnut Lodge Sanitarium, and consultant at Saint Elizabeths. According to Robert Jay Lifton (2011), who knew him well, Rioch was an imposing figure with a somewhat gruff manner but was, "unusually kind" and took a particular interest in assisting young physicians in whom he perceived potential (p. 30). Though he did not know Otto well, Rioch approached him one day. As was his custom, he was direct. Referring to Otto's functioning, he commented: "This is not working — you're not getting anywhere." He suggested psychoanalysis. Otto knew of an analyst he respected — Edith Weigert — who in addition to psychoanalytic training, had an existential bent. Otto remembered that Weigert "was kind of a mother of the analysts" around Washington and served as a training analyst for several. Rioch was again direct: "Edith's fine, but why not see Sullivan?" Otto restated his admiration for Weigert, but Rioch was adamant that Sullivan was the wisest choice.

Courtesy of the Washington School of Psychiatry

Harry Stack Sullivan, M.D. (1892-1949)
circa 1935

Sullivan inspired Otto because "he talked about people, not cases." Otto accepted Sullivan's description of psychotherapy as the "plain hard work" of being present with patients.

# Chapter Eleven:
# A Somewhat Witty Irishman

Harry Stack Sullivan stood five feet, eight inches and weighed approximately 150 pounds. His build was slight, and he had thinning brown hair. The color of his eyes was debated, some calling them brown (including Sullivan himself), others green, and still others, gray. He wore round glasses with a slightly yellow tint that may have interfered in accurately perceiving his eye color (Perry, 1982). Whatever their color, his eyes were distinctive and may have been his most apprehending feature. A nurse who worked with him during his years at the Sheppard and Enoch Pratt Hospital described those eyes as "piercing," but they also contained a subtle twinkle (Forbush, 1971). His preferred attire was brown or gray tweed suits. He smoked heavily, sometimes sporting a cigarette holder in the style of Franklin Delano Roosevelt. He had a sonorous baritone voice, and, indicative of his Irish descent, spoke with a subtle brogue (Perry, 1982).

Sullivan was charismatic and intense; some found his intellect intimidating. In a one-on-one interaction, Sullivan was direct, sometimes arousing discomfort — anxiety and resentment — in the other person. Others found Sullivan a man who could hear honesty and sought mutual understanding. Talking with Sullivan could be both an anxious and profound experience. Further, unless one was a patient — the people to whom he directly communicated his caring — Sullivan fit descriptions of other brilliant but schizoid men. Nathaniel Hawthorne was one such man, described as: loving "humankind in the abstract, not the particular" (Wineapple, 2003, p. 382); and Ralph Waldo Emerson who was "so wary of intimacy at close quarters, [that he] found it much easier to love people at a distance" (Marcus, 2024, p. 135). H.P. Lovecraft described the schizoid personality when he described himself as "relatively indifferent to people" (de Camp, 1975, p. 64). Finally, to demonstrate that not all schizoid men are the product of American culture, there is a description of Søren Kierkegaard by a contemporary who noted, "he always wants to be different from other people, and he himself always points out his own bizarre behavior" (Garff, 2000, p. 207).

Emerson (1844/1993) wrote in *Experience*: "As I am, so I see; use what language we will, we can never say anything but what we are" (p. 98). Harry Guntrip (1975) suggested that a clinician's theoretical orientation is created from his own problems in living (see also Frankl, 2000). Certainly, men with schizoid dynamics shaped innovations in psychoanalysis. Candace Orcutt (2018) has suggested that schizoid theorists like Fairbairn, Guntrip, and Winnicott introduced the importance of relationships into psychoanalytic thinking. This group, of course, represents British object relations theorists. Among the American group that explored the importance of human relationships were members of the interpersonal viewpoint including, of course, Sullivan and Otto. Sullivan's schizoid features posed dilemmas for those around him — as they did for Otto who also demonstrated such schizoid features. Yet, without those features, we might still be thinking of human beings as instinctually driven, self-contained bundles of energy. Guntrip (1975) remembers Donald Winnicott once saying to him: "We differ from Freud. …. We are concerned with living persons, whole living and loving" (p. 153).

Sullivan was controversial in his own time and remains somewhat mysterious. Some believe that he was the most creative and original American psychiatrist of the twentieth century (e.g., Cortina, 2020; Havens & Frank, 1971). He called psychiatric disorders "problems in living." Further, he (1953a) resisted the reductive tendency to view people as "other" and proposed that everyone has problems in living. Erich Fromm (1994) echoed this, "There is nothing in the patient which I do not have in me" (p. 100).

As Mauricio Cortina (2020) points out, Sullivan also brought "a democratic and egalitarian sensibility" to his clinical work (p. 103). This sensibility still pervades the interpersonal point of view and is demonstrated in a heightened humility about the limits of our knowledge (Lurie, 2008, pp. 173-174). Otto maintained this humility.

## "I Do Not Feel that I Really Know Dr. Sullivan"

What is known about Harry Stack Sullivan is that he was born in Norwich, New York in 1892 to Irish parents. His father, Timothy Sullivan, born around 1857, was a factory laborer and his mother, Ella Sullivan (neé Stack), born around 1855, kept the family home. Within two years of Harry's birth, Timothy Sullivan lost his job at the Maydole Hammer Factory in Norwich, and the family relocated to Harry's maternal grandmother's farm in Smyrna, New York. The Sullivans were one of only two Catholic families in a solidly Protestant area (Evans, 2024).

Harry was a bright and imaginative boy but socially isolated and lonely (Rioch, 1985). He was successful at school and earned a scholarship to Cornell University, which he attended for only one semester. Suspended after involvement in an illegal activity with some older students, he left Cornell permanently after one semester (Evans, 2024).

In 1911, Sullivan enrolled at the Chicago College of Medicine and Surgery. Though it was not a medical school of outstanding reputation, Sullivan apparently received an adequate medical education — although, ironically, the school was weak in psychiatry. He graduated in 1915, but because he owed the school money, he did not receive his diploma until 1917 (Chapman, 1976; Evans, 2024). Sullivan described himself as an autodidact in psychiatry, and, by any measure, this is accurate (Kuklick, 1980; Levenson, 2017).

Sullivan's real education in psychiatry began with a year-long position at Saint Elizabeths Hospital in Washington, DC in November 1921 as a liaison officer with the Department of Veteran's Services. The superintendent at Saint Elizabeths was William Alanson White, a psychiatric clinician, researcher, educator, and innovator. He was also a humane human being (D'Amore, 1976a). Sullivan learned a great deal from White, particularly regarding applications of psychoanalytic theory and methodology to hospitalized, seriously mentally ill persons (Evans, 2024). When Sullivan's position ended, White wrote an ambivalent letter of recommendation to those considering hiring him.

White wrote that during Sullivan's time at Saint Elizabeths "our relations were eminently cordial and we got along nicely." He added, however, that "I do not feel that I really know Dr. Sullivan very well." He described Sullivan as "keen" and "alert" and a "somewhat witty Irishman." Yet despite these qualities he also described Sullivan as having "a façade of facetiousness" that was "difficult to penetrate" (D'Amore, 1976b, pp. 78-79).

Whatever the extent of White's ambivalence toward Sullivan, Sullivan admired the older man, adopting some of White's concepts into his own thinking. One of these was White's differentiation of the *self* and *not-self*, which became for Sullivan a differentiation between *me* and *not-me*. Both "not-self" and "not-me" refer to qualities that are split-off from awareness because of overwhelming anxiety (D'Amore, 1976b).

Another concept that Sullivan incorporated from White was what Sullivan termed "The One-Genus Theorem." In his 1938 autobiography, White wrote that he hoped readers would come to think of the patients he described (referring to them as "our friends") as — "very much like the rest of us, in fact, very much more *like* the rest of us than they are *different* from us" (White, 1938, p. 58, emphasis in the original). Sullivan's (1953b) One-Genus Theory stated: "*everyone is much more simply human than otherwise*" (p. 16, emphasis in the original; see also Sullivan, 1953a). This idea reappears in and forms the foundation of Otto's work.

Ultimately, Sullivan was hired by Ross McClure Chapman, superintendent of the Sheppard and Enoch Pratt Hospital in Towson, Maryland, a suburb of Baltimore. Douglas Noble (1976) described Chapman as a "tolerant, intelligent man with an empathic clinical sense" (p. 96). According to Noble, Chapman and Sullivan "made a good team," inspiring the hospital staff with their conviction that psychotic patients could be successfully treated if approached with "understanding and respect" (p. 96). Though often obstreperous and sometimes overtly combative with other staff members, Sullivan retained the trust and support of Chapman during his tenure at Sheppard Pratt between 1922 and 1930 (Evans, 2024).

Sullivan was particularly interested in the treatment of men with schizophrenia (Ralph, 2004). At Saint Elizabeths Hospital Sullivan worked with Edward Kempf, who believed that the recognition of one's homosexuality could lead to overwhelming panic. Ultimately, such panic, resulting in psychotic symptoms, would become known as "Kempf's Disease" (Chuang & Addington, 1988; Perry, 1962). Twenty years later, psychoanalytically oriented clinicians still considered homosexual panic as playing an important role in psychosis (Karpman, 1943).

Probably beginning around 1926, Chapman and the Trustees of Sheppard Pratt decided to create a new 75-bed reception building, Chapman North, named in honor of the superintendent (Ralph, 2004; Schulz, 1987). Within this reception facility, Sullivan created a small, six-bed unit for young male schizophrenics that combined milieu therapy, or what he termed "socio-psychiatric research," and individual therapy — which he called "participant-observation" (Chapman, 1976; Perry, 1962).

Sullivan picked the staff himself and most —if not all — were, in the parlance of the time, "overt homosexuals," though Sullivan was careful to avoid this description publicly. He (1962) instead wrote that he employed personnel who had been at risk for schizophrenia themselves but found other solutions — based on the principle — *similia similibus curantor* ("like cures like") (p. 262). The unit emphasized a democratic milieu in which staff members were encouraged to interact with patients in an honest, open, and self-disclosing way. They were particularly encouraged to share their experiences with homosexuality. Sullivan (1962) spent much time training them in therapeutic interactions with patients. Further, hugging and other non-genital touching was encouraged. CEO Emeritus of Sheppard Pratt and past president of the American Psychiatric Association, Robert Gibson, informed me that a colleague had toured Sullivan's unit and found "everyone on the unit, staff and patients, involved in a transvestite party. ... such parties took place periodically on Sullivan's unit" (personal communication, March 16, 2007).

Sullivan described the fundamental goal of the unit as the creation of an empathic and warm environment where patients could interact with unit personnel who were relatively more functional, though still flawed human beings. Patients and staff members strove to create a community — and a safe space that supported the young men's feelings of adequacy and self-esteem (Chuang & Addington, 1988; Sullivan, 1962). Otto (1983) described the goal as creating a loving and respectful environment in which patients could reorganize their personalities more quickly and fully than could be done in an indifferent, hostile, or humiliating environment. This conformed to Sullivan's belief that "intimacy was not essentially sexual but was instead the desire for humans to be close and to receive validation of self-worth" (Evans, 2024, p. 30).

Sullivan routinely used self-disclosure to make contact with patients. He employed his own experiences to aid patients in making sense of their experiences (Schulz, 1987). He tolerated aggression from patients — even being assaulted, without retaliation — viewing it as a desperate attempt to make some form of contact (Gibson, 1989; Perry, 1962).

Chapman North was opened on May 18, 1929, just five months before the stock market crash of October 1929 ushered in the Great Depression (Forbush, 1971). The trustees had been forced to borrow for the completion of this expansion. Sullivan, tone deaf to institutional politics, was pushing for improvements to the newly constructed building. He was also pushing Chapman for a salary increase and full authority over the entire building's programs. As the national economic situation deteriorated, the income available from patients also decreased. The trustees could not grant Sullivan a salary increase. Further, Sullivan's relations with other staff members were problematic. Will Elgin, a resident at Sheppard Pratt, described Sullivan's reputation as critical and demanding (Cornett, 2008).

Toward the end of his tenure at Sheppard Pratt, Sullivan became involved with faculty members at the University of Chicago. According to Darnell (1990), Sullivan was viewed as an outsider by most of the faculty because he held no faculty position. Among those who rose above this prejudice, however, his ideas were valued. These included the linguist and anthropologist, Edward Sapir, and the political scientist, Harold Lasswell. Lasswell probably made the initial contact with Sullivan; Sapir would be among Sullivan's closest friends until the former's death in 1939. The contact with this interdisciplinary group broadened Sullivan's outlook. He began to integrate sociology, linguistics, semiotics, and anthropology with his understanding of psychoanalysis (Ralph, 2004). This integration of the social sciences with psychiatry is what initially attracted Otto to Sullivan's work.

Sullivan resigned from the Sheppard and Enoch Pratt Hospital in the spring of 1930 (Forbush, 1971). Because of his pioneering work with schizophrenic patients, Sullivan left Sheppard Pratt, "a legend in the world of clinical psychiatry" (Evans, 2024, p. 31).

Sullivan considered two possibilities as he planned to leave Sheppard Pratt. The first was relocating to the familiar city of Chicago to work with Sapir and Lasswell researching personality and culture. The other option was New York City, where he hoped to open a private practice on Park Avenue. Funding for the position in Chicago did not materialize, so Sullivan left Towson in 1930 for America's preeminent metropolis (Perry, 1982).

## The "Other"

The country was still in the Great Depression, and Sullivan only wanted to work with patients who had obsessive problems. He believed that obsessional illnesses were prodromal syndromes of schizophrenia. He was saddled with debt, having borrowed money from Sheppard Pratt and assumed the debts of his deceased father (Forbush, 1971). He was soon forced to declare bankruptcy ("Business Records," 1932).

After the bankruptcy, Sullivan established a lucrative practice on East Sixty-Fourth Street in a five-story townhouse in which he lived with Jimmie Sullivan — his life-partner and adoptive son. They also employed a housekeeper. His practice was soon filled with artists like the African American dancer, Katharine Dunham, and the young *Life* photographer, Margaret Bourke-White, as well as writers and a variety of mental health professionals.

Sullivan was a remarkably accepting and affirming man of those viewed as "Other" or "inferior" by most of society (Jackson, 2002). It was an era when African Americans were anathema to white professionals. Institutions like Chestnut Lodge, the Menninger Clinic, and Sheppard Pratt would not accept them for treatment (Friedman, 1990). At Chestnut Lodge there was a sign that read, "we do not take colored people" (Hornstein, 2000, p. 91). Sullivan did not respect any racial barriers and was intolerant of anti-Semitism (Waugaman, 2012). In unintegrated America, he employed at least one Black man in a sensitive job.

On August 17, 1936, a 22-year-old gay African American man applied for a temporary job with Sullivan. His name was Ralph Waldo Ellison and he had come to New York from Tuskegee, Alabama to study the arts and writing. He found his way to Sullivan through Richmond

Barthe, a gay sculptor (and probably through a network of gay men and women). The job with Sullivan was extraordinary for the time. White professionals simply did not hire African Americans for jobs involving contact with the public (Rampersad, 2007).

Ellison worked for Sullivan greeting patients five days a week. He was paid $12.50 a week. As Sullivan worked with patients, Ellison filed, typed, and ran errands for him. However, his duties went well beyond those limited roles. During these four months, Ellison helped Sullivan with his writing. During the months that they worked together, Sullivan often lunched with Ellison and asked him to read whatever he was writing (Jackson, 2002; Rampersad, 2007). For the hypersensitive Sullivan, this was a demonstration of rare trust that was not lost on Ellison. On December 31, 1936, Ellison left Sullivan's employ. The young man had learned from Sullivan to become more emotionally open. In 1952, Ellison's novel, *The Invisible Man*, was published (Rampersad, 2007).

In 1939, Sullivan spent a few weeks in Greenville, Mississippi to study the effects of race on personality development at the behest of the American Council on Education (Rose, 2005; Samway, 1997). For part of this time, Sullivan stayed with William A. Percy, the uncle of the writer, Walker Percy. As Percy (1972) described the visit, Sullivan made his headquarters in the family pantry and sipped what was previously an unknown concoction in Mississippi, the martini. He would chat with people of both races who stopped by.

In Alabama, there was another form of research being carried out. In 1932, a study called the "Tuskegee Study of Untreated Syphilis in the Negro Male" began. Syphilis, caused by the bacterium *Treponema pallidum*, is probably as old as tuberculosis and, because it is sexually transmitted, has been a source of ignorance and shame. The so-called study of the disease in African American males took place without the subjects' full knowledge of what was being studied and without treatment being administered, even when antibiotics became available. The "research" continued for 40 years, the longest period of time of any non-therapeutic study in American medical history and ended only when all the subjects had died — after never having received treatment for syphilis. For many white physicians, particularly those who began the research, this was not noteworthy because they viewed Black men as just a part of a "syphilis-soaked race" (Krishnan, 2022, p. 240).

Sullivan had experienced being looked upon as "Other" — "different" from "normal people." In childhood he was a Catholic in a region of protestants. His father did not understand his interest in books and lack of interest in the farm. He (1942) wrote that his mother, who was probably mentally ill: "never troubled to notice the characteristics of the child she had brought forth, and 'her son' was so different from me that I felt she had no use for me except as a clotheshorse on which to hang an elaborate pattern of illusions" (p. 813).

Part of Sullivan's controversial nature involved his sexuality. It is known that Sullivan had sexual relations with other men, though it is still debated among Sullivan scholars as to whether he was, in modern parlance, "gay" (Alexander, 1990; Allen, 1995; Chapman, 1976; Evans, 2024; Perry, 1982). The relevance of this knowledge for our discussion is that it demonstrates another way in which Sullivan was "Other." As described above, Sullivan had few friends as a child. Indeed, he may have had only one who was a bully to him. His name was Clarence Bellinger, and he was a few years older than Sullivan. Bellinger also became a psychiatrist. As Sullivan reached celebrity, Bellinger remained an unknown mediocrity. As the differences in status grew apparent, Bellinger deprecated Sullivan to colleagues, denouncing him as "a homosexual and a son-of-a-bitch" (Perry, 1982, p. 313); both descriptions were meant as insults. To be "a homosexual" was to be inherently inferior.

Sullivan had one primary intimate relationship in his life. Whether it was also sexual remains a question. He and James H. (Jimmie) Inscoe met in 1927. Sullivan was 35 and Jimmie was 15. There is much about their relationship that is not known with any certainty. Inscoe may have been a prostitute in Washington (Allen, 1995). They moved in together soon after they met. Jimmie took the name "Sullivan" through common usage (Allen, 1995; Perry, 1982). Theirs seems to have been a relationship of love for twenty-two years.

One of Sullivan's most controversial positions was set out posthumously in a 1950 paper entitled "The Illusion of Personal Individuality." The title succinctly conveys the main contention of the paper; however, he also challenged the concept of the unconscious mind, writing that, "the mind is coterminous with consciousness" (p. 319). After being challenged on this idea by a member of the audience to which the paper was originally presented, he responded somewhat obliquely, "I tried to say nothing about the unconscious except to suggest that it was not phenomenologically describable" (pp. 329-330).

The body of the paper, though, concerns the development of the self in an interpersonal matrix. In a statement that aroused much ire then but remains a cornerstone of the interpersonal point of view, he proposed that, "you will find that it makes no sense to think of ourselves as 'individual,' 'separate,' capable of anything like definitive description in isolation, that the notion is just beyond the point" (p. 329). Sullivan concluded the paper with an almost casual — even if, for some, incendiary — thought, "For all I know every human being has as many personalities as he has interpersonal relations" (p. 329).

Finally, Sullivan described himself as different from the average person by alluding to his own problems in living. Helen Swick Perry (1982) reported being told by Sullivan that he had once been hospitalized as the result of a schizophrenic break. Though others who knew Sullivan well dismiss this claim as a type of exaggeration to which Sullivan was prone (see Rioch, 1985), some have taken that description as a truth that warrants dismissing Sullivan and his work (Jacobsen, 1955; Kohut, 1994).

Sullivan knew loneliness and alienation from his own experience. Such experience offered a channel of communication with other alienated souls. As Rainier Maria Rilke suggested to his correspondent in *Letters to a Young Poet* (1905/2002),

> do not think that the man who seeks to comfort you lives untroubled among the simple and quiet words which sometimes do you good. His life has much hardship and sadness and lags far behind you. If it were otherwise, he could never have found those words (pp. 40-41).

One of the alienated people with whom Sullivan would make contact was Otto Will.

# Chapter Twelve: I'm Not Here to Give Interpretations

Otto took Rioch at his word. In the summer of 1946, he began what turned out to be an arduous enterprise. The initial challenge was simply reaching Sullivan on the telephone. Otto recalled trying repeatedly without success, Sullivan's number being continuously busy. "I finally got to talk with him, and I said Dr. Rioch suggested that I see him about therapy."

Sullivan asked, "Where do you live?"

"Southeast Washington."

Sullivan, who had moved with Jimmie from New York in late 1938 to early 1939, and saw patients at his home in Bethesda, Maryland, responded, "That's too far a trip."

Otto remembered countering, "No, I can handle that alright, Dr. Sullivan."

Sullivan proffered a further question: "What's your rank in the Navy?"

"I'm a lieutenant commander."

Sullivan was direct: "You can never afford me; I charge $10 an hour, $15 for an hour and a half."

Otto was not deterred. "I can handle my expenses, Dr. Sullivan."

The older man finally relented: "Alright, I'll see you in consultation."

It is not clear — and Otto offered no hypotheses as to why Sullivan was resistant to scheduling an appointment — however, sometime later he described an interaction with Sullivan that might give some perspective. He (1979) wrote: "I once spoke to Sullivan about a man known to both of us. To my surprise he replied irritably, 'He's only a patient.' He paused, and then rather sadly added, 'Everyone in my life is now a patient'" (p. 570). Having experienced such a form of isolation in my own work, I understand that it represents a particular kind of loneliness. Conversations may be — perhaps should be — spontaneous and mutual but the therapist must also be mindful of what is said in a way that is not required in casual conversation. As Otto pointed out in his (1979) paper, the "continuing exposure to the pain of others is itself painful" (p. 569).

The day scheduled for Otto's consultation arrived, and he made his way to Sullivan's home. It was not an easy journey, requiring both a bus and a streetcar. Constructed of brick and located several hundred feet from the road, the house, at 9003 Bradley Boulevard in Bethesda, was in the colonial Williamsburg style (Perry, 1982). Although he does not say so in describing the scene, it seems that he might have been surprised to see Sullivan "out in the garden, puttering around." He later learned that Sullivan "loved his flowers." He was greeted by one of Sullivan's five Cocker Spaniels barking at him. Sullivan invited him in. The two of them moved inside — along with the dogs — and Sullivan suggested, "Tell me about yourself." Otto was unsure of what he told Sullivan but remembered that Sullivan said something that remained with him.

"I hope I am not violating the Aesculapian Oath or drawing the curtains to reveal a scene that should not be seen, but you should know that every therapist, no matter how well trained or how experienced, is always anxious at a first interview." In the casual way that Sullivan had of doing so, he acknowledged something personal and simultaneously normalized anxiety as a part of the first meeting. Otto related, "I'll never forget [that]."

"After a while I said, 'Dr. Sullivan, would you be willing to work with me?' Sullivan's response was immediate: 'You began an hour and a half ago.'"

Otto began a routine of two 90-minute sessions a week. Sullivan did not suggest that the younger psychiatrist assume a reclining position on a sofa or couch but had chairs arranged at 90-degree angles which allowed both to see each other if desired while not requiring that they look directly at each other. Otto remembered many of his interactions with Sullivan. I will describe some of these with an eye toward understanding Sullivan's clinical style, particularly those aspects that became part of Otto's own repertoire.

To understand Sullivan's style, it is helpful to consult his writing. With the exception of *Conceptions of Modern Psychiatry* (1953a), originally published in 1940, most of us read very little of Sullivan's work as originally written. His other works are edited collections from lecture notes, teaching materials, and other sources. This is particularly true of his clinical works — *The Psychiatric Interview* (1954) and *Clinical Studies in Psychiatry* (1956). Otto was one of the editors of these works and wrote the introduction to *The Psychiatric Interview* (1954). There is at least one paper, however, that Sullivan (1949) made available for publication in the journal *Psychiatry* — though it was published posthumously. This paper, entitled "The Theory of Anxiety and the Nature of Psychotherapy," was originally presented to the neuropsychiatric section of the medical and chirurgical conference in Baltimore, Maryland in 1948. In the following paragraphs, I will outline aspects of Sullivan's clinical approach, relying heavily on this posthumously published paper, as well as *The Psychiatric Interview*, for an intellectual understanding of what working with Sullivan would have been like and how Otto might have developed his own ways of working from this experience.

## The Principal Instrument is the Self

Sullivan (1954) asserted that the therapist must be present with the patient as an observer and participant — the former impossible without the latter: "His principal instrument of observation is his self — his personality, *him* as a person" (p. 3, emphasis in the original).

Otto described Sullivan as present, even when ill. In 1945, Sullivan suffered a subacute bacterial endocarditis, an infection of the inner cardiac lining and valves (Crowley, 1971). Because of this heart disease, some days Sullivan did not feel able to sit up for the entirety of a session and was himself recumbent on a sofa. Otto was continually reminded of Sullivan's illness by the oxygen tanks kept in the area in which they worked (Rioch, 1985; Thompson & Thompson, 1998). Despite this, Otto remembered, "I had the feeling that he was pretty much present — he wasn't somewhere else."

One of the qualities that Otto emphasized in working with patients was the simple but profoundly important one of being physically and emotionally present — that psychotherapy cannot take place with the therapist in absentia (1964, 1968b, 1973). He asserted that, "a therapist doesn't have to be a great success always — maybe never has to be a great success — the therapist just has to be there."

It is worth noting that, when Sullivan was present, so were his five cocker spaniels. Otto found them a significant distraction. They barked at noises outside the house like trash collection, or a knock on the front door. At tense moments, they also growled at Otto until calmed by Sullivan. Otto remembered addressing his distraction with Sullivan whose response was: "But doctor, what can I do?"

## Stop Talking and Say Something

Sullivan's (1949) central contention was that "[t]herapy works through or as a function of interpersonal communication" (p. 5). Otto recalled several instances in his work with Sullivan in which communication was the focus. Once, Otto arrived for a session somewhat distracted. He began speaking and after a few minutes noticed that Sullivan seemed bored and inattentive.

"Dr. Sullivan, are you listening to me?" Otto asked.

Sullivan's reply was immediate, "No, Dr. Will, are you?"

Otto found this very powerful. Sullivan was reinforcing the idea that he was not the fountain from which insight flowed; "He was saying 'I don't know any more than you do.'" Additionally, he believed that Sullivan was suggesting that it is fruitless to expect others to be interested in our communications when they do not even interest ourselves. Edgar Levenson (2017) maintains that the patient must develop the capacity to listen to herself as a part of successful psychotherapy. Indeed, he (2018) wrote that it is only when the patient begins to listen to herself that change can occur. Morris Schwartz (1996) captured the importance of the patient listening to herself when he wrote: "The whole thrust of psychotherapy, as well as psychoanalysis, is to get outside and look at the way you repeatedly act and think" (p. 100).

Otto remembered other instances during which Sullivan said something like: "For Christ's sake, stop talking and say something!" Sullivan (1949) wrote: "there are many things about which much is said and exceedingly little communicated" (p. 6). Some years later, Otto (1961a) wrote: "[The patient] has before him the task of increasing his ability to be an observer as well as a participant" (p. 158). Clarence Schulz told me that Sullivan was seldom prepared to accept "I don't know" as an answer; it often met with Sullivan's response: "Now, having told me that you don't know, go ahead and answer [the question posed]" (personal communication, February 10, 2007).

The art of communication might be described as an art of selective omission. Jargon and words used to highlight the therapist's (and/or patient's) erudition often interfere with communication. As the biographer, Clark Davis (2023) notes: "modern, clinical explanations offer little in the way of genuine understanding … too often they simply translate basic description into a specialized vocabulary" (pp. 5-6). Otto recalled learning this from his son, Patrick.

> Pat was a little boy. [Les Farber] and I were having a cup of coffee and Pat came in and joined us. He must've been about nine or something. He began talking about a little friend of his, and how this kid was kind of difficult and so on. Then he went on to say, "Well, this kid's mother was thus and so, and his father was thus and so." And I began to realize that he was trying to tie all this together in a sort of pseudoanalytic way — mother and father leads to this and that. And Les finally looked at Pat and said, "Jesus Christ, Pat, cut it out. Why don't you just say it — the kid's a prick."

## Think About It

Once meaningful communication is established, the therapist works as an educator by providing information that the patient may not have or has not considered (Sullivan, 1949). Otto recalled an instance of this in his work with Sullivan. At the time, Otto's parents were still living in Colorado Springs, and his mother wanted him to move back and practice there. While discussing the matter in a session, Sullivan offered his perspective.

> I remember Sullivan said: "If your mother or father needed some money and you could provide it for them, I'd say do it. If your mother or father were sick and needed to see you, I would say, by all means go back and do it. You're talking about maybe moving back there and trying to cure your mother or something. If there are some practical things that'd

> be helpful to your mother or father, by all means do it. But, if you just think you're going back there and settle down, somehow or other to deal with your mother's whatever it is, go ahead. But think about it."

Otto incorporated that into his own way of working. "I sometimes say to patients, 'You know, if I felt that you were going to do something hurtful to yourself — make a damn fool of yourself — I sure would say so, and nothing would keep me from saying it.'"

## They'll Have the Bright Idea

In the therapist's role as an educator, Sullivan (1949) proposed that: "The correction of misinformation, therefore, is not too readily achieved by pouring correct data into the person but instead has to be sought by studying the role in the personality of that which is intact and correct" (p. 4). One builds on the patient's strengths. Yet, there are erroneous beliefs that are so pervasive that they must be addressed.

Leston Havens was probably the most eloquent of Sullivan's followers in articulating how Sullivan addressed misinformation. For Havens (1989), this work involved disconfirmation of the patient's erroneous beliefs — not only in the therapist's words but in her whole being. Such beliefs are given life in the patient's expectations of the world and of the therapist as a part of the world. Havens wrote: "The greatest power of psychotherapy may be precisely … [the] power not to confirm the patients' expectations" (p. 17). He (1979) called this work "kicking at the underpinnings of ideas" (p. 26). In his early work at Sheppard Pratt, Sullivan would often confront patients when he thought that they were operating on misinformation. Clarence Schulz suggested that this represented Sullivan's approach, before he developed his theory regarding anxiety. As Schulz put it: "[Sullivan] was like a bull in a China shop" (personal communication, January 8, 2011). The mature Sullivan understood that directly confronting mistaken beliefs was more likely to entrench rather than weaken them. He developed what Havens (1979) termed "counterprojective" interventions that were more subtle, oblique (p. 29). When the therapist perceives a powerful, though mistaken, belief, she simply registers a note of skepticism to the patient. Quiet responses such as "Really?" or "I've not heard that before" can be powerful counterprojective interventions. As Havens (1979) wrote, "The important thing was not letting the idea pass without comment" (p. 27).

In an interview with Jon Frederickson (2001), Donald Burnham remembered learning from Sullivan that he did not have to present fully formed ideas to the patient, "If you're fortunate you can sort of drop an apple on their head and they'll have the bright idea" (p. 39).

Clarence Schulz told me of an example of this that had been related by Dexter Means Bullard when he had been in therapy with Sullivan.

> Dexter had announced one day to Sullivan that he had been to a cocktail party with a tuxedo and came home about ten o'clock and decided to make rounds. Dexter said that he could walk a straight line and his speech was not impaired. He believed that no one could tell that he'd had a drink. Just as he finished, he said Sullivan remarked, "and smelling like a brewery." Dexter said, 'I've never been on a unit of the Lodge after having had a drink since" (personal communication, February 6, 2007).

Sullivan did not observe this caveat in his own work. Otto recalled that Sullivan was never without a glass of brandy during their sessions. He inferred that Sullivan used this as both a stimulant for his heart and an anesthetic for angina. He described one session in which Jimmie interrupted to bring Sullivan a fresh glass of brandy. "You've just saved my life" Sullivan told the young man.

## Perfection

Every human being measures herself against standards, some very reasonable, others impractical or frankly impossible. The result either maintains self-esteem or damages it. Sullivan (1949) suggested that addressing self-defeating evaluations by the patient is an integral, but complex aspect, of psychotherapy.

For many people, the standard against which they measure themselves is perfection. Perfection, of course, is impossible to achieve. I spent much time in my personal psychotherapy learning this. To address perfectionism and other self-esteem defeating systems, we return to Havens (1979). Oblique comments rather than direct confrontation are again the most effective path. If the patient expresses the expectation of herself that she will only accept perfection, the therapist might gently inquire: "Oh, do you know someone who has done that perfectly?" Again, the goal is not to increase the patient's anxiety or "catch" her being impractical, but to sow some doubt that the patient may consider when approaching goals.

## Learning and Observing

Otto emphasized that Sullivan was generally quiet:

> I don't remember him saying very much. I don't think he felt bound by analytic silence or something like that. It seemed to me that he would ask questions and try to get information. If he thought he didn't know enough about some particular thing, he'd ask what else you knew about it.

Sullivan rejected interpretation as a technique. Otto suggested, "A lot of interpretations are designed to make the therapist feel more comfortable — that's your mother, not mine." He (1964) wrote: "A therapist works within a particular frame of reference whereby he attempts to 'explain' (perhaps 'justify') that which he does" (p. 6). Erich Fromm (1994), who also rejected interpretation as a technique, wrote, "I don't interpret; I don't even use the word interpretation. I say what I hear" (p. 98). In this sense, what some call an interpretation is intended as a confirmation that the therapist is hearing the patient's material in a useful way, thus diminishing the anxiety of both participants (Guntrip, 1975). Otto's view of interpretation seemed very much in this mode. He was careful to avoid what he described as the therapeutic situation of being "awash with interpretation."

Commenting on his memories of Sullivan in a 1981 paper presented at Chestnut Lodge, Otto related:

> Sullivan seemed to me to be always learning and observing. He did not appear to be fixed in a theory from which he could not be moved. I must say I had the feeling that I was not alone in going on a voyage of discovery; if I was to learn about myself, then Sullivan could learn about me. As a sort of mariner, he knew how to navigate alright, but for him there was always something new to be learned about the sea (Will, 1981a).

Too much interpretation interfered with Sullivan learning from the patient. It might even be argued that Sullivan was dismissive of the value of interpretation.

Otto described an incident with Sullivan involving the efficacy of transference interpretation.

> I don't know if he said some things, but I was awfully angry. And there he was sitting in the chair, and I said, "I could pick you up and throw you out the window!" Sullivan calmly responded, "No doubt you could." And I was ashamed of myself and I said, "I'm sorry, you're not really like my father but [he] would sometimes talk the way you do — reminds me of him, so I suppose this is father transference." And he [Sullivan] said, "Oh no, doctor — it's not." He said, "At the moment, I think you thoroughly dislike me and at the moment I don't care very much about you" (for another version, see Thompson & Thompson, 1998, p. 292; Morris Parloff also touches on this in Frederickson, 2002, p. 109).

Otto explained to Kim Chernin that, with Sullivan, it was more important to deal with concrete here and now realities than abstract concepts.

## In It Together

Otto found Sullivan "gentle and compassionate without many words. I felt that he cared about me — he had my welfare in mind as far as I could see." Sullivan would acknowledge this periodically, but only indirectly. "[Sullivan] said to me one day, 'You know why I decided to work with you? Because Little Lady [one of his dogs] liked you.'" Otto's daughter, Deirdre Will Vinyard, recounted to me another instance of Sullivan using ironic humor to communicate with her father. During one of their sessions Sullivan volunteered that he had been thinking about Otto. Otto was interested and Sullivan concluded the thought by stating, "It was this morning while I was shaving and holding the razor to my throat." It may have sparked a mutual laugh and Otto understood it to be a playful expression of affection. On this occasion, Sullivan (1954) did not follow his warning in *The Psychiatric Interview* to other practitioners to avoid "being ironic" (p. 120).

Unfortunately, Sullivan had a well-earned reputation for condescension and cutting criticism. Otto remembered a typical refrain about him: "Some people tolerate fools lightly, Sullivan not at all." Writing in the *New York Times*, David Elkind echoed this: "Sullivan never learned to 'suffer fools gladly' and he could publicly demolish a pretentious colleague or an ill-prepared student" (Elkind, 1972, p. SM 18). Otto experienced that side of Sullivan, as well:

> I found him critical, and, at times, his criticism seemed harsh and unpleasant in all places, but I understood that it was in the service of my personal development. I recall his criticism of my presentation of an initial interview in a seminar in which such matters were considered. Many members of the seminar commented on my presentation, some favorably. Sullivan had only one thing to say; he sighed and said, "Well, now I think you know why the patient did not return for a second meeting" (Will, 1981a).

Otto remembered Sullivan saying: "I don't mind reassuring people — it's just that I don't know how;" yet, another one of his memories of Sullivan involved such reassurance. He described a good friend, also in therapy with Sullivan, who was "having a very bad time" (though what exactly this meant, he never revealed). His friend told him that at the conclusion of a very difficult session, Sullivan remarked: "'Doctor, I sure would like to give you a helping hand, but right now I don't know how; so, I guess we just have to totter along together.'" Otto related that his friend found this remark very helpful, and Otto thought it of profound importance because as a therapist "there are lots of things in a person's life that I don't have a solution for." He admired that Sullivan avoided "any magical stuff like … some kind of so-called interpretation." Talking with Gerard Fromm, who knew Otto at Austen Riggs, I asked about Otto's clinical priorities. Fromm responded: "He conveyed the sense that you and the patient were in it together. He placed his full weight behind the therapeutic relationship" (personal communication, August 22, 2007). Like Sullivan, Otto often reassured the patient that he was in it with her. Particularly, when he felt that he was not being of much help, he (1989b) wrote: Often all I can say is, 'I wish I could give you a helping hand. But since I'm not being very good at that — at least for now — let's go on together, and see what we can find'" (p. 140). No matter how desolate things looked, you could depend on him to totter along with you.

Otto acknowledged that simply being with a patient could itself be very powerful. He (1961a) wrote: "Sometimes the most that a therapist can do is be with his patient; for the moment this may be enough, and should not be neglected" (p. 80).

Courtesy of the Washington School of Psychiatry

## Harry Stack Sullivan, M.D.

circa 1945

Otto learned a great deal from Sullivan about being with patients. Sullivan emphasized the importance of communication and challenging the patient's projections. Sullivan rejected the traditional emphasis on transference interpretation.

# Chapter Thirteen: A Clinical Study from Saint Elizabeths

Shortly after his abdominal surgery, Otto decided to take a gamble with his career. Rather than continue in the safe role of physician, he gradually entered the practice of psychotherapy. He downplayed the motivation for this as simply having the time to explore a new aspect of psychiatric practice, but no doubt some inspiration came from Sullivan in this regard. Over his long career, Otto illustrated his clinical papers with vignettes designed to give the reader a sense of what he did and why he did it. Clearly, one of the most important patients with whom he worked was his first about whom he wrote in at least two papers (1965, 2021). He also described this experience to Kim Chernin toward the end of his life. As was and is common practice, Otto referred to this young man with a pseudonym, "John."

## "John"

John was a 22-year-old Ensign in the United States Navy originally from New Orleans, Louisiana. He had been transferred to Saint Elizabeths from the psychiatric unit on Mare Island in California. While stationed on a destroyer that was bound for the Aleutians, John had approached his commanding officer (CO) claiming that the Holy Spirit had spoken to him and encouraged him to withdraw from the war. War was "evil." After approaching his CO, John began attempting to convert his fellow officers to his newfound view that war must be abolished and that they should lay down their arms. On a combat vessel, this behavior posed the simultaneous dangers of undermining morale and mobilizing other officers to take action against John as a traitor.

His behavior and sensorium began to quickly deteriorate, and his CO ultimately had the young Ensign transferred for psychiatric treatment. Over the next several months, John was hospitalized in several institutions and diagnosed as schizophrenic. According to Otto, the only treatment he had received was electroconvulsive therapy (ECT) which had not resulted in any significant changes. Ultimately, he was transferred to the naval unit at Saint Elizabeths. There he was assigned to "a ward for regressed patients" (Will, 1965, p. 11).

At this point in his career, Otto remained ambivalent about the role of "psychiatrist;" he largely focused on the medical treatment of patients with physical complaints, using his skills as an internist. One of the patients he saw in this capacity was John who was by this time — about seven months after the initial display of symptoms — both suicidal and self-mutilative. Otto met John who was under close observation and restrained on his bed. Verbally, he alternated between barely audible mumbling and cogent articulation: "Let me die ... Let me go free to die" (Will, 1965, p. 12). He was incontinent, suffered from bedsores, would not eat, and required nasal tube feeding. He also suffered from a pharyngeal infection. His psychiatric symptoms had been treated with hydrotherapy and barbiturates, but the nursing staff was convinced that he would end his own life. This was not a promising patient for a man already deeply ambivalent about his professional role and identity. Otto (1965) described "a great urgency to do something to be of help to him" (p. 13). Yet, overwhelmed with anxiety, the repellent nature of John's physical condition, and his basic incomprehensibility, Otto withdrew to the safe distance of a medical practitioner. He considered ordering another ECT treatment.

John might have paid dearly for this course of action. Otto remembered calling John's parents in New Orleans to apprise them of the plan for further ECT. He remembered telling them, "I have to tell you, it might kill him."

John's parents gave Otto permission to "do what you think is best." Otto (1965) wrote that John responded remarkably well to the shock which astonished and relieved the ward staff. Yet, he had a nagging concern — he did not know or understand this young man. Within a few days, John's symptoms began to return. Because his respiratory system was compromised, further shock and tranquilizers were prohibitively dangerous.

It was at this point that Otto asked Sullivan for a recommendation. "Sullivan suggested, 'Why don't you pay some attention to him — you might learn something.'" Otto remembered that he approached John in his room, determined simply to be present with him.

Before settling into what must have been an anxious and lonely silence with John, Otto (1989b) wrote that he hoped for control of the situation and John by being "an authority" (p. 132). Otto ruefully related: "Finally I noted — I said a lot. I know that one session I'd given him at least six theories about mental disorder." He also recalled that he offered John suggestions about how he might live "a better life. I decided I was more likely to be confusing — so I shut up." Within this silent world of two, Otto (1965) discovered a profound truth — every suggestion for improvement, was, at least partially and simultaneously — well-intended and defensive. "I was declaring that the man in his present state was unacceptable to me. I came to believe that 'desirable' change could come only as the 'undesirable' could be accepted" (p. 23). Further, his suggestions on how John might live an improved life frustrated the young man, who confronted Otto about "trying to convert him."

Armed with this new understanding and the hope imparted by figures such as Sullivan and Fromm-Reichmann, Otto related: "I just sat there, and he was mute. I sat there hour after hour, and nobody said anything." He recalled that he sometimes took a book to these sessions until he realized that, in so doing, he was not fully present. When he focused on being present — enduring the anxiety and loneliness that accompanied it — John began to show improvement. Otto (2021) wrote that John: "altered his behavior, speaking and no longer requiring restraints. My guess is that he found my words of little value, but he was able to tolerate my presence" (p. 6). John's lonely world was less lonely.

Otto was recalled to the Mayo Clinic for a post-surgical check-up. When he returned, he was astounded by John's response: "I'll never forget, I came back and walked into the room where he was sitting. He said, 'Hello Dr. Will' — first thing he'd ever said. I said, 'Hello.'" Otto remembered experiencing a wave of anxiety and thinking: "For Christ's sake, shut up — you've been getting along fine without saying anything, now we've got to talk about it." Though anxious about this development,

Otto again began to sit with John and something akin to conversations gradually developed. Sessions became more reciprocal. For two and a half years, Otto saw John three to five times weekly (1965). He recalled that John: "finally got better and went home to Louisiana. The last I heard he was a fisherman down there."

The time that Otto spent with John was formative in his development as a skillful psychotherapist. In the papers listed above, Otto articulated some of what he learned with and from John.

First, he noted the importance of the therapist's *presence*. The situation was initially uncomfortable for him, and he retreated in both subtle and obvious ways. Among the subtle forms of retreat, he set out to change John. He (1965, 2021) recalled spending a great deal of time explaining to John the origin of his distress and how he might attain a "better life." Under such circumstances, the therapist's presence can become a burden to the patient. The therapeutic relationship is one that must always be concerned with "acceptance and understanding," these qualities superseding attempts at change, whether by interpretation or other techniques (Will 1965, p. 26). Otto (1954) would assert in his introduction to *The Psychiatric Interview* that the therapist must demonstrate "a very simple and serious respect for the other person" (p. xxii). He (1960) emphasized that a demonstration of respect means that "the words 'we respect you' must be confirmed in action and environment" (p. 211).

A second subtle way that he retreated from the relationship was by being present physically but not emotionally. As John was generally non-communicative, Otto would bring a book to read during their sessions. He (1965) suggested that being distant in such a way distracts the therapist from learning about the patient by becoming aware of her own emotional reactions. Feeling lonely and isolated (particularly to the point that one wants to flee) may suggest some of what the patient feels.

Under these circumstances, the therapist's presence can become important to the patient. Otto was fond of quoting Dexter M. Bullard's definition of psychotherapy: "You put two people in the same room frequently enough and over a long enough period of time and something's bound to happen — sometimes it turns out good." This is a basic statement of attachment in psychotherapy that would later infuse Otto's point of view (Will, 1968b, 1970c, 1973, 1981b).

In addition to therapeutic presence, he (1965) suggested that the effective therapist is pragmatic, willing to accept the possible rather than demanding the ideal. Therapeutic ambition must be monitored, lest the patient be burdened with the unrealistic expectations of the therapist. Indeed, Otto discovered that he lost touch with John's goals and became overly focused on his own.

Otto echoes the humanism that so impressed him when he heard Sullivan speak, writing that "[t]o the therapist ... the patient must become a person; he cannot remain a 'case' of dementia praecox or of anything else" (p. 25). Otto (1970c) wrote that his point of view: "requires that we discover ourselves in our fellows" (p. 6). Neville Symington (2006) also puts this quite well: "this person sitting opposite me in my consulting-room is what I am" (p. 79).

Finally, Otto (1965) suggested that authenticity is required of the therapist. This authenticity is demonstrated in a congruence between what the therapist feels and thinks and that which is communicated to the patient. If the patient perceives a discrepancy between these two aspects of the therapist, the patient may experience "a repetition of an all-too-familiar situation in which the words 'I love you' are not in accord with the behavior which says, more or less clearly, 'I love you not'" (p. 27). John Sutherland (1989) identified this congruence as an imperative of the first object relations theorist, Ronald Fairbairn as well:

> He believes a caring attitude is basic to the whole process of analysis; it is a requirement dictated not only by sentiment but by ... infant development. The patient's original experience was of not being "loved" for himself, and it is the need for such an attitude that he will inevitably sense (p. 154).

Such an incongruence is also a relatively simple formulation of what R. D. Laing (1969) called *mystification* (p. 27). Though Otto seldom used this term, he viewed the phenomenon as a key dynamic in most problems in living and certainly in the schizophrenic reaction.

# Chapter Fourteen: Belief Enriched by Doubt & Question

In 1946, while beginning intensive psychotherapy/psychoanalysis with Sullivan and working with John, Otto enrolled in the Washington School of Psychiatry (WSP). The WSP was a program of the William Alanson White Psychoanalytic Foundation, both having been created in 1936 (Rioch, 1986). The foundation was meant to honor its namesake and to advance the field of psychiatry through education and research. The school boasted an impressive Board of Trust and faculty. The Board of Trust included White, Adolf Meyer, and Abraham Arden Brill. White and Meyer were two of the most esteemed men in American psychiatry and Brill was an acknowledged leader of American psychoanalysis (Richards & Mosher, 2006). However, after White's death in 1937, both Meyer and Brill left the governing body. Meyer cited tension with the administration of Johns Hopkins University which was concerned about divided loyalties. After White's death, the trustees decided that "Psychiatric" should replace "Psychoanalytic" in the foundation's name, a move Brill found unacceptable. Within a short period, the leadership lost its three most recognizable figures (Bever, 1993).

The most energetic of the remaining trustees were led by Harry Stack Sullivan and included Lucille Dooley, Frieda Fromm-Reichmann, Ernest Hadley, and Lewis Hill. This group was determined to create a multidisciplinary, post-graduate institution for the training of mental health professionals from all disciplines (Burnham, 1978). The loss of White, Meyer, and Brill reduced the fundraising potential for the school, especially as America was still deep in the Great Depression. The school had no building of its own and classes were held at Saint Elizabeths and other federal facilities. The faculty and students were something of a nomadic tribe, with many suffering from an "edifice complex" (Frederickson, 2002; Rioch, 1986).

The faculty of the school was, nevertheless, composed of a core of 29 of the most distinguished, creative, and innovative professionals of the era. The curriculum was structured around three areas of study. Sullivan directed the school and the division of psychobiology. Ernest Hadley, a traditionally oriented psychoanalyst, directed the division of biological sciences, and Edward Sapir, an anthropologist and linguist from Yale, directed the social sciences division. The faculty also included clinicians like Clara Thompson, Erich Fromm, Frieda Fromm-Reichmann, Lucille Dooley, Margaret Rioch, and Dexter M. Bullard. Margaret Mead and Edward Sapir taught anthropological approaches to psychiatry, as did Edward T. Hall. David McKenzie Rioch and Alfred Stanton taught clinical research. Charles Johnson, a sociologist and President of Fisk University in Nashville, Tennessee, provided a sociological perspective (Bever, 1993). Sullivan spent much of his time commuting between New York and Washington. In late 1938 and early 1939, he and Jimmie made a transition to Bethesda, Maryland (Chapman, 1976). In Bethesda, Sullivan served as a training analyst and supervisor. He supervised the first analytic case of Robert Cohen, later clinical director at Chestnut Lodge and director of the National Institute of Mental Health (R. Cohen, personal communication, March 3, 2007).

The WSP arranged with the training division of the Washington-Baltimore Psychoanalytic Institute to provide graduates of the WSP's three-year program with credit toward a certificate in psychoanalysis as well as a certificate from the WSP. By 1948, the WSP, which qualified under the G.I. Bill, had approximately 400 students enrolled (Evans, 2024).

The WSP was unusual among post-graduate psychotherapy training centers in the United States. It was willing to accept non-medical practitioners. Another contemporary training program for non-medical professionals was available at the National Psychological Association for Psychoanalysis (NPAP). This program was created in 1948 by Theodor Reik, a psychologist and close colleague of Freud (NPAP 2021). At present, psychotherapy turf wars — where they exist — are among the different professions (e.g., psychiatry, psychology, social work, etc.).

During the early part of the twentieth century, the central conflict was between those with medical degrees and those without. In the United States, psychoanalysis was considered the province of medical professionals. Non-medical psychoanalysts were referred to as "lay analysts." The WSP's stance regarding the training of non-medical professionals was not popular within institutional psychoanalysis.

In 1943, the trustees of the William Alanson White Psychiatric Foundation created a branch of the school in New York City, now the William Alanson White Institute of Psychiatry, Psychoanalysis, and Psychology, under the direction of Clara Thompson (Kwawer, 2012). Conflict regarding the admission of medical and lay analysts briefly resurfaced. There was a new dimension to this conflict, though: were non-medical analysts qualified to teach at the institute?

Hilde Bruch (see Chapter Fifteen) was an Associate in Psychiatry at the Columbia University College of Physicians and Surgeons and was invited to join the faculty at the White Institute. She was astounded that non-medical professionals were admitted (this had apparently been more tolerable to her in Washington) but became enraged when she was asked to teach a course with a psychiatric (clinical) social worker. She complained to Thompson, and, receiving no satisfaction, fired off letters to Sullivan and Fromm-Reichmann: "Who are these lay people, anyway? Certainly it's hard to envision any educational background that can be considered adequate equivalent for admitting non-medical professional workers into clinical courses" (J. Bruch, 1996, pp. 190-191). Sullivan never responded to this missive, while Fromm-Reichmann mildly reproached her: "I am a little disconcerted about your attitude;" Bruch quietly resigned from the faculty (J. Bruch, 1996, p. 194).

However, at least in the Washington program, there were minor differences in the training medical and non-medical professionals received. Beatrice Liebenberg, a social worker, who attended the school beginning in 1947 (and was involved in its activities until her death in 2024) told me that non-medical practitioners, for instance, could not attend the seminars on dreams. There were two programs open to the school's students. One, for physicians, was a certificate in Intensive Personality Study. The other, for non-physicians, was a certificate in Applied Psychiatry (Bever, 1993; Evans, 2024). She, however, was most struck by the differences between Sullivan's treatment of the men and women at the school. She related:

> I thought Sullivan was absolutely brilliant, truly brilliant. I was so excited by his ideas ... I loved the fact that he actually had a social science background .... The lecture hall held well over 100 people when he spoke. ... I never talked with him directly ... I don't know that women ever really got to talk with him at any length. Helen Swick Perry ... [his assistant at the journal *Psychiatry* and biographer] said he never looked at her directly the whole time that she interviewed him (personal communication, March 30, 2011).

Sullivan's relationships with women were complex, but he did value the friendship of Frieda Fromm-Reichmann, Edith Wiegert, and Clara Thompson; he also held Thompson in high enough esteem that he undertook an analysis with her (Perry, 1982).

Liebenberg remembered Otto fondly from the time they shared at the WSP. She recalled that they shared classes with Sullivan, Frieda Fromm-Reichmann, and Edith Weigert. She related: "I think what struck me most about Otto ... was his openness, his willingness to listen — there was no dogma in [him]" (personal communication, March 30, 2011). She did not feel any prejudice from Otto toward non-medically trained professionals.

Around 1949-1950, Liebenberg described an ironic development in Otto's practice.

> There was one day ... on the front page [of the *Washington Post*] an item about a patient having committed suicide and it was Otto's patient. I remember talking with Otto ... and he thought that was going to be the end of his practice. Instead, he ... got many calls in the days following from people who wanted to begin therapy with him. He finally asked one of them "... [Why] do you want to do this?" [The caller] said he'd always wanted to see a psychiatrist but didn't know any (personal communication, March 30, 2011).

Having Otto's name from the paper gave him someone to call.

Liebenberg remembered Otto as "such an original person and so was Sullivan." Otto was "an extremely intelligent, gentle person, who was reflective and who pretty much followed ... the Sullivan approach to therapy" (personal communication, March 30, 2011).

During this period, Otto's relationship with Sullivan expanded. Because of his heart disease, Sullivan could not drive, and Otto often drove him to appointments. He recalled that, after one of his sessions, he and Sullivan shared a meal. He detected no difference between Sullivan the therapist and Sullivan the dinner companion. Patrick Will said that his father had "clearly … found a soul mate in Sullivan" (personal communication, January 16, 2011). Michael Guy Thompson, a colleague of Otto's on the West Coast, confirmed this view: "He [Will] talked about Sullivan a lot. Clearly, Sullivan was the one who changed his life. He revered and adored Sullivan and was very open about that" (personal communication, June 29, 2007).

Perhaps one of the most important things that Otto remembered Sullivan telling him was that: "it takes about five years for a doctor … to get over analytic training." He approached psychoanalytic theory particularly skeptically.

## Psychoanalytic Education & Training:

Otto maintained a respectful, but wary view of traditional psychoanalysis. He related, "I didn't go along very much with the instinct theory." Reflecting on his own analytic training, Otto (1962) wrote that it was stimulating and generally satisfying. He related, however, that this satisfaction was, in large measure, the result of the curriculum being rich in the social sciences — sociology, anthropology, and linguistics — the indisputable influence of Sullivan. Yet, he described a variety of potential weaknesses in psychoanalytic training. These weaknesses began with the process of identifying candidates "suitable" to the program. He noted that analytic faculty seemed to want candidates who would confirm their own views and proffered the question: "Had we developed skill in selecting the non-troublesome … [and] the conventional …?" (Will, 1962, p. 87).

Though Otto may not have known it, his concerns were played out at the Topeka Psychoanalytic Institute, which was heavily influenced by Karl and Will Menninger and Robert Knight. Lawrence Friedman (1990), in his study of the Menningers and the Menninger Clinic, described a system in which those applicants who presented themselves as friendly and cooperative to the admissions committee for psychoanalytic training were assessed as having the necessary "psychological mindedness" to be advanced over other applicants in the admission process. Conversely, "[s]tudent rebels who prized neither cooperation nor rapport with senior analysts tended to have less favorable interviews and were less likely to be approved" (p. 186). Applicants among the latter group were also generally viewed as less psychologically mature.

Otto wrote and taught that much of what analytic candidates were taught were *theories*, not *facts*, though that differentiation was seldom made. He (1946) described some of these theories as overly facile. He (1962) perceived an element of authoritarianism in institutes in which candidates were encouraged to become copies of faculty members, particularly their training analysts, rather than being guided toward the "recognition and realization of … [the candidate's] own potential and values" (p. 93). He was also concerned that candidates were not encouraged to think freely and creatively.

The authoritarian nature of psychoanalytic training was a part of the process from the beginning. Robert Jay Lifton (2011) wrote that Erik Erikson had described his earliest contacts with psychoanalysis. Because his formal education had been truncated, he described gratitude for the education he received but that "the atmosphere was so 'unhealthy' that he would have found it necessary to leave [Vienna] even without the Nazi threat" (p. 51).

Otto told Kim Chernin a possibly apocryphal story about delivering a speech to a graduating class of candidates, which he ended by saying, "Well, once again I congratulate all of you on finishing a long course of studies and let me remind you of one thing: you are now — at last — free to think." Otto could also be flippant about training analysts, characterizing them as "training people to keep their thoughts to themselves."

The training analysis held other dangers. Within institute hierarchies, training analysts sometimes breached the confidentiality of their analysands to ensure that they would not progress beyond a point the analyst thought appropriate. Professional positions could also be affected by such breaches (Friedman, 1990).

There was one aspect, however, of identification with an analytic faculty member that Otto (1962) viewed as potentially helpful. This was an identification with their authenticity. This, though, required faculty members "to live to some extent the lives we advocate" (p. 100). Otto believed authenticity to be a goal of both psychoanalytic instruction and practice. As Ralph Waldo Emerson wrote in *Spiritual Laws* (1844/2009c): "[a] man may teach by doing, and not otherwise" (p. 90). "[W]hat the best teachers embody ... [is] a way of living" (Davis, 2023, p. 133).

Otto similarly found some of the clinical concepts of psychoanalysis questionable. Among these were "neutrality" and "anonymity." Neutrality, he believed, was not possible in any real sense. Every action, just like every lack of action, influences the patient (Will, 1972). The therapist must deal with the sometimes-unforeseeable consequences of both. He (1966) cautioned that in the preoccupation with maintaining neutrality the therapist "may lose sight of all else ... and thus jeopardize the work" (p. 20).

In a similar vein, Otto (1970c) believed that anonymity, even if considered "relative," was impossible; the therapist is often "revealed as a real person, unshielded by a professional front" (p. 11). For him, the pursuit of anonymity was undesirable (1960, 1970a, 1970b, 1973, 1975). He (1970a) wrote: "The therapist (his training, technique, and his whole past and present self) is an instrument for the patient to explore, learn to use, mold, discover its limitations, see how it can grow, teach, and learn" (p. 389). He (1960) believed that revealing aspects of himself aided the patient in discovering what was true about herself.

Otto, like Sullivan, sometimes used counterprojective interventions to deal with transference phenomena. He (1961a) built on the patient's strengths describing his approach to perceptual distortions as reinforcing accurate perceptions, "... having no hesitancy in attempting to clarify my attitudes, behavior, and views of the current scene" (p. 82).

In working with analytic candidates, he often found that they felt so surrounded by rules that they became paralyzed. He recalled that a candidate attending one of his seminars was presenting a patient study. He asked this young man, "How'd this patient happen to come to see you?"

The candidate stammered, "Well ..."

"Don't you know?"

"Well, [he named a training analyst] referred her to me."

"Was that her problem?"

There is a quality to this interaction that seems Sullivanian in its critical tone, and Otto remembered being frustrated. "He hadn't found out [why she had come for treatment]. What the hell?" He perceived some of the candidates as "anti-historians." "To get information was bad business; they believed that 'It'll all come out in the transference.' I used to say to some of them, 'You should live so long. It won't hurt you to know about somebody a little bit.'"

Otto described his own practice of scheduling an initial session for 90 minutes to two hour's duration and developing a picture of the patient. While he did not formally take notes, he would ask questions about what prompted the patient to seek psychotherapy, her symptoms, and other relevant information. At the conclusion of the initial session, he attempted "to take out a piece of paper and write up a little outline." He would also tell the patient something about himself in the initial interview.

Otto seemed to have also been ill at ease with psychoanalytic technique. It was probably, at least to some extent, because a prescribed technique implied certainty. For a uniform technique to be applicable, all therapists and all patients would have to be the same. Therapists would need to be interchangeable — like cogs in an impersonal machine (see also Strupp, 1968). Otto believed that each unique therapeutic dyad creates the tools needed to accomplish their work.

During the era when Otto first became an analyst, it was felt that the primary technique of analysis and psychotherapy based on dynamic principles was interpretation — the explanation of the present by reference to the past (Wallerstein, 1986, 1988). Otto did not completely eschew interpretation as Sullivan did, but he preferred to observe and comment on the here-and-now rather than the there-and-then of genetic interpretation. While he did not rely solely on the technique of *interpretation*, he did recognize the centrality of the relationship (not just the transferential elements) between therapist and patient. One of his goals was to increase the patient's awareness of the characteristics of that relationship.

Outcome studies have not supported the differences between psychoanalysis and psychotherapy originally predicted by researchers. Psychoanalysis accomplished less than was predicted and psychotherapy accomplished more (Di Donna, 2011).

Otto did not subscribe to Sullivan's (1954) notion that the therapist is an "expert." He (1977a) asserted that the therapist could not be an expert "in the sense that a mechanical engineer can be expert" (p. 13). He (1961a) acknowledged that, early in his practice, he had assumed a particular role (i.e. as therapist/physician) and expected that his partner in the endeavor would assume the complementary conventional role of "patient." However, he quickly learned that such roles can be injurious to the person expected to fulfill the patient's role. This came to be an expectation he attempted to abandon.

Near the end of his life, while living in California, Otto seemed to view formal psychoanalytic training as superfluous. As I wrote in the preface, I did not pursue a traditional psychoanalytic training experience. I once shared my ambivalence about this with Kim Chernin. She told me that she had been considering applying to the San Francisco Center for Psychoanalysis when she first began working with Otto. When she shared with Otto her own ambivalence about doing so, Otto's response was: "You don't need a certificate to demonstrate that you know how to listen in a way that is helpful to people" (she also described this interaction in Chernin [2017, p. xvii]).

Courtesy of the National Library of Medicine

## Hilde Bruch, M.D. (1904-1984)

circa 1955

Hilde Bruch idealized Sullivan and Fromm-Reichmann. Initially interested in schizophrenia, she became an expert on eating disorders. She and Otto were friends for over thirty years. Uninterested in theoretical schools of thought, her approach to psychotherapy has been called "The constructive use of ignorance."

# Chapter Fifteen: The Constructive Use of Ignorance

## Inquisitive & Easily Frustrated

Otto considered his most effective teachers to be: Harry Stack Sullivan, Hilde Bruch, Dexter Bullard, and Frieda Fromm-Reichmann. He felt that all four, to a greater or lesser extent, shaped his professional life, and he held all in affectionate esteem. Brunhilde Bruch, who shortened her first name to Hilde, was a dear friend, and a helpful teacher — a pioneer in the field of eating disorders and a skilled psychotherapist. In the latter endeavor, she, like Otto (1970b), emphasized curiosity and discounted interpretation (Skårderud, 2009).

Hilde was born in 1904 to Hirsch and Adele Bruch (neé Rath) in the German village of Dülken on the lower Rhine near Holland. The couple met at a synagogue dance. She had two older siblings: a brother, Rudolf, and a sister, Auguste; she also had four younger siblings, three brothers and a sister: Artur, Erna, Ernst, and Kurt. Auguste was beautiful and graceful. Hilde tended to be overweight and her brothers tormented her with the nickname "die dicke" ("The fat one"). For much of her life she would struggle with her weight (J. Bruch, 1996; Rosen, 2022).

From the beginning of her life, Hilde was inquisitive, difficult to satisfy with easy answers, easily frustrated, and aggressive. The German education system at that time did not correspond exactly to the American system, but the two can be approximately correlated. Hilde moved through *grundschule* (elementary school) for four years, then *volkschule* (a continuing primary school) for another four years, *septa* (emphasizing science), and then *gymnasium* (high school). Though she received high marks, she was often a frustration to her teachers. Her father, a cattle rancher, died of cardiac complications from diabetes when she was sixteen, and his role was assumed by his brother who was a physician (J. Bruch, 1996; Rosen, 2022).

Initially, Hilde wanted to become a mathematician. Her uncle counseled against this choice and encouraged her to become a physician. She enrolled at the Albert Ludwig University in Freiburg and graduated with her medical degree in 1929. She began her *praktische jahr* (internship) at the Hospital for the Medical Academy of Dusseldorf, spending three months studying obstetrics and three months studying gynecology. She finished the year as a research assistant at the University of Kiel. The next year, she began a residency in pediatrics at the University of Leipzig (J. Bruch, 1996; Rosen, 2022).

By 1931, Germany was tottering between chaos and authoritarianism. Adolf Hitler, and his brown-shirted supporters were almost ubiquitous, inciting hatred against the Jews. Hilde began preparing to leave Germany, which she did in 1933. She left for England under the pretext of attending the International Pediatric Congress. Once in England, Hilde took a position as a research assistant at the East End Child Clinic. However, Germany was not the only country with antisemitic elements, and some in England refused to let her treat their children because she was a Jew. In 1934, Hilde left England for the United States. After landing in Boston, she made her way to New York City and completed her residency in pediatrics at Babies Hospital of Columbia Presbyterian Hospital in 1935 (Rosen, 2022).

By 1935, Hilde was exhausted, disillusioned, and depressed. She attempted to take her life with an overdose of barbiturates. She was in a coma when admitted to Columbia Presbyterian Hospital where she spent a week recovering. She was then transferred for care to the Bloomingdale Psychiatric Hospital in White Plains, New York (J. Bruch, 1996).

At Bloomingdale, something quite remarkable occurred. The experience did not break her as some of her colleagues thought it might. The psychotherapy to which she was exposed kindled a curiosity in her about the psychological aspects of pediatrics. She decided to study child and adult psychiatry and psychoanalysis. She contacted and scheduled time to participate in lectures given by Frieda Fromm-Reichmann at Chestnut Lodge (J. Bruch, 1996).

In 1941, she contacted John C. Whitehorn, the newly appointed Henry Phipps Professor of Psychiatry and director of psychiatry at the Phipps Clinic of Johns Hopkins University, who had succeeded Adolf Meyer in these positions (Baxter, 1986). According to rumors at the hospital, Whitehorn had been hired because of his research background in biochemistry at Harvard. The Board of Trust had been concerned when Meyer, a pathologist, had begun to promote psychobiology, with its emphasis on psychotherapy. The trustees hoped that Whitehorn would return the department of psychiatry to a physiological foundation (Young, 2012).

Instead, they got a psychiatrist interested in psychotherapy with schizophrenic patients (see Whitehorn, 1950, 1955). He and Otto frequently regaled residents with stories about their work with patients (Yalom, 2017). One resident, Barbara Young (2012), believed that Whitehorn's basic communication to the residents was: "*bear in mind that patients are people just like you. Don't teach them. Listen to them and they will teach you*" (p. 2, emphasis in the original).

Whitehorn permitted Hilde to attend lectures at Phipps. She also arranged to attend lectures at both the Washington-Baltimore Psychoanalytic Society and the Washington School of Psychiatry. She was still curious and could still be aggressive in seeking answers. She said what was on her mind; Whitehorn noted: "Her honesty sometimes outstrips her tact" (J. Bruch, 1996, p. 162). She relocated once more, from New York City to Baltimore.

Once in Baltimore, she began supervision with Harry Stack Sullivan while working with a young patient diagnosed as schizophrenic. Sullivan found her sensitivity toward her patient so exquisite that he suggested that she might be schizophrenic herself. Both appreciative of Sullivan's comment and disturbed by it, she talked with Frieda Fromm-Reichmann about it. Fromm-Reichmann reassured her that she was not schizophrenic — Sullivan had simply given her his ultimate compliment.

She idolized Sullivan for his innovative thinking about the nature of psychotherapy. He was different from many of the psychoanalysts she knew, who were willing to place blame squarely on their patients for any lack of progress. Sullivan accepted responsibility for his part in a process that was seldom easy and sometimes unsuccessful. When her patient improved and ended psychotherapy, he presented her with a carton of

Lucky Strike cigarettes — not her preferred brand. She informed Sullivan of this and he laughed, responding, "he communicates what you and I already know, that he was *lucky* to have you as his therapist" (J. Bruch, 1996, p. 191, emphasis in the original). In working with Sullivan, Hilde became convinced that "working psychotherapeutically with schizophrenic patients could lead to insights into fundamental problems of human existence and of psychopathology not readily gained from neurotic patients" (Skårderud, 2009, p. 84).

In 1940, Hilde became a naturalized American citizen (Rosen, 2022). While she was in Baltimore, she began analysis with Frieda Fromm-Reichmann (Skårderud, 2009). She returned to New York City in 1943, interested in working with schizophrenic patients (Rosen, 2022). 1943 was also the year that Otto returned from the Pacific to undergo training in psychiatry at Saint Elizabeths Hospital. The two met and began a lifelong friendship. They shared common interests, including a fascination with schizophrenic people and a desire to improve their lives, a guarded, perhaps schizoid, approach to relationships, and high regard for both Sullivan and Frieda Fromm-Reichmann. They also shared clinical priorities. Both maintained a commitment to open-mindedness toward theories. Hilde's niece, Joanne Hatch Bruch (1996) wrote that Hilde: "emphatically refused to identify with any particular school of thought" (p. 256). She believed that, ultimately, each perspective had a rigidity that interfered with understanding patients. Like Otto, she felt that listening to patients in an open-minded way yielded the wisdom to help.

Gradually, Hilde began to observe similar processes in patients with eating disorders and schizophrenia. These included: perceptual distortions, lack of understanding of bodily sensations, a lack of clarity about emotional states, the inaccurate use of language, and anxiety about interpersonal disapproval (Skårderud, 2009).

In 1964, Hilde was invited to teach psychiatry at Baylor University in Houston, Texas. As a teacher, she was sensitive, though perhaps overly involved with her students. Stuart Yudofsky (1996) wrote that mothers of young women with eating disorders often lack respect for their child's boundaries, telling their daughters how to feel and pressuring them on important life decisions. It was a version of the concept of mystification. Perhaps Hilde discovered in these mothers one of her own characteristics, albeit less extreme. Yudofsky (1987), who knew Hilde for eighteen years, never felt confident that he understood her because she had a place for everyone in her life and they were seldom allowed to stray from that place.

While at Baylor, Hilde was highly productive. She wrote several books, including the classic *The Golden Cage: The Enigma of Anorexia Nervosa* in 1978. She also developed an approach to intensive psychotherapy that came to be called "the constructive use of ignorance" (Skårderud, 2013, p. 174). This approach emphasizes what is unknown about each patient and attempts to engender the patient's curiosity so that she may understand herself more fully. Hilde was convinced that an interpretive, rather than inquisitive, approach often led to defining the patient externally and recreated harmful family dynamics (Skårderud, 2013).

## *Learning Psychotherapy*

Of most relevance to this book, however, was Hilde's 1974 text, *Learning Psychotherapy: Rationale and Ground rules.* Though described as an introduction to psychotherapy, it is, nevertheless, a sophisticated treatment of the subject. She begins with a definition of psychotherapy as an interaction in which two people attempt to understand each other. Her definition suggests that it may be impossible to understand oneself without understanding others — to see oneself in another.

Throughout, Hilde emphasizes that psychotherapy offers the patient a new experience of being listened to rather than told how to feel and what to think. She also encourages the therapist to avoid preconceived ideas, holding in abeyance what she thinks she knows, so that the patient may experience her own understanding. She believed that the patient has an innate tendency toward health.

Hilde's approach eschews interpretation in favor of comments on what the therapist sees occurring in the interaction. The therapist must take care to avoid labeling the patient's anger, resentment, or suspended movement as "resistance" and consider that it may be a communication to the therapist about an error made. The therapist is best served by communicating clearly and with warmth. She suggested that a patient's silences often convey that the patient does not feel understood.

Hilde encouraged the establishment of the relationship's "ground rules" with flexibility. The fact that therapist and patient meet together regularly aids in the development of attachment. Patients may get more from each session if its duration is negotiated with the patient's needs fully considered. Additionally, the fee is negotiated rather than imposed by the therapist.

Ultimately, Hilde described learning psychotherapy as a process that continues throughout a lifetime. It is never completely mastered and requires a willingness to explore both successes and failures. On the cover, Otto endorsed *Learning Psychotherapy* … as "a masterpiece of succinct and clear statements about the major and fundamental issues of psychotherapy."

Hilde and Otto remained in contact for the rest of her life. In their correspondence, they often shared information about unidentified patients with whom they were working. In one instance, in 1971, Otto wrote to her about a young woman he had treated who might have been anorexic. He wrote:

> The patient to whom I refer … was variously diagnosed before finally being defined as schizophrenic. There had been a problem of severe weight loss mainly associated with her apprehension about taking in any food and her need to regurgitate that which was given to her. I had heard from someone that she had been considered at one time to be a "case of anorexia," but I do not have the official records on that. She was in and out of various hospitals and was an inpatient at the Lodge for about eight years. I was her therapist for seven years. We stopped work about seventeen years ago after which she finished college ….

Long after her treatment ended, he was still curious about this young woman and something he might have missed.

Hilde referred patients to both Chestnut Lodge and the Austen Riggs Center. She congratulated Otto on his retirement from the latter institution. Each letter ends with a personal note. Otto wrote, in closing his 1971 letter: "We are having a cold and snowy winter and a beautiful one. Gwen joins me in sending our very best wishes to you."

In 1982, members of the Austen Riggs staff organized a conference to honor Otto. Entitled "Illuminations of the Human Condition," the conference represented Otto's fifty years of relationships with the luminaries in the fields of psychiatry and psychoanalysis (Moore, 1982). Though she had begun to turn down invitations to present papers, Hilde was excited to honor Otto and immediately agreed to present a paper on "The Changing Picture of an Illness: Anorexia Nervosa" (Bruch, 1987). However, as the date drew near, she was hospitalized and forced to cancel. As a demonstration of her importance to Otto, her paper remained in the conference schedule and Otto's third wife, Beulah Parker, presented it. Hilde died in December 1984, after years of struggling with several maladies, including metastasized cancer. (J. Bruch, 1996). The conference papers were collected in a book entitled, *Attachment and the Therapeutic Process: Essays in Honor of Otto Allen Will, Jr., M.D.* published by the International Universities Press in 1987 (Sacksteder, Schwartz & Akabane, 1987).

Courtesy of Peerless Rockwell

Dexter Means Bullard, M.D (1898-1982)

circa 1950

Dexter Bullard owned Chestnut Lodge and functioned as the institution's medical director. He emphasized respect for patients and permitted the staff a wide latitude in creative thought and expression. His approach has been called "humane pragmatism" and "hospitality" (i.e. warm acceptance without expectation).

# Chapter Sixteen: Humane Pragmatism

To employ an overused truism, the only constant in life is change. For Otto, the decade between 1947 and 1957 would be a period of extensive change, affecting all aspects of his life.

Otto began 1947 as a lieutenant commander in the United States Navy Medical Corps. He was still titular head of the naval unit at Saint Elizabeths Hospital, though his assistant was running the day-to-day operations. He continued to recover from the gastric resection that, no doubt, saved his life, but required significant modifications in his style of living. He was single, divorced from Adeline Rowe after the death of their child. He was a student at the Washington School of Psychiatry, and he continued his intensive psychotherapy with Harry Stack Sullivan, which began the year before. All those parts of his life — and more — would change over the next ten years.

In 1947, he resigned from the navy and accepted a position with the Chestnut Lodge Sanitarium (the "Lodge") in Rockville, Maryland. He was attracted to the atmosphere of the Lodge. He recalled it as "renowned on the Eastern Seaboard for its psychoanalytic orientation and commitment to treating schizophrenics." He also recalled that the Lodge was "quite small and very human." The therapists carried a maximum of six patients. Therapists were required to have undergone analysis or to be currently in analysis. Some were in or had been in analysis with Fromm-Reichmann. The psychotherapists were supervised both individually and in groups. The medical director, Dexter M. Bullard, and the director of psychotherapy, Frieda Fromm-Reichmann, encouraged the psychiatrists to maintain private practices so that they could work with "less difficult" patients (and to supplement relatively low salaries at the Lodge). The Lodge had been in operation for thirty-seven years when Otto joined the staff.

## 125 Chestnut Trees

Dexter Means Bullard was born on August 14, 1898, in Waukesha, Wisconsin. His father, Ernest Luther Bullard, was a physician in general practice. His mother, Rosalie Bullard (neé Means), was a vivacious young woman from Kentucky. Ernest and Rosalie met at a summer resort in Northern Illinois, and, married, after a short courtship. Dexter was their only child (Rioch, 1984).

Dexter's father, Ernest Bullard, started his career as a general practitioner in Wisconsin. Though Ernest had no formal training in psychiatry, the governor of Wisconsin, Robert LaFollette, named him Superintendent of the Wisconsin State Hospital for the Insane at Mendota in 1902. It was an appointment bestowed on political friends and loyalists. It was also the kind of gift that came with expectations of further service. Ernest Bullard managed the hospital for about two years before colliding with LaFollette over the limits of his gratitude (Bullard, 1961).

The Bullard family left Mendota for Milwaukee where Ernest practiced and taught neurology and psychiatry at the Marquette University Medical School. However, he discovered that he was not an academic. He missed his previous administrative work at Mendota and wanted to administer a hospital. He did not, however, want to feel indebted to anyone else; he wanted his *own* hospital. As a shrewd man with some understanding of economics, he began to search for a property near Washington, DC. Because that city's primary business was government, it was more insulated than most cities from economic fluctuations. In 1908, Ernest found what he was looking for and bought the Woodlawn Hotel, a second empire structure in Rockville, Maryland, about twenty miles northwest of Washington. The Woodlawn Hotel consisted of one building with four floors and eight acres of surrounding property. The grounds were adorned with 125 Chestnut trees and Ernest rechristened it "Chestnut Lodge Sanitarium" (Rioch, 1984).

Opened in 1886, the Woodlawn Hotel had initially been a successful enterprise; however, over the years the owners had become overburdened with debt. When Ernest Bullard bought it, the building had been closed for eight years and required considerable work before it would again be functional in a new role. The Bullards spent two years renovating it and in 1910 reopened it as Chestnut Lodge. They had one patient (Silver, 1997).

For almost twenty years, the Bullard family shared the former hotel with the patients. Family quarters and Ernest's work area were on the first floor; patients were lodged on the upper three floors. By the summer of 1911, the Lodge had six patients. Within a few years, there were 22 beds available for patients. Ernest Bullard was the entire medical staff, on-call 24 hours a day, seven days a week. Rosalie Bullard managed the non-clinical aspects of the Lodge. There were no holidays and no vacations (Rioch, 1984; Silver, 1997).

The Lodge had a relatively simple treatment philosophy. Ernest Bullard believed in personal, individualized care. Patients received a great deal of attention. In the moral treatment tradition, he also believed that rest, healthy food, exercise, and productive work were curative (Hornstein, 2000; Rioch, 1984; Silver, 1997).

Dexter Bullard, in describing his childhood, seemed to have enjoyed his time at Mendota and at the Lodge. Dexter enjoyed people and made no distinction between "people" and "patients." As a young man, Dexter rode horses and loved dogs, particularly Great Danes (Rioch, 1984).

Having enjoyed such experiences, Dexter Bullard was predisposed to pursue a medical education and to help those with problems in living. He began his education in a Milwaukee public school. When the family relocated to Rockville, Dexter was accepted to the prestigious Sidwell Friends Select School, a Quaker institution, in Washington, DC. After graduating from Sidwell, Dexter studied at Yale, earning a Ph.B. (Bachelor of Philosophy), and then completed his medical education at the University of Pennsylvania in 1923 — just as the ideas of Otto Rank began to dominate the school of social work and influence other departments, as well. (Lieberman, 1985; Rioch, 1984).

Dexter learned a great deal by watching his father administer the Lodge and deal with the patients; in particular, he learned that running the Lodge would be hard, isolating work, devoid of many chances for travel. After receiving his medical degree, Dexter undertook postgraduate training at Queens Hospital in Honolulu, Hawaii (Rioch, 1984).

Perhaps more in keeping with his Ivy League education was the brief period he spent with the Scottish psychoanalyst, Charles MacFie Campbell, at the Boston Psychopathic Hospital (which later became the Massachusetts Mental Health Center). This training experience lasted only two months because in 1925 Ernest Bullard suffered a coronary, and

Dexter returned to help run the Lodge. In 1926, Dexter spent a day a week at the Henry Phipps Psychiatric Clinic of Johns Hopkins University. Though he did not study directly with Adolf Meyer, he learned much about Meyer's psychobiological approach to psychiatry (Bullard, 1961; Hornstein, 2000; Rioch, 1984).

From 1925 until 1931, Dexter was the assistant physician at Chestnut Lodge. During this period, the hospital had 20 beds. In 1927, Dexter married Anne W. Wilson. Almost immediately, the couple bonded not only as marital partners, but also as business partners. When Ernest and Rosalie left on a vacation, Dexter was responsible for the medical care of the patients and Anne was responsible for the day-to-day administrative functions of the Lodge. According to Hornstein (2000), the only thing that Anne asked of Dexter was that he avoid second-guessing her decisions in her areas of responsibility and Dexter agreed. Dexter and Anne turned out to be an effective team. For 40 years, until Anne's retirement in 1967, they efficiently administered the Lodge (Rioch, 1984).

In 1931, while on vacation in Florida, Ernest Bullard suffered a second, and fatal, coronary. Dexter's inheritance was Chestnut Lodge. He decided that he would spend five years considering what to make of it. He and Anne had already built a cottage on the grounds, about 100 feet from the main building, to serve as their family home. This came to be known as the "Little Lodge." The Lodge had beds for 22 patients and Dexter began to expand. Initially, he bought two small adjoining farms and later other land surrounding the Lodge (Rioch, 1984).

David Rioch (1984) described Dexter Bullard's clinical approach at this time as warm, humane, and pragmatic. Dexter had always been interested in Freud's ideas and was now considering psychoanalytic training (Hornstein, 2000; Silver, 1997).

Yet, before he could commit himself to psychoanalytic training — or much else — he had to remedy the problem of staffing. He did not want to be the sole physician responsible for all the patients at the Lodge. As a partial remedy to this situation, he began hiring medical students. According to Rioch (1984), Dexter also found professional help in a way that might be frowned upon today; he hired medical personnel who were well-trained, but in need of respite care themselves. Bullard had now cobbled together enough support that he could pursue psychoanalytic training with its requisite four sessions weekly.

Harry Stack Sullivan and Ernest W. Hadley founded the Washington-Baltimore Psychoanalytic Society in 1930. For over 15 years Sullivan and Hadley would be a successful team. Sullivan provided the mercurial genius and Hadley the capacity for practical planning — and the patience. Hadley had also undergone the best training available for a psychoanalyst in that era and was the third psychoanalyst in private practice in the Washington area (Bever, 1993). Bullard completed a training analysis with Hadley, though he would later be one of Sullivan's patients, as well.

During those years, psychoanalytic training consisted primarily of the student's own psychoanalysis, conducted by an analyst approved by the local Society, and the supervision of cases by an approved control analyst; the training and control analysts were required to be different people (Hale, 1995).

## The First Psychoanalytic Hospital for Schizophrenics

In 1931, the Great Depression was ravaging the economy. Dexter was aware that competitors up and down the Eastern Seaboard were declaring bankruptcy and closing their doors. Dexter and Anne were facing a similar fate unless Dexter could distinguish Chestnut Lodge in some way from competing hospitals. He devised a plan to turn the Lodge into the world's first psychiatric hospital specializing in psychoanalytic psychotherapy for schizophrenics (Hornstein, 2000). The plan paid off. He hired Marjorie Jarvis, another psychiatrist with some psychoanalytic training, and together they began treating some of the most difficult patients in the world.

The Lodge slowly began to grow; by 1934 it had 30 beds. In 1935, Frieda Fromm-Reichmann, a German-Jewish psychoanalyst, fleeing Nazi persecution, came to the United States (Bullard, 1959; 1961; Hornstein, 2000; Weininger, 1989). In September 1935, Fromm-Reichmann became a full-time staff member at the Lodge. She initially lived in the main building with the patients and Dexter's mother, Rosalie. The quarters were cramped. Eventually, Frieda received offers from other facilities, particularly the Menninger Clinic, which she leveraged to obtain her own living space. Dexter built her a cottage on the Lodge grounds, and she took occupancy in 1936 (Hornstein, 2000; Rioch, 1984). By the 1940s,

Chestnut Lodge became the clinical laboratory of the interpersonal perspective (Kwawer, 2019).

Dexter completed his training analysis with Hadley in 1937. Shortly after, he was elected to membership in both the Washington-Baltimore Psychoanalytic Society and the American Psychoanalytic Association. Bullard's involvement with psychoanalysis did not change his fundamental approach to patients or the language used by the staff at the Lodge, which remained simple and descriptive (Rioch, 1984).

Robert Gibson told me that Dexter, a chain smoker with a fondness for bourbon, maintained an eclectic orientation and encouraged multiple philosophies at the Lodge (personal communication, March 9, 2007). He had a rare non-competitive personality and was comfortable with what he called "letting people run their own show" (Langs & Searles, 1980, p. 74). The motto at the Lodge, applicable to both staff and patients, was "Be Yourself" (Waugaman, 2019, p. 5). The freedom this philosophy offered produced some of the most exceptional therapists of the time, including Robert Cohen, Harold Searles, Clarence Schulz, Benjamin Weininger, and Otto (Hornstein, 2000; Katchadourian, 2012). Gerard Fromm (2011) wrote that early interpersonal views of treatment, especially at Chestnut Lodge, were focused on the basics of establishing relationships.

After initially publishing in 1940 *Conceptions of Modern Psychiatry* (1953a), Sullivan hoped to continue expanding his ideas about interpersonal psychiatry, particularly a theory of personality development. Dexter saw an opportunity. He invited Sullivan to present to the medical staff at the Lodge. The staff would have the experience of interacting with a truly original theorist and Sullivan would have the opportunity to receive feedback from a small group of bright clinicians who could help advance his ideas. From 1940-1941, Sullivan held a seminar on the principles of interpersonal psychiatry; this was discontinued when Sullivan began to work for the Selective Service System (Bullard, 1956).

In October 1942, Sullivan's consultantship with the Selective Service System ended after conflict with a new director (Perry, 1982). Sullivan was again available to consult at Chestnut Lodge and Dexter Bullard was still interested. From 1942 until 1946 Sullivan met with the medical staff and Dexter's Great Dane two evenings a week in the basement of the Rose Hill

Mansion, previously part of a farm purchased by the Bullards (Bullard, 1956; Hornstein, 2000). During the winter months, Sullivan positioned himself near the hearth and held forth on a variety of topics. According to Dexter (1956), he was sometimes spellbinding and at other times muddled. The tone of the seminar could be affable and enlightening but could also be contentious. Dexter emphasized, however, that "no one ever went to sleep — one did not when Sullivan held the floor" (1956, p. xi).

## Hospitality

Henry David Thoreau (1863/1993) wrote in his essay, "Life Without Principle," that "The greatest compliment that was ever paid me was when one asked me what *I thought*, and attended to my answer. I am surprised, as well as delighted, when this happens" (p. 75, italics in the original). Thoreau's comment alludes to how seldom others listen to and respect us.

Respect toward patients was a foundation of the approach at Chestnut Lodge. David Rioch (1984) was particularly impressed with what he called Dexter Bullard's "hospitality," a quality of warmth given without obligation. Former Lodge staff member, Marvin Adland, told Jon Frederickson (2003) that Dexter's basic philosophy was that if a therapist met with a patient, and treated her with compassion and respect, a connection would occur. A helpful relationship would then develop.

According to Fromm-Reichmann's colleague and friend, Edith Weigert (1959), Bullard provided "an atmosphere of open-minded, enthusiastic understanding" and opportunities for Fromm-Reichmann and the many young psychotherapists drawn to her (p. vi). "For the Lodge patients, Dexter was equally open-minded and non-dogmatic. That was his philosophy" (p. 3). Dexter called it "humane pragmatism" (Rioch, 1984, pp. 2-3). Otto (1981b) echoed Bullard's view that, "If therapist and patient meet together over a long enough period of time at regular and frequent intervals, relational bonds — the foundation of understanding, growth, and betterment — will form" (p. 208).

Dexter published only a handful of papers during his career. One that exemplified what Rioch referred to as Dexter's "hospitality," was published in 1939 in *The Psychoanalytic Review*, and entitled "The Application of Psychoanalytic Psychiatry to the Psychoses." Early in the paper, Dexter suggests the theoretical limitations of classical psychoanalytic theory, by dethroning sexuality as the primary focus of psychotherapy and equating it with *all* the experiences that have contributed to the patient's strengths and difficulties.

While Dexter was not a theorist by nature, his paper is practical, emphasizing the demonstration of respect in the relationship between therapist and patient. He (1939) suggests that respect is reflected in the therapist's attitude. Further, he admonishes that the therapist's attitude itself may "spell the difference between recovery and chronicity" (p. 529). Most of the paper is focused on the importance of communication that is both respectful of and arouses minimal anxiety for the patient. His recommendations include the following: 1) Introducing only those subjects to which the therapist perceives the patient can respond (a plea for common sense); 2) reassuring the patient that she need not talk about anything too anxiety-provoking; 3) maintaining an awareness that questions from a stranger can be frightening, feel accusatory, and arouse anger; 4) insuring that both participants have a similar understanding of words and phrases used; and 5) immediately and clearly attempting to rectify missteps made. It is a wise and humane paper.

Dexter and Fromm-Reichmann began to attract residents interested in psychoanalysis. The Lodge nurses underwent personal psychoanalyses, and the professional staff grew. According to Benjamin Weininger (1989), a resident physician and then staff member at the Lodge, Bullard and Fromm-Reichmann did most of the supervision but encouraged the staff to get supervision outside the Lodge, as well. Weininger (1989) wrote that he had supervision in New York, first with Harry Stack Sullivan and later with Karen Horney.

Weininger (1989) related that the focus of supervision at the Lodge was countertransferential reactions (what might now be called "enactments") that seemed to be interfering in the therapy. Sullivan (1954) taught that the therapist should keep the therapeutic situation simple enough so that the interpersonal field remained relatively clear of obstacles, including destructive countertransference, thereby allowing the patient's natural growth tendency to move the therapy in a positive direction. Otto entered this environment in 1947. The Lodge required a two-year commitment (though five years was highly encouraged) from staff psychiatrists (Waugaman, 2019). Otto stayed for 20 years.

## Sullivan's Death

Sullivan's health inexorably deteriorated, and his range of activities contracted. He continued teaching at the Washington School of Psychiatry and was engaged in clinical supervision. His work with Otto continued. Sullivan was also involved in the United Nations International Tensions Project and, at the invitation of Canadian Major General and psychiatrist Brock Chisholm, served as a consultant to the International Congress on Mental Health (Evans, 2024; Perry, 1982).

Sullivan's weariness grew more pronounced over 1948, and many suspected the end was near. Otto remembered being present when Sullivan received a visitor who implored him not to die, "Oh, Dr. Sullivan, don't die now."

Sullivan responded, "Why not?"

"Because I need you," replied the guest, who then chastised himself, "Oh, that's so selfish."

Sullivan reassured him: "I don't know of a better reason to keep living than somebody needs you."

As Sullivan prepared for his final trip to Europe, he met with Chisholm at the Hay-Adams Hotel in Washington, DC. Otto drove him and was present for the meeting. Toward the end of their discussion, Otto remembered Chisholm urging Sullivan to remain in the United States. "Harry, I don't think you ought to go."

Sullivan asked, "Why not?"

"Because I don't think you'll survive the trip," Chisholm replied.

"Do you think I'll live much longer if I don't go?"

"No, Harry, I don't."

"Well, I'm going."

The end came in a room of the Hotel Ritz in Paris on January 14, 1949. The French authorities ruled the cause of death a meningeal hemorrhage (bleeding in the meninges, the membranes that cover the brain and spinal cord, frequently called "a stroke") (American Foreign Service, 1949; Perry, 1982). Although he was well-aware of Sullivan's deteriorating health, Otto was surprised by his death. He recalled, "I was sitting in my office one night at the Lodge, and Dexter Bullard, walked by. I had my door open. He said, 'Got bad news; Harry's dead.' And I didn't know who he meant by Harry."

The official explanation of Sullivan's death co-exists with a rumor that Sullivan took his own life (Perry, 1982). Sullivan died on his mother's birthday. This, and an ambiguous note that he left his life partner, Jimmie, form the basis of these rumors. Before he departed for Europe, he left a note with Jimmie, who by then had adopted the surname Sullivan, that he did not expect to return (Evans, 2024). Was the date of his death a strange coincidence or a determined act? The uncertainty surrounding Sullivan's death will probably remain. Otto dismissed rumors of Sullivan committing suicide by asserting that such rumors were used to detract from "the great and good."

When Harry Stack Sullivan died at the age of 56, he was one of the most celebrated and controversial psychiatrists in the United States. He was loved and hated, admired and detested, considered a genius by some and a fraud by others (Farber, 2000; Gaarder, 2006; Silverberg, 1952; Waugaman, 2012). As Dexter noted, Sullivan brought out the most passionate and ambivalent of emotional reactions in others (Cornett, 2008). Very few who knew Sullivan could separate his ideas from the man. Martin Cooperman, Otto's colleague at the Lodge and later, Austen Riggs, was one who could. While he described Sullivan as "a son of a bitch" he found his ideas full of potential (Pepper, 2019, p. 106).

Ironically, on August 21, 1949, a few months after Sullivan's death, *The Washington Post* favorably compared the Washington School of Psychiatry to Freud's psychoanalytic study group in Vienna at the turn of the twentieth century (Rioch, 1986). Through the Washington School of Psychiatry and the journal *Psychiatry*, Sullivan had, prior to his death, refined and disseminated his thinking to a large audience. *Psychiatry*, under Sullivan's editorship, became an interdisciplinary study of what it means to be human (Bazerman, 2005).

# Chapter Seventeen: Endings & Beginnings

## Gwen Tudor

Otto formally graduated from the Washington School of Psychiatry in 1950 and was elected to the faculty. There was a new addition to his life, as well. Bea Liebenberg remembered that, around this time, Otto began dating "a psychiatric nurse, whose first name was Gwen. Gwen was just lovely! He was so happy during that time" (personal communication, March 30, 2011).

Gwen Elizabeth Tudor was born just outside Iowa City, Iowa on February 23, 1918. She was the daughter of Milton J. and Mary Grace Tudor (neeé Ryan). Married in December 1914, the couple owned a farm. About 1928, when Gwen was ten, their farm was destroyed by a devastating fire. Gwen's parents bought another farm in Olin, Iowa, a village of about 700 people (U.S. Census Bureau, 1920b). Gwen had one sister, Mary Ruth, two years her senior. She also had two younger siblings — a brother, John Milton, born in 1922, and a sister, Abbie Ann, born in 1928 (U.S. Census, 1930b). The farm employed three laborers and a housekeeper (U.S. Census Bureau, 1920a). It was a "working farm." It is speculative, but I wonder if this was part of Otto's initial attraction to her — the bucolic background with a fantasy of a close and sane nuclear family. One, at least, saner than his own.

Gwen worked on the farm and attended the local public schools. The family was Episcopalian. According to Deirdre Vinyard this was one difference between her parents — Otto had no religious affiliation or real interest in religion (personal communication, June 2, 2025). Gwen was a bright and curious student. She attended the University of Iowa, earning a bachelor's degree in nursing in 1941. Following graduation, she became a Registered Nurse. She remained affiliated with the University of Iowa as an instructor and in 1945 she became an assistant professor and director of nursing (Sullivan, 2007).

Soon after establishing herself at the university in 1945, Gwen married Jose Puig-Guri, M.D., an orthopedic surgeon on the faculty of the State University of Iowa, who had also been a surgeon with the Republican Army during the Spanish Civil War ("Licenses to Wed in Iowa," 1945). He was 31 and she was 26. In 1942, he co-authored an article entitled, "General Principles in the Treatment of Wounds and Fractures in the Spanish War" in the journal *The Military Surgeon*, which brought him recognition. Puig-Guri was a Spanish national, and, probably because of his involvement with the leftist Republican forces in Spain, he could not become a permanent resident of the United States. He ultimately relocated to Mexico, and the couple divorced.

In 1955, Gwen testified before the House Un-American Activities Committee (HUAC) as a condition of employment with the World Health Organization (WHO) where she would be consultant to the United Nations' Expert Committee on Psychiatric Nursing. This was the height of the Red Scare and no doubt her former marriage raised the eyebrows of a few committee members. She was called to testify before the committee as to whether Puig-Guri had been affiliated with the communist party. She testified that she had no knowledge of such an affiliation (Sullivan, 2007). HUAC accepted her testimony and she accepted the position at WHO. While that ended her involvement with the benighted HUAC, the experience had been stressful and, as for so many Americans coerced to testify, an unwarranted intrusion into her life.

In 1950, Gwen relocated to New York City to study nursing education at Columbia University Teacher's College. Developed in 1899, the Ivy League program was one of the most prestigious in the field (Christy, 1969). The development of formal nursing education programs was part of the advancing professionalization of nursing as a vocational discipline. In 1951, she received a Master of Arts degree in psychiatric nursing, education, and administration (Sullivan, 2007; Tudor, 1952).

After taking her degree, Gwen left New York for Washington, DC and the position of chief of psychiatric nursing at the National Institute of Mental Health. She was also a consultant at Chestnut Lodge, where she and Otto probably met. She was 29 years old with wide-set and intelligent eyes, a generous smile, and a fashionable pageboy haircut; he was 37. She would become a real partner with him, though a partner he would not always fully appreciate.

As a nurse consultant at Chestnut Lodge, she undertook a six-month research project which would have a lasting impact on the profession of nursing (Slavinsky & Krauss, 1980). The research was coordinated with Morris Schwartz, a sociologist who became an icon through Mitch Albom's (2002) book, *Tuesdays with Morrie*. In 1959, he became a professor of sociology at Brandeis University. Patrick Will related that, "Morrie Schwartz was over at our house all the time; he was one of my mother's best friends" (personal communication February 26, 2011).

This study is a remarkable piece of participant observational research which also includes detailed case studies of two women at Chestnut Lodge (Tudor, 1952). Gwen introduced a hybrid paradigm that she called "sociopsychiatric nursing," which integrated the tools of the social scientific approach with those of psychiatric nursing. As Slavinsky and Krauss (1980) point out, one of the values of the study was an explication of the sociopsychiatric model as evolving from the roles of observer and participant undertaken in the study. In other words, the theoretical model was developed from the data, rather than imposed upon it.

The theoretical material is well-illustrated in two detailed case studies in which Gwen courageously shared her own experiences and reactions. From a ward of 14 women diagnosed as schizophrenic, she identified two — Mrs. Smith, a 43-year-old and Miss Jones (primarily called Marian), 28 — as the most avoidant and from whom the nursing staff withdrew most clearly. She illustrated the concept of selective inattention with observations concerning her own behavior.

## "Mrs. Smith"

For several days, she set herself the task of interacting with Mrs. Smith, only to discover that the day passed without any interaction. In exploring this phenomenon with Schwartz, who was trained in the principles of intensive psychotherapy and had experience as a patient, she discovered that she was anxious around Mrs. Smith, who seemed to covertly communicate a sexual longing for Gwen. She was able to understand both her own anxiety and instruct the unit staff on the role of anxiety in relationships. She became much more comfortable in interactions — which increased — with Mrs. Smith. She also observed deepening levels of reciprocal interaction between the other unit personnel and this patient.

## "Marian"

A similar pattern was observed with "Miss Jones (Marian"). Marian was highly avoidant of contact, often remaining in bed throughout the day. The staff had very little contact with her, rationalizing their withdrawal as the result of Marian being "hopeless" and "unresponsive." Gwen worked with a student nurse who cared for Marian as her primary responsibility. Gradually, Marian became less avoidant and more integrated into the unit. Gwen outlined the process of systematic observation, evaluation of such observation, and interruption of the mutual withdrawal. She also described the integration of individual psychotherapy (defined as "the intensive investigation of the patient's difficulties in living") with the nursing care of the patient on the unit (Tudor, 1952, p. 217).

In a separate paper (Schwartz & G. Will, 1953), she again worked with Morris Schwartz to conduct perhaps the earliest study of nursing "burnout," though this is not a term used in the paper. This immersive study focused on one nurse, called "Miss Jones," and on the dynamics of low morale on a unit for women diagnosed as schizophrenic at the Lodge. They offered a concise description of why "low morale" can affect the nursing staff on such a unit: "It is inevitable in the course of working with patients that ward personnel will become discouraged at times and that the burden of caring for these patients will sometimes be too heavy to bear" (p. 339). They also identified a cyclical pattern involving both patients and nursing staff that ultimately led to the two groups withdrawing from each other; the pattern included: 1) feeling resentment for not being valued, 2) having guilt for the resentment, 3) feeling discouragement with a sense of being uncared for, 4) noticing only the worst of events on the unit, and 5) giving up and withdrawing.

One of my mentors shared his notes from a seminar led by Frieda Fromm-Reichmann in 1950, in which one of the participants suggested, "One doesn't become psychotic without a partner" (L. Lurie, personal communication, November 29, 2007) Whether that is always accurate is unclear, but Schwartz and Will did discover that nurses and patients had a reciprocal influence — if the nurse was indifferent or hopeless, so were the patients with whom she interacted. The authors suggest that a system develops and establishes equilibrium. The system can only change if its equilibrium is disturbed.

In this study, the unit equilibrium is disturbed by giving Miss Jones an opportunity to process her feelings with one of the authors, by encouraging her to approach herself and the patients with curiosity (i.e., to become a "participant-observer"), and by redefining the goals she sought to accomplish. The authors assert that this affected the entire unit and reestablished an equilibrium with higher morale.

## My Mother's in Trouble

In 1951, Otto remembered assisting his mother in obtaining psychiatric care. He did not reveal why, after so many years of distress, she picked this time to reach out for care. I presume that Otto had some hand in it because he coordinated that care.

His parents were still living in Colorado Springs, and he first contacted a local psychiatrist. After meeting with Otto's mother, he called Otto and told him that he thought Florence was "quite disturbed." He suggested that she be hospitalized.

Otto asked, "What are you going to do?"

He responded, "I think we'll give her a little electric shock."

"What if that doesn't work?"

"Well, we can do a prefrontal lobotomy."

Otto recalled simply saying, "No," and dismissing him.

Otto then contacted a psychoanalyst in Denver. He remembered that the analyst was one of the first and few practicing there. According to the Denver Institute for Psychoanalysis, there was only one psychoanalyst in Denver in 1951 — John D. Benjamin, a Zurich trained psychiatrist and a graduate of the Chicago Psychoanalytic Institute with an interest in schizophrenia (Groth, n.d.). That same year, Benjamin was appointed a consultant to the National Institute of Mental Health (Lewin, 1966). Benjamin would also become a consultant for the Psychotherapy Research Project of the Menninger Foundation (Di Donna, 2011). Sixteen years earlier, in 1935, suffering from tuberculosis, he moved to Denver for treatment (Lewin, 1966). It is not certain that it was Dr. Benjamin who Otto contacted, but it is likely.

Otto remembered calling him and telling him that, "My mother's in trouble." According to Otto, he responded immediately by driving from Denver to Colorado Springs. Florence Will told Otto that his first comment to her was, "What's an Irish Colleen [an Anglicized version of the Irish word '*cailin*,' meaning girl or young lady] like you doing behaving like this?" After this gentle reproof, he began to take a more detailed history. Otto later learned his father was an obstacle and "was always speaking for her."

Dr. Benjamin told her, "I want to see you in my office tomorrow." When she told him that her husband would need to drive her, he rejected that idea, "You have to come alone." She reportedly expressed a fear of public transportation, and he reassured her. The next day she traveled to Denver, and, after meeting with him, stayed in a hotel. It was a far cry from her ordinary routine — sitting in her room, behind a closed door, crying. She continued to make regular visits to Denver which Otto recalled empowered her.

She later told Otto, "Sometimes we [she and Dr. Benjamin] don't do anything, if the weather is nice, but sit outside and drink tea." Otto related, "My mother got better." His mother's improvement continued, and, after the death of his father in 1958, she became more independent and, Otto sensed, she enjoyed her life.

Otto and Gwen married in 1953 (Sullivan, 2007). Otto graduated from the Washington-Baltimore Psychoanalytic Institute in 1952. Both Otto and Gwen were on the faculty of the Washington School of Psychiatry, and both continued their work at Chestnut Lodge. According to Patrick Will, Gwen was much better known in her profession than Otto was in his (personal communication, February 23, 2011). After her death in 2007, *The Journal of Psychosocial Nursing and Mental Health Services* ("Tribute," 2007) described her as both a pioneer and a progressive force in the nursing field in the last half of the twentieth century. In 1956, Gwen worked with Joan Doniger, an occupational therapist at Saint Elizabeths, to create a new form of psychiatric care — the country's first halfway house for the mentally ill. Designed for those with serious psychiatric disorders who did not need hospitalization, but who required support to live in the community. Woodley house opened in northwest Washington. The creation of other such facilities would remain one of her professional passions. After moving with Otto to Stockbridge, Massachusetts, in 1967, she worked with Austen Riggs, the Elms Halfway House, and the University of Massachusetts to create three more halfway houses in the Berkshires (Sullivan, 2007). Though they were separated by this time, Otto publicly supported her work in this area. Residential communities were highly resistant to such facilities in their neighborhoods. In Berkshire County, her attempts to create halfway houses were defeated three times. Otto wrote a passionate letter to the Berkshire Eagle in which he noted that psychiatric patients were, like delinquent adolescents and older people, frequently stigmatized and rejected. He (1977b) reminded his readers that "All of these [groups] are products of our own living, and we are in one way or another responsible for them and to them as well as ourselves" (p. 20).

Patrick Will told me that throughout their time together, his father had great faith in Gwen's clinical acumen and spent many hours each evening with her going over his cases and getting her thoughts. Her collaboration with Otto had a great influence on his clinical work (personal communication, February 23, 2011).

Patrick also told me that his mother resigned from the Lodge in frustration:

> My mother was furious with the doctors … because they treated the nurses as if they were completely neutral, as if they had no impact whatsoever, as if they were just caretakers. The doctor's relationship with the patient was the only thing that moved things one way or the other. She felt very strongly that the nurse's relationship had a very strong impact. She wanted nurses acknowledged for their therapeutic impact (personal communication, February 26, 2011).

Courtesy of the National Library of Medicine

Frieda Fromm-Reichmann, M.D. (1889-1957)

circa 1955

The "giant" who stood four feet, ten inches, Fromm-Reichmann offered Otto compassion and supported him in the lonely process of becoming someone he could recognize as himself.

# Chapter Eighteen: A Natural Psychotherapist

In 1949, when Sullivan died, Otto had not completed his analysis. Frieda Fromm-Reichmann became his new analyst. At four feet, ten inches tall, she was physically diminutive, but a professional giant (Silver, 2000). Otto recalled her telling him that to become recognized as a bona fide psychoanalyst by the American Psychoanalytic Association, he would need to complete his training analysis with four weekly sessions. In addition to being his analyst, she would also be his clinical supervisor at the Lodge.

Fromm-Reichmann was born in 1889 in the city of Karlsruhe, to Adolf and Klara (neé Simon) Reichmann. Her parents were Jewish and middle class. Frieda had two younger sisters, Grete and Anna (Hornstein, 2000). Based on anecdotes from Frieda's childhood, her colleague, Edith Weigert (1959), considered her to have been a "natural" psychotherapist.

Fromm-Reichmann completed her medical training in 1914. She received her psychoanalytic training at the Berlin Psychoanalytic Institute, a progressive institute founded and, (until his death in 1925), directed by Karl Abraham. Her training analyst was Hanns Sachs, a lawyer and lay analyst. Fromm-Reichmann's biographer suggested that Sachs became an important, but conflictual, figure in her life. She viewed him as a model for "what not to do" as an analyst (Hornstein, 2000).

## A Haven for Lost Causes

Early in her career, Fromm-Reichmann was introduced to Sandor Ferenczi's ideas and found them compelling. She also received supervision from Ferenczi, a Hungarian psychiatrist who became one of Freud's closest collaborators and — to the extent that Freud had friends — closest friends (Kwawer, 2019). They viewed clinical psychoanalysis, however, very differently. Freud was certain that schizophrenic patients were not amenable to psychoanalytic treatment. Ferenczi accepted people with schizophrenia as patients and became known as the "haven for lost causes" (Kwawer, 2019, p. 89). Ferenczi's explorations in this area opened the way for the development of interpersonal psychoanalysis. However, his deviations from Freud's views on psychoanalysis came at a price.

Freud was ever vigilant against attempts to amend his theory and brooked no revisions. As Ferenczi extended his explorations with a more active technique and non-traditional patients, Freud became increasingly alienated. Additionally, Ferenczi was the object of Ernest Jones's enmity. Jones was one of Ferenczi's former analysands and, Freud's first biographer, who aided Freud in leaving Vienna for England. He was also one of the truly shadowy figures in the history of psychoanalysis — petty and vindictive (Di Donna, 2011; Maddox, 2007).

Freud and Ferenczi ended their relationship when the latter wanted to democratize the therapeutic relationship, included the child's relationship with the mother in psychoanalytic theory, experimented with shortening the duration of analyses and developed a more active approach to technique (Breger, 2000; Haynal, 2002).

## Oddly Asexual

After completing her Berlin Institute training, Fromm-Reichmann founded her own psychoanalytic sanitarium in Heidelberg (Hornstein, 2000; Weigert, 1959). Her experience in administering a psychoanalytic hospital would later be invaluable as she and Dexter Bullard developed Chestnut Lodge.

At 36, Fromm-Reichmann met Erich Fromm. The relationship began as that of analyst (Fromm-Reichmann) and patient (Fromm). However, Fromm-Reichmann fell in love with the younger man (who, at 26, preferred older women), and the two began an affair. As a young woman, probably while in medical school, Frieda was brutally raped (Friedman, 2013; Hornstein, 2000). Erich may have been her first sexual experience after the rape (Friedman, 2013). Both recognized that they could not continue their dual professional and personal relationships and agreed to end Fromm's analysis. In 1926, the couple married, which soon began to fail. Erich was dismissive of her, particularly when she thought she was pregnant, telling her "Having a child is nothing; even a cow can do it" (Friedman, 2013, p. 22). She began engaging in extramarital affairs. In 1932, Frieda underwent surgery, and two days after, she saw what was removed. It could have been a stillborn, but Frieda told Erich and others that it was a benign tumor (Friedman, 2013).

It is interesting that Otto recalled Frieda as oddly asexual. She seemed "asexual" to Robert Gibson, as well (personal communication, May 9, 2007). During this period, the term "asexual" was used loosely to convey something about sexuality that seemed beyond understanding or that violated cultural norms. Sullivan was also described as "asexual," though we know he had sexual partners (Allen, 1995). Whatever the reason(s), Frieda did not complicate her relationships with men by involving sex.

After their marriage crumbled, Fromm worked with Fromm-Reichmann at her sanitarium and, together, they founded the Psychoanalytic Training Institute of Southwest Germany (Hornstein, 2000; Weigert, 1959). Adolf Hitler's rise to power and the increasing barbarity of his followers toward Jews forced both to leave Germany. When Hitler was named Chancellor of the German Reich, Frieda moved to France. After about a year in Strasbourg, she moved to Palestine. From there, she contacted Erich, already in the United States, and asked for money to make the voyage and assistance in locating work. Though their marriage was over in all but name, Erich loyally began to search for positions for Frieda. Frieda arrived in New York on April 16, 1935 (Friedman, 2013; Hornstein, 2000).

Erich had been in the United States for about a year when Frieda arrived. During that time, he made important contacts within the psychoanalytic community and was directed to Ernest Hadley, Dexter Bullard's analyst. Fromm-Reichmann's introduction to Bullard was inauspicious. Bullard described himself as in a state of "resistance" with Hadley at this particular time, and, unfortunately, Fromm called during one of Bullard's sessions. Hadley answered the phone. Bullard had been complaining to Hadley about his inattentiveness and interruptions of his flow of free association. Even though Fromm-Reichmann's recommendation came as another interruption by Hadley, Bullard considered her for a summer replacement for himself and Marjorie Jarvis (Hornstein, 2000). As Dexter (1959) later wrote, the original plan was two months of coverage for a vacation. Fromm-Reichmann stayed 22 years (p. xi).

## Clinical Priorities

Robert Cohen (2010) wrote that, early in her tenure at the Lodge, Frieda conducted psychoanalysis in a traditional manner — sitting behind the reclining patient. Sometime before 1945, she moved her chair to the foot of the couch so that patients could see her (Fromm-Reichmann, 1950). Silver (2000) wrote that Fromm-Reichmann's philosophy was that all patients — all human beings — want to be treated with respect, care, and without fear.

In addition to her direct clinical work, she provided an hour of supervision for all the psychotherapists weekly. Robert Gibson remembered that staff growth and Fromm-Reichmann's involvement in other activities eventually led to group supervision — meeting with dyads of staff members once a week. Gibson was paired with Clarence Schulz, and their supervision hour took place over lunch. Gibson recalled that Frieda held oversimplified stereotypes about men: "Fromm-Reichmann said that it was no use asking men what they wanted to eat, all men want roast beef" (personal communication, May 9, 2007).

Cohen (2010) wrote that Frieda was more attracted to object relations theory than to traditional drive-conflict theory, rejected the universality of the Oedipal complex, and believed that patients should have the choice of the couch or a chair. He compared her clinical work to that of a guide in unfamiliar terrain. As that guide, Fromm-Reichmann was both resourceful and fearless. She also did not hold interpretation in the reverence typical of the analyst of that era. She believed that successful analysis provided a new and ameliorative experience for the patient, and asserted that, "The patient needs an experience, not an explanation" (Abzug, 2021, p. 203). Cohen (2010) described her interactions as infrequent and focused on clarifications rather than interpretations. He related that she was warm and intensely focused during their sessions (see also Weigert, 1959). Alberta Szalita (1976/2015) described her as communicating directly and simply: "She taught … [her patients] to convert complex communications into ordinary thoughts and more or less sound actions" (p. 104).

There was, of course, an ambivalence towards Fromm-Reichmann at Chestnut Lodge. She was a powerful woman in what was still a man's field. Robert Gibson related to me that an oft-heard joke at the Lodge was that "Erich Fromm's book should not have been named *Escape from Freedom*, but *Escape from Frieda*" (personal communication, May 9, 2007). Her deviations from the Freudian canon and her interest in schizophrenia brought out derision from the larger analytic community. And yet, Sullivan was concerned that her approach was too near the traditional. Otto recalled Sullivan commenting to him that, "she [Fromm-Reichmann] never can quite grasp what interpersonal means — too much Berlin."

## A Decided Distrust of Psychoanalysis

In 1944, Joan Erikson gave birth to her and Erik's fourth child, Neil. She had been heavily sedated during the birth. Before she regained consciousness, her physicians informed Erik that his child had been born with Down Syndrome. They recommended institutionalization. After hastily consulting with the anthropologist, Margaret Mead, and the analyst, Joseph Wheelwright, Erikson had his son transferred from the hospital to an institution. After Joan Erikson came to, he informed her of what he had unilaterally done. He also went home to tell his other three children that their newborn brother had died (Friedman, 1999).

Sue Erikson Bloland (2005), Erikson's daughter, wrote that her mother had never really made peace with Erik's decision. To try working through her guilt, grief, and anger she discreetly consulted Fromm-Reichmann on one of the latter's annual New Mexico vacations. I asked Bloland why her mother might have chosen Fromm-Reichmann. She related that:

> Mom had a very *decided* distrust of psychoanalysis and would probably not have consulted anyone on a purely professional basis. Frieda must have been selected because mother liked her personally and felt safe enough with her to talk about Neil (personal communication, April 11, 2005).

## *Principles of Intensive Psychotherapy*

In 1950, the University of Chicago Press published *Principles of Intensive Psychotherapy*, Frieda's most celebrated and, now classic, work. In a clear and readable style, she described the priorities of her work. According to Szalita (1976/2015) Frieda was highly critical of the book and dismissed it as "a cookbook" (p. 105).

Like her friend, Sullivan, she defined mental health as a perception of oneself as others perceive one. The goal, then, was to clarify distortions in interpersonal functioning that obscured perception and awareness. She referred to such efforts at clarification as "interpretation," though not in the traditional sense. She did not strive to make the unconscious conscious. Instead, she (1950) wrote that: "The central part of all intensive psychotherapy is therefore the interpretive clarification of the connection between a patient's early pattern of interpersonal relationships and his present experiences" (p. 98). She also believed that this clarification was more effective if the patient arrived at it for herself. She worked on the clarification of resistance and security operations — those defenses, such as selective inattention, denial, rationalization, and so forth, which minimize anxiety by obscuring the perception of what is occurring and the patient's role in it (see Chapter Twenty-Five).

In all the operations of the therapy, she considered it imperative to avoid shaming or humiliating the patient who, she believed, was already burdened by deficits in self-esteem. She (1950) focused on behavior, proposing that "It is more bearable to feel hated for what one *does* than for what one *is*" (p. 53, emphasis in the original). She had known hatred for simply being who she was as a Jew in Hitler's Germany.

Again, like Sullivan, she believed that every human being is endowed with a "tendency toward health" similar to eating when hungry and drinking when thirsty. She suggested that patients dissociate during experiences that arouse overwhelming anxiety; accordingly, another priority of intensive psychotherapy is to carefully aid the patient in discovering disassociated elements and integrating them into awareness.

When I first read this book, I was struck by the flexible way she addressed boundaries in the therapeutic relationship, often referred to as "the frame." For instance, she did not believe that a patient should be charged for a missed session due to illness or an emergency.

Though *Principles of Intensive Psychotherapy* was admired by many, it also energized detractors. Senior analysts like Robert Waelder and Edward Bibring attacked her vehemently for attempting to apply psychoanalytic principles to the care of psychotic patients, and such attacks wounded her deeply (Hornstein, 2000; Szalita, 1976/2015).

## Final Years

Frieda played important roles in both Otto's professional and family life. In 1956, Gwen and Otto's son, Patrick, was born. Frieda was his godmother. He related that Frieda "was sort of a grandmotherly figure to me. She was incredibly gentle, and she loved me. I bonded with her when I was quite young" (personal communication, February 26, 2011). Otto remembered that, when she had a break in her schedule, Frieda would call Gwen and ask her to take Patrick to her cottage at the Lodge. She also frequently had dinner with the family to spend time with Patrick (Will, 1989b).

As Otto described memories of his analysis with Frieda, he noted her support at moments when he felt lonely; Fromm-Reichmann's compassion was of the greatest import. He also noted that she offered support in his search to become himself. As had been the case with Sullivan, Otto found himself engaged, at times in obsessive talking that reflected only his anxiety. However, rather than challenge this as Sullivan had, Frieda suggested, "Doctor, the next time you come in, why don't you have a couple of stiff drinks." If not meant sarcastically, this was not helpful guidance for Otto, who recalled that he did not follow through on it. He remembered developing a competitive relationship with another of her patients, a psychotic young woman. Otto (1989b) wrote that he confronted her once about her relationship with this patient — suggesting that if he had become psychotic, she would value him more. Her response seems to have been oblique, implying that it would not have been worth it to Otto to be cared about in the same way. Otto also remembered that, as was the case with Sullivan, Frieda's cocker spaniel, Munie, was always present during his sessions. Munie was an offspring of Sullivan's dogs.

In 1954, Frieda reduced her clinical and supervisory duties by half. Otto assumed some of the supervision that she had provided. The next year, Frieda was invited to spend a year at the Ford Foundation's Center for the Advanced Study in the Behavioral Sciences located in Palo Alto, California, near the Stanford University campus. Involvement with the Center was by invitation only. Making it even more prestigious was the fact that Frieda was the first woman ever invited to become a fellow. The year in Palo Alto provided a needed break from a crowded schedule of clinical work (Hornstein, 2000).

As she aged, Fromm-Reichmann was increasingly burdened by a loss of hearing (Silver, 2000). Toward the end of her life, she felt isolated and lonely, often despairing (Szalita, 1976/2015). She required barbiturates to sleep and amphetamines to get started in the mornings (Hornstein, 2000). When she died in 1957, she was working on a paper concerning loneliness. Though it was not finished, she (1959) had written that intense loneliness could take the form of psychosis.

The evening before her body was discovered in her bathtub, she joined the Wills for dinner. Otto remembered that Frieda made an overture for physical contact with Patrick that he rejected. Otto wondered, with some guilt, if this contributed to her death. Like Sullivan, there were rumors that she had taken her own life. Though the official cause of death was recorded as an acute coronary thrombosis, her friends and those who knew her well believed she had committed suicide (Bullard, 1959; Hornstein, 2000). Otto rejected this idea, but Gwen suspected that Frieda had taken her own life. Patrick Will told me, "That was her suspicion but she never said it to me unequivocally…; I think my mom strongly suspected that she took her own life." (personal communication, February 26, 2011). Otto never discussed her death with Patrick.

Chestnut Lodge, with its freedom from dogma, was a helpful environment for Otto. After Fromm-Reichmann's death, he succeeded her as director of psychotherapy. As with Sullivan, he had not finished his own therapy with Fromm-Reichmann when she died. He would never again enter psychotherapy (Will, 1989b).

It is difficult to know the role that Fromm-Reichmann played in Otto's professional life. In his interviews with Kim Chernin, Otto noted that Frieda was his analyst (eight years), far longer than Sullivan (three years) had been. To everyone I interviewed I posed the question, "Who do you think had the greatest impact on Will's life: Sullivan or Fromm-

Reichmann?" Without exception, the response was "Sullivan." Otto told Kim Chernin, "I don't think I would have gone into analytic training if it hadn't been for [Sullivan]."

Otto (1989b) had never had a non-traumatic termination of therapy and responded by determining not to engage in therapy again. He would learn about himself from the insights of friends. He had also learned the skill of self-observation, and, as it does for many of us, therapy continued with the internalized Sullivan and Fromm-Reichmann. It was not until after he ended formal psychotherapy that he came to an important realization: "My father didn't like me. It was a great relief to say 'My father didn't like me. He was proud of some things I did, but he never showed any feeling of really liking me and I can see why.'"

## Director of Psychotherapy

Chestnut Lodge was an environment that supported Otto's growth. He quickly gained a reputation as a psychotherapist and supervisor more loyal to his patients than any theory.

It was during the years at the Lodge that Otto established himself as an authority on the psychotherapy of schizophrenia, though he wrote about depression, as well (Will, 1963b, 1966). Some who interacted with him during this period also perceived *his* schizoid qualities. Joseph Abrahams (2007) described attending a seminar at the Lodge taught by Otto. Otto discussed schizoid people as living outside conventional relationships, in a type of other space — "out there." Abrahams formed the idea that Otto was speaking both about the patient and himself. Otto's reputation as a therapist also brought, mostly young, therapists who hoped to learn from him. Herant Katchadourian (2012) described consulting Otto around this time in his private practice. He was impressed that Otto did not encourage use of the couch, instead, they sat in chairs. He found the distance between their chairs remarkable — Otto sitting in one corner of the room and he in the other, the whole office length between them. Though Katchadourian felt mildly put off by the questions Otto asked — he thought them more appropriate to a schizoid character — he appreciated experiencing Otto's much discussed style of psychotherapy.

As Director of Psychotherapy, Otto was considered an excellent supervisor. John Kafka, one of Otto's supervisees, described the intensity of Otto's presence and attention, both during his own supervision and in his observations of Otto's work with patients:

> It was as if nothing else existed at that moment and at that place; I should add, however, that I felt the intensity of his engagement contrasted with a pronounced disengagement of which he was capable outside of a supervisory or therapeutic situation (J. Kafka, personal communication, November 30, 2008).

It is noteworthy that such a state of presence and attention can have a cost. One cannot be present with such intensity during all interactions. Social interactions, which are potentially more reciprocal and affirming, are often given less importance. Otto (1971b) acknowledged this form of isolation as a potential source of loneliness to the psychotherapist. It is a form of isolation easily denied or discounted. Some years ago, Irvin Yalom (2002) described isolation as one of the occupational hazards of being a psychotherapist. The therapist's worldview is in itself isolating. Seasoned therapists view relationships differently, they sometimes lose patience with social ritual and bureaucracy, they cannot abide the fleeting shallow encounters and small talk of many social gatherings (p. 252).

As Kim Chernin (2017) related, Otto often shared stories of his experiences with his supervisees as a means of offering alternative perspectives on the clinical material they brought to him. He remained non-dogmatic in perspective. In 1961, he stepped out of Sullivan's shadow, writing that he was not a Sullivanian and describing himself as a psychiatrist interested in theory and psychotherapy (1961c).

## Jungle Warfare

The Lodge could be a conflictual environment. Many of the staff were accomplished professionals with the egos to match. Staff meetings and clinical seminars could bring out their querulousness. Harold Searles (Langs & Searles, 1980) likened it to "jungle warfare" (p. 37*n*). Otto observed, however, that neither Dexter nor Frieda discouraged open conflict and Otto found that overt disagreements were less likely to disrupt patient care than covert ones.

This was apparently not the way all conflicts were resolved, though. Patrick Will related: "There were some colleagues of my mother who were infuriated by my dad and that … came out after … [both parents] passed away; there was some sense that he was indebted [without acknowledgement] to my mother's work" (personal communication, February 26, 2011).

Chestnut Lodge was also an environment of fellowship and camaraderie. Patrick Will remembered:

> We'd do a big party at least once a year for all the doctors and nurses at Chestnut Lodge — it was a big deal! We'd have it catered and have tiki torches all over the lawn. We'd play a game of softball in the afternoon, and it would always end with a big square dance (personal communication, February 26, 2011).

Otto continued to play the flute. Frieda had a piano in her cottage; Otto recalled his enjoyment of meeting with her and Leslie Farber, who played the violin, to engage with Baroque music. Both Patrick and Deirdre remembered that their father loved music. "Our entire family was musical," Patrick related. Otto, Gwen, and Deirdre played the flute while Patrick played the piano. His father was "a phenomenal sight reader!" he noted, but Patrick's real interest was improvisational jazz. His father "couldn't improvise to save his life" (personal communication, February 26, 2011).

Courtesy of Patrick Will

Otto
date unknown

At Chestnut Lodge, Otto became a recognized expert on psychotherapy with schizophrenics. He did not allow "analytic niceties" to interfere in making contact with patients.

# Chapter Nineteen: Clinical Studies from Chestnut Lodge

It has been standard practice since Freud began writing to illustrate clinical papers with vignettes about patients that describe conceptual points made. Many experienced clinicians have pointed out that such vignettes do not always closely adhere to what actually transpires in the therapist's office, with presentations being tailored to fit the theoretical and political expectations of the audience (Binder, 2004; Bion, 1965/2018; Bruch, 1974; Hirsch, 2015; Levenson, 2018; Rubin, 2014, Strupp, 1968). However, even if clinical vignettes cannot be relied upon for unfailing accuracy, they can give some idea about how a particular psychotherapist views her work and can depict in broad strokes what she does.

How Otto thought about his work is also somewhat compromised because he was indifferent to theory. To the best of my knowledge, Otto described himself as interested in theory only once in a paper (1961c) after he seemed to defensively reject the description of himself as a "Sullivanian." As colleagues have described his work, they tend to imbue it with the outlines of what they expected to perceive. For many years, I perceived him as simply a "stand-in" for Harry Stack Sullivan. That was the result of my sometimes-idealized (sometimes overly-idealized) view of Sullivan, and at other times it was from lazy reductionism. Colleagues would tell me how much of Frieda Fromm-Reichmann they saw in his work. Still others perceived the fundamentals of the attachment theory of John Bowlby (1987), Holmes (2014), and Scott (1987) in his clinical presentations. The upshot is that we were all correct (except when I was reductionistic). All of his mentors and respected colleagues contributed to his understanding of the human beings we call "patients."

Again, some years ago, my supervisor, who had known most of the figures I have written about, suggested that Otto worked intuitively and was most guided by what he had learned about the mechanics (for lack of a better term) of relationships. He followed his gut, applied common sense, and attempted to repair any damage that resulted from errors in judgement. He also relied on respect for the patient, attempted to make therapy as anxiety-free as possible, and diligently tried to avoid embarrassing or degrading the person. I have described a few vignettes below that Otto remembered in some detail or abstracted some published vignettes from his time at Chestnut Lodge.

## "Anne": Magic and its Limits

Otto recalled Anne as his first patient at the Lodge. In her early twenties, she had already been hospitalized at the Menninger Clinic and the Institute for Living in Hartford, Connecticut (between 1822 and 1943 the Hartford Retreat for the Insane) — both highly respected facilities. Otto recalled that she had received many ECT treatments and just as many insulin coma treatments. One of her physicians, who viewed her as a deteriorating schizophrenic, had suggested a prefrontal lobotomy, to which a colleague had asked, "Why don't you send her to the Lodge?"

Otto remembered that she had to be locked in a room without anything but a rubber mattress because she destroyed everything. During his first session with her she questioned him:

"This has never worked before, why should it now?"

Otto responded, "Well, I don't know. I don't ask you to trust me, I don't ask you to believe anything I say. The only thing I ask you is that we meet seven days a week."

Anne had run away from every hospital she had been in, and she ran away from the Lodge. Each time, the police were notified, and they would pick her up and return her. After running away, she would begin hitchhiking toward home with the expressed intent to kill her mother.

Otto's wife, Gwen, who he described as "a wonderful psychiatric nurse," was assigned to help provide care for Anne. He described Gwen reading a well-known children's book to Anne called *The Runaway Bunny* (Brown, 1942).

> Well, the bunny is going to run away, and the mother says, Well, I'm going to come after you.
>
> The bunny says, I'll be a little fish.
>
> Mother says, I'll be an angler and catch you.
>
> The bunny says, I'll be a little bird.
>
> Mother says, I'll be the mother in the nest. And so on and so on.

Anne asked Gwen to read this over and over, and Gwen read it again and again. Then one day, Gwen offered Anne "a special nickel, a magic nickel. If you run away again, you can use this nickel to call me or the doctor [Otto]." She did, indeed, run away again, and this time the police were not called.

Otto related, "And she came back. I went to see her."

Anne asked, "Did you notice anything?"

"What?"

"I was away."

"Oh, I knew you'd come back."

Otto explained that, after running away, Anne had gone to the Howard Johnson's to have a soda. She sat down beside a woman at the counter and talked with her. Anne explained that she had run away from a hospital and the woman invited her to stay overnight at her house. "The next morning, she called us up. That was the end of her running away."

As Otto worked with Anne, he discovered that her difficulties began when she was a senior in high school. She was working as an aide at a hospital with a young man who had broken his arm in an auto accident. Otto recalled:

> They fell in love and wanted to get married — the parents said that they were too young. They sent her on a cruise around the world with her grandmother; when she returned home, they planned a sort of coming out party. Before the party, she took an overdose; *the parents revived her to attend the party*. It was only after the party that they found a pistol under her pillow.

They took her to a local hospital which, in turn, transferred her to the Menninger Clinic which then transferred her to the Institute for Living. After that, her caregivers gave up on Anne.

Otto worked with her as an inpatient for six years and then as an outpatient for two years. One of the experiences he and Anne enjoyed was walking. However, he noted, "She never walked beside me — she would always have me walk twenty steps behind her." When she was an outpatient, Otto saw her walking down the street near his home. He drove by to pick her up, and she casually explained, "My car broke down and I thought I'd walk over to your house and phone Triple A."

Otto responded, "It's lucky I was here."

"I knew you'd be here."

"Anne, this could get you killed. Be careful — the magic is gone."

He related, "I think that was very important to have said to her, because magic is wonderful, but you've got to be careful with it."

Anne ended her therapy after eight years, enrolled in college and graduated. Otto noted, "I still hear from her every Christmas."

There are several interesting elements to this vignette. First, Otto agreed to work with a patient who others had given up on. Further, despite her frequent flights from the Lodge and from him, he remained in the relationship with Anne.

Second, the vignette demonstrates how well Otto and Gwen worked together and, frankly, how skilled Gwen was. As he related Anne's story, he complimented Gwen. He (1971b) would do so again, describing her as, "a psychiatric nurse of long experience and great skill" (p. 18). Beneath these compliments, however, lay a fundamental truth — he depended on her clinical acumen. As I talked with both Deirdre and Patrick, they emphasized this dependence.

A third facet of the vignette worth considering is the fullness of Anne's recovery. She graduated from college. It is an outcome that a prefrontal lobotomy might have denied her. While speaking with Deirdre, I once asked her what she thought her father was most proud of. Without hesitating, she replied, "He was the therapist who cured schizophrenia."

## "Miss A": Communication & Countertransference

Earlier I described a potential limitation of clinical vignettes. They cannot be relied upon for total accuracy, because therapists are human beings and are therefore concerned with rejection. To compensate for this tendency, particularly when conducting research on psychotherapy, audio and later video recordings were employed. Recordings are now used in training as well as research. However, in the late 1940s and early 1950s those who recorded their work were often criticized for violating the sanctity of the consulting room and, at some institutions, recordings were strictly forbidden (Di Donna, 2011).

Despite such criticisms, in 1947 Otto collaborated with Robert Cohen at Chestnut Lodge in publishing an audio recorded session with a young woman who they called "Miss A." Miss A was in her late twenties and like many Lodge patients, she had been treated previously at other institutions and undergone ECT (Will & Cohen, 1947).

Miss A had been in intensive psychotherapy with Otto for "several months" prior to her sessions being recorded. This published recording was the eighteenth of 50 sessions made on a Gray Audograph recording device, which created plastic records of 30 minutes on each side (Will & Cohen, 1947).

Miss A was a college graduate employed in a clerical position with a large firm. The authors write that she had an active social life and was successful professionally and socially. Despite this, when she began psychotherapy, she expressed a lack of interest in her job; she also noted an inability to establish long-term intimate relationships. She was described as a guarded person (particularly in what she said and how she said it), lonely and isolated. She was also described as deferential to Otto, though in a formal way that seemed distant. On occasion, however, anger and even rage, would be apparent despite her superficial deference.

Though Miss A was often critical of Otto, her criticisms were couched in passive, ambiguous language. Among her complaints was that he did not intuitively grasp her inner experience and could not respond to her feelings before she shared them. A pattern that Otto clarified in this regard was her tendency to offer such criticisms but quickly reverse the blame from him to herself.

At the time of his work with Miss A, Otto was in analysis with Frieda Fromm-Reichmann, as Cohen had also been previously. Somewhat more traditional than Sullivan, who generally dealt with transference as a nuisance, Fromm-Reichmann found exploration of transference phenomena helpful. Cohen (2010) described Fromm-Reichmann's technique in this regard: "The therapist's task, she thought, was to identify these [transference] distortions, to convey very clearly both verbally and nonverbally that she was not the figure the patient took her to be" (p. 212). This approach is evident in Otto's work with Miss A.

One notable moment in the session occurs when Miss A describes her experience of dissociation; "a lot of things I know, I don't know in words. I just *know*" (p. 268, emphasis in the original). As Breger (2000) maintains, memories accumulated prior to symbolic speech are retained as physical and emotional sensations, not easily brought into awareness.

Otto (Will & Cohen, 1947) highlights his own experiences with countertransference throughout the vignette, particularly when he felt accused of being unsupportive of Miss A, prompting him to be kinder at such times. As Otto and Cohen explored Miss A's criticisms, they discovered that some were based on accurate perceptions, and Otto gradually acknowledged his human frailties. Interestingly, there are multiple references to transference, a phenomenon that Otto did not treat in-depth in other clinical reports. During one such interaction, he presented a non-interpretive thought:

> what we have to do, I think, is to get … clear so we have some kind of consensus about … [what we are both attempting to communicate] — not that one of us is right or wrong, but that we at least know how the other person feels about this thing (p. 272).

This is Sullivan's (1953a) concept of *consensual validation*: "symbolic activity [that] involves an appeal to principles which are accepted as true by the hearer[s]" (p. 29*n*).

As Otto (1954) emphasized in his introduction to Sullivan's (1954) book, *The Psychiatric Interview*, he made careful note of variations in communication during the interview, hypothesizing that when Miss A became anxious, her use of qualifying words (e.g., "might," "perhaps") increased. At one point during the session, he shares this hypothesis with her:

> one might theorize that language was for communication … to make things clearer between people … But … as we grow up, we also learn something else — we learn to be somewhat afraid of some people, and we often use language to obscure what we feel (p. 274).

Otto and Cohen close the article by acknowledging that this interview did not fulfill the "ideal standard" for which they strove. From their point of view, Otto erred by being overly active when attempting to assuage his anxiety; he was too willing to converse about material that might have been better interpreted; finally, he allowed himself to be distracted from the process of the interview in favor of the content. Yet, they also point out that this interview demonstrates that "the personality of an effective therapist is a deep curiosity about himself and other people" (p. 281).

Unfortunately, there is no satisfying end to this vignette as there is no follow-up on Miss A's treatment. There are no records left to bring closure to the discussion of the case. This is not an unusual aspect of the psychotherapist's experience. We must often accept uncertainty as the final word. There are also three recordings (i.e. January 7, 1952, February 28, 1952, and March 21, 1952) of Otto working with an anonymous female patient between 1952 and 1954 in the University of Chicago Library Archives. These, too, emphasize his informal style (McQuown, 1955).

What is available in this vignette is a broad outline of how Otto worked. Though Cohen proposed that the ideal form of intervention would have been interpretation, this was not Otto's primary way of working. He often wrote that a key task for the therapist is education (1970c). This is the task with which he seems most comfortable, in the discussion of communication. He pays close attention to the flow of communication during the session, noting when it becomes more abstract, which is probably an indication that the anxiety in the room has increased. Finally, he seems to monitor his own anxiety (i.e., countertransference) and is aware of much of it. He does not, however, share what he notices about his anxiety with Miss A, often a component in other descriptions of his approach.

## "Miss B": An Introduction to Love

In several papers, Otto (Will, 1968b, 1970b, 1971b, 1972, 2021), described his work with another patient he called "Miss A." For the sake of clarity, and since the patient just described was also given this pseudonym, I have identified the current patient as "Miss B."

Otto wrote that Miss B was 20 years old when she first entered the hospital. Before that, she had been a sophomore in college, studying literature with the hope of becoming a writer. Her family and friends regarded her with ambivalence. She could be appealing and amiable, though also arrogant and unconcerned with others' feelings or needs. She was considered intelligent and competent.

Initially, her past functioning seemed largely successful, but, on careful review, there had been ominous signs since childhood. She was fearful of relationships and had no intimate friends; she considered her body to be "evil," and avoided touching others. She engaged in self-mutilation (cutting and burning), which helped her experience sensations that were otherwise absent. She perceived the world as devoid of color and form. When she began college, her relationship with her parents and sister deteriorated; they had little contact. Miss B spent most of her time alone in her room fantasizing about a world in which other people were under her control. She was critical and aggressive to the real people in her environment, and they began to withdraw from or abandon her. She began to engage in unsatisfying and compulsive sexual contacts.

As she began her sophomore year, she seemed depressed, which she denied, and her sleep was riven by nightmares. During a brief visit with her parents, she became embroiled in an argument with her mother and struck her. She ran away from the house and was later discovered in her car after overdosing on barbiturates.

After her suicide attempt, she was hospitalized and was treated with ECT and insulin coma. She was released, and she consulted several therapists for outpatient psychotherapy. She found each of these professionals unacceptable for one reason or another. After giving up on the idea of psychotherapy, she again attempted suicide by cutting her wrists and taking a combination of medications. She was subsequently admitted to the Lodge in a florid psychotic state — hallucinating, delusional, as well as self-mutilating and assaultive.

Assigned to Otto upon admission, Miss B made it clear that she did not want to work with him. Initially, Otto perceived her as "a schizophrenic;" he knew, however, that he must see her as a person — lonely and afraid. He learned that she felt estranged from everyone and everything — being a part of nothing. She attempted to avoid her time with Otto, but he sought her out. They met for five sessions a week, of which Otto (1972) wrote: "I frequently wished to escape from the situation" (p. 33). When they were together, Otto remembered sitting on the floor in her room, sometimes sensing that she was aware of his presence and, at other times, not. She was tall and slender, with dark hair, her face was covered with self-inflicted scratches, and her dressing gown was disheveled. She often paced when they met. At other times, she sat on the floor with her back to him. She mumbled and refused to respond to questions. In the fourth month of therapy, when Otto decided to be more determined in his questioning — she walked out of the room. She proclaimed that she did not want him or anyone else in her life and told him that he was not there to help, but to destroy her. During one session, she crawled to Otto on her knees, took his hands in hers and told him: "You have come to kill me. No one will get out of here alive" (Will 1968b, p. 555). However, after several months, he felt a bond developing.

During this period, Miss B attempted suicide by medication overdose. When he learned of it, he tried to contact her father but was told by the father's assistant that he was busy with a board meeting and could not come to the phone. Next, he phoned Miss B's mother. She asked, "Is she [Miss B] going to live?" He responded that he did not know yet. "Well," her mother replied, "I don't think there's anything I can do, so there's no point in my coming down." Otto then went to the hospital. In and out of lucidity, Miss B asked him if he cared about her, to which he replied that he did. She then asked him if he loved her. He seems to have felt "put on the spot" and embarrassed. He recalled at first thinking "No, of course not. I'm your therapist — I'm your analyst — I'm here to try and help you with your problems." He said nothing. After this interaction, he described thinking about what she had asked in relation to Harry Stack Sullivan's definition of love. Sullivan (1953a) defined love as existing only in situations in which one values the growth and satisfaction of the other as much as her own. Otto (2021) found this definition somewhat perfectionistic and added the words *almost as much* as her own. After this consideration, Otto spoke with her about the process of his thinking and told her, "that her welfare did mean a great deal to me; I told her that I hoped I had demonstrated that." He related becoming increasingly comfortable with the word "love" when applied to psychotherapy. When Miss B asked again whether he loved her, he simply said "yes" (p. 2). He (1971b) decided that an attachment develops during psychotherapy reflecting affection and love, no matter how uncomfortable that may be for the therapist. Perhaps, given her parents' responses to her suicide attempt, it was important that someone loved her.

Love was not "the cure" for her difficulties, and Miss B continued cutting her arms (one episode required sixty-eight sutures to repair). Otto discussed this with her as an automatism, behaviors that seem to be automatic and unrelated to other people, but that are actually symbolic actions involved with past, present, or anticipated future experiences. The ward staff were becoming impatient and angry with her, sensing that she was "hopeless." Otto felt increasingly stressed and inadequate. She was also criticizing him as incapable of a "real relationship." "She may go to a swami," he wrote, "'Go ahead' is my answer, but she doesn't" (Will, 2021, p. 11). She accused Otto of not seeing or understanding her and he agreed that that was the case. He (1971b) wrote, "She sought out my personal idiosyncrasies and defects … with remarkable perceptiveness and precision" (p. 16). He validated these accurate perceptions, though it was painful. He then told her that she did not see or understand him either. He proposed that they were both operating from misperceptions and stereotypes. Otto described working with her to further an understanding of the commonalities they shared as human beings, particularly troubling feelings.

As their bond deepened, Miss B became resistive to it, telling Otto that she preferred a lack of attachment to loss when the therapy ended. Otto emphasized that this is a phenomenon that all human beings share — there is no real life without relationships, but all relationships end in loss and thus pain. After much improvement, Miss B was discharged from the Lodge and went to New York City and engaged in outpatient psychotherapy with Otto's good friend, Hilde Bruch.

## "Miss M": Combat & Caring

Miss M was not a patient who Otto wrote about in any of his papers, however, he discussed her at length with Kim Chernin. Brief references to her can be found in Hall (1992) and Hornstein (2000). Otto offers little background material about her, except to describe her as "an artist" (painter) prior to hospitalization.

Once she was hospitalized, Miss M assaulted Otto and the ward staff. He (1971b) noted that the desire for touch is often disguised in physical aggression. During his time at the Lodge, Otto grew inured to the threat of assault. In one instance, a newly admitted 17-year-old, who did not want to be at the Lodge, picked up a marble ashtray and "wondered" what might happen if he threw it at Otto's head. According to the young man, Otto impassively replied that such an action would simply confirm his impression of the patient as a very angry person (Carlson, 2019).

Miss M destroyed the furniture in her room and had only a mattress on which to sleep. Initially, Otto would only see her when she was restrained in a wet sheet pack. Of course, she could not be so restrained the rest of the time, but Otto does not explain how the nursing staff dealt with her violence.

He recalled that he came one day for her appointment. She had not been restrained in preparation, but Otto had not been informed of that. As he made his way across the ward to her room, she suddenly appeared with a chair above her head preparing to strike him with it. He grabbed her arm, and she smashed the chair on the wall. Gail Hornstein (2000) described Otto as angry, wrestling Miss M toward her room. As they reached her room, they stumbled and fell to the floor. Miss M was on her back and Otto fell on top of her. In the moment they laid there, she calmly said to Otto, "Well, doctor, you've finally touched me."

In a session that soon followed, Otto went to her room. She was not restrained, but neither was she assaultive. He remembered them sitting quietly together, she smiling and seemingly enjoying herself.

The next day, Otto mentioned this unusual session to Dexter Bullard. Dexter responded, "She's paranoid and that's the wrong way to deal with a paranoid person — you've got to keep your distance." Later, when Otto went for his next session with Miss M he remembered, "she was terribly assaultive and upset. I thought, 'Well, that proves Dexter's point.'" She quieted for a moment, and he asked her, "What the hell's the matter — You talked nice yesterday and you're upset today?"

She replied, "I knew what you'd do."

"Well, what did you know?"

"You can't stand that kind of closeness, I can tell." She described Otto's routine when he came to see her. Based on that routine — primarily on how he tapped on her door — she could predict whether the session would be satisfying or not. Otto acknowledged that "She was exactly right."

He recalled that she ended her combative behavior. However, she replaced it with smearing her feces on herself, the walls, and floor. For a period of time, the nursing staff would clean her and the room and always did so when she had an appointment with Otto. After considering this, Otto asked the ward staff not to clean up after her. He recalled thinking that, while overseas, he often had to bathe his patients before he could perform surgery on them.

The next time he came for a session, he brought a mop and other cleaning supplies. "I came into her room, and mopped the floor, wiped down the walls and windows and then I sat down on a chair with a pail of [clean] water." He removed her gown (she was now nude): "I washed her hair and bathed her. She was quiet throughout." Otto recalled wondering if she was quiet because "she felt I was so compassionate" or because she thought, "I'd better stop acting this way or the crazy man will come in and give me another bath." Miss M did not smear after this interaction and returned to painting. Sessions became conversational and both Otto and Miss M felt that she was approaching discharge and outpatient psychotherapy.

Otto described a visit from Miss M's mother about this time. "I told her mother that things looked good, and that Miss M would be able to leave soon, maybe go back to college or continue her painting." Her mother returned home and two days later she called Otto and told him that her daughter was to be transferred to another hospital. When Otto inquired about why this decision had been made, "She just said she'd made the arrangements and that's all there was to it."

Otto took his patient down to the train station. "She cried, put her arms around me, and kissed me; she got on the train to go." A week later, Miss M's mother called again and "she wanted to know what happened to her daughter."

"I said, 'What do you mean?'"

"I went to see her," she responded, "and she didn't recognize me. She just sat on the floor, [and wouldn't] pay any attention to me and she had two black eyes."

"Did you sign anything for treatment?"

"Yes, they had a new treatment, and I signed [for] it."

"Well, she's had a prefrontal lobotomy."

Miss M's mother explained that after she returned home from her final visit to the Lodge, the family chauffeur was at the station, but her husband was not. When she asked the chauffeur where he was, he replied that Miss M's father "said he had something he had to do and would meet her [at home]." The chauffeur drove her home, and, together, they searched for her husband. When they did find him, "[he was] hanging in the basement." After that, she made the arrangements for Miss M to be transferred.

In a rare nod of appreciation to Harry Stack Sullivan, Leslie Farber (2000) wrote that, "Sullivan worked with his bare hands, alone, inside the cages where the beasts were wild and real" (p. 66). Despite Farber's turning Sullivan's patients into "the Other," his point captures a quality of desperation as well as emotional and physical danger that often accompanies work with people during psychosis. This quote describes Otto's work with Miss M.

I believe that Otto's decision to bathe Miss M might foster disagreement among reasonable clinicians as to whether it was primarily designed (covertly) to meet his needs or to give her an experience of loving care that one might give to an infant. I tend toward the latter interpretation while acknowledging that it was — as all actions are — overdetermined. Yet, if his version of events is accurate, his intuition that Miss M needed touch led to successful interventions. Unfortunately, *she* was not capable of working bare-handed with the wild beasts in her world — whether family or medical professionals.

## "Professor M": One & One

Otto wrote far less about his male patients than he did about his female patients. One is a richly detailed study of a paranoid man that Otto (1961b) called "Mr. X." However, he described to Kim Chernin another man with whom he worked that illustrates his technical flexibility and the extraordinary lengths to which Chestnut Lodge would go in making care available.

Otto described Professor M as "a genius," who, from an early age, showed himself to be a savant in mathematics. At the age of 12, he began working out mathematical formulae on his bedroom walls. By 14, he was in correspondence with celebrated mathematicians around the world. By his late teenage years he was at Princeton University, working with Albert Einstein on his unified field theory.

Professor M married, had two children, and settled in on the faculty of a college in California. At 40, he displayed psychotic symptoms, delusions and visual hallucinations. He was hospitalized twice at the university hospital within a four-year period. With each hospitalization, he received 50 ECT treatments, showed no improvement, and continued to deteriorate. After the second hospitalization, he was transferred to a state hospital; he was mute and physically limited.

While in Palo Alto on her fellowship at The Center for Advanced Study in the Behavioral Sciences, Frieda Fromm-Reichmann learned about this man. She visited him in the hospital, and, seeing the potential for improvement, began contacting mathematicians around the United States to raise money for him to become a patient at Chestnut Lodge. Her fundraising efforts were very successful. American mathematicians contacted European colleagues, and they donated money, as well. He was admitted to the Lodge and remained there for eight years, seven of which were fully funded — including spending money — by Frieda's efforts.

He became Otto's patient. He thought the prognosis was positive because of a subtle interaction during their first session. Professor M took a chair opposite Otto. Although he did not smoke cigarettes, Otto kept some in his office for patients. He offered Professor M one and the mathematician nodded and took it. "I lit a match to light his cigarette and held out my hand and my hand touched his. He did not withdraw his hand." Otto thought that this was a good prognostic sign.

Professor M's mother died when he was an infant, and he lived with an older, married sister. (Otto gave no indication of why he did not remain with his father.) Until he began to display his extraordinary capacity for math, his development seemed unremarkable. As his talents emerged, he also developed the ability to "visualize" mathematical problems and formulae.

Otto recalled that a mathematician at Johns Hopkins heard about Professor M and scheduled a time to visit him at the Lodge. They spent an hour together. Afterwards, the visitor sought Otto out and thanked him for allowing the visit: "It's been one of life's great privileges to talk with that man." He continued, "It's hard to explain, but this man sees things — and he can tell us about them. We can put mathematical formulae around them, but we can't see them."

Otto noticed that Professor M had a sense of humor. After being transferred from "the disturbed ward," Otto often took his patient off campus. He related that, during one session, they had gone for a drive in Washington. "We stopped at a little place near the canal to have a hamburger. We sat at the counter and Professor M got to talking with the counter man [he was obviously no longer mute]. I wasn't talking and the counter man asks, 'Who's your friend?'" Professor M replied, "Oh, he's okay, but he's terribly shy in company and can't say very much." Otto noted, "There was a little role change — very funny, very dear."

On another excursion into the city, they stopped near the Potomac River where there was a waterfall. "We sat and watched, and then he turned to me and asked, 'How many gallons per second do you think goes over that waterfall?'

"I haven't the faintest idea," Otto replied.

"I didn't think you would."

Otto appreciated these displays of Professor M's sense of humor — often at his expense.

One process that made Professor M very angry, yet still has a humorous quality, involved him dropping little pieces of paper.

> A nurse would pick them up and throw them away. I later learned that at the university, he'd write little formulae on bits of paper and drop them. His secretary would pick up every little piece carefully in case he had a formula he wanted to see.

After eight years, Professor M was discharged from the Lodge. Otto believed that he even returned to teaching. "I got a letter several years after we stopped work. I remember it just said, 'Dear Otto, how are you doing? Love, M.'"

# Chapter Twenty: I & You

## The Cheerful Mystic

From 1955 to 1962, Leslie H. Farber was chairman of the faculty at the Washington School of Psychiatry. An existential analyst, Farber and Otto enjoyed a long friendship. Like Otto, Farber graduated from the Stanford School of Medicine, though two years ahead of Otto in 1938. Also, like Otto, he attended the Washington School of Psychiatry and received his psychoanalytic training through the Washington-Baltimore Psychoanalytic Society. During his training, he had been supervised by Sullivan but found this experience unsatisfying. More than that, Farber had apparently been offended by Sullivan in some deep way and seldom missed an opportunity to degrade Sullivan's memory after his death (see Farber, 2000). What Sullivan did to arouse such enmity in Farber remains a mystery, to me, at least (see also Frederickson, 2001). Speaking with his widow, Anne, shed no light on the issue (personal communication, March 19, 2011).

Farber had long been interested in the work of the philosopher and theologian, Martin Buber. From the beginning of his term as faculty chair, Farber wanted to bring Buber to Washington to give a series of lectures at the Washington School. In May 1956, Margaret Rioch (1986), the sister of David MacKenzie Rioch and a skilled analyst in her own right, made initial contact with Buber in London. He expressed interest, but when she met with him, Buber reminded her of his age (78) and acknowledged that he had to expend his energy in the most efficient ways. He reported excitement, though, about speaking at the Washington School of Psychiatry because that institution did not pretend to have answered all the important questions about the human condition. Thereafter, he and Farber corresponded and began arranging the visit. Farber extended a formal invitation to Buber to give the Fourth Annual William Alanson White Lectures (Friedman, 1991). Buber accepted the invitation, his topic entitled, "What can Philosophical Anthropology Contribute to Psychiatry" (Agassi, 1999, p. xii).

Like all complex arrangements involving people, planning proceeded with negotiation and compromise. Farber wanted a series of four new lectures; Buber was on a lecture tour in Europe and felt that he could not prepare four. They agreed to two new lectures and to two existing lectures that were unfamiliar in the United States (Buber, 1999; Friedman, 1991). As planning progressed, the Washington School received $25,000 from a private foundation to produce a film of the lectures. Buber diplomatically turned down the request. He believed that the recording of his lectures might interfere in a genuine dialogue between himself and the participants (Friedman, 1991).

Buber was curious about Harry Stack Sullivan and Farber was relatively less critical of Sullivan than was generally the case. In a March 1956 letter, he informed Buber that "there ... [was] an unpleasant discrepancy between his [Sullivan's] theories and his practice." He also asserted that Sullivan's writing was "overcome by pomposity and pedantry" (Buber, 1999, p. 193). He did send Buber material concerning Sullivan's ideas and Buber believed they were quite compatible with his own (Friedman, 1991).

In 1956, the year before Buber was scheduled to come, Farber (1956) wrote an overview of Buber's theory, "Martin Buber and Psychiatry," which was published in the journal, *Psychiatry*. After reviewing other dynamic theories and what he believed to be their flaws, Farber wrote, "I now turn to the theories of Martin Buber — theories which, I think, provide an answer to the question, *What is man*?" (p. 110, emphasis in the original). This paper, no doubt, served as an excellent introduction to those unfamiliar with Buber's work.

---

Born in Vienna in 1878, Martin M. Buber's childhood was, like Otto's, one of loss and confusion. When he was three years old, Martin's mother disappeared (Friedman, 1991, p. 3). The child was sent to live with his paternal grandparents. His father eventually remarried, and Martin later discovered that his mother had gone to Russia to marry another man. This early loss was devastating to the young boy (Friedman, 1991, pp. 3-4).

A 1956 *Time* article ("Religion: I & Thou," 1956) paints the philosopher as prone to deep thought during which he lost track of what was happening in his immediate environment. According to the magazine, he sat down in a New York barber's chair and lost much of his traditional beard before realizing it. He is also portrayed as a *Zaddik* (derived from the Hebrew meaning "righteous" or "just"), a "cheerful mystic" who found absolute devotion to Hasidic law too confining. Like Otto, he distrusted formal philosophical structures and tenets, believing that an understanding of God came through a personal relationship.

Though Buber had no formal training in psychology or psychoanalysis, he met Freud in 1908 and requested a monograph by Freud for a series that he was editing. Freud declined the request. It turned out that both felt they did not share enough values or common views. Buber found Freud's moral hierarchies (physician and patient, well and neurotic, etc.) off-putting and believed that Freud's developmental schema was moral in nature (Roazen, 1999). Nevertheless, he followed developments in psychoanalysis and by the mid-twenties Buber could fully describe his views and clarify his disagreements with Freudian psychoanalysis. Buber had an interpersonal view of the human condition; he postulated that the woes of the psyche are the result of dysfunction in relationships. He also believed that the primary prescribed activity of psychoanalysis, interpretation, was an obstacle in the two participants truly meeting because of the hierarchical relationship and the supposed greater objectivity of the analyst (Agazzi, 1999).

## *I and You (Ich und Du)*

Buber wrote his first draft of *I and Thou* (*Ich und Du*) in 1916, during the height of the carnage of the First World War. Between 1919 and 1923 Buber finished the statement on his philosophy of dialogue. Until the translation by Walter Kaufmann in 1970, Buber's seminal work was translated as *I and Thou*. Previous translators argued that God was considered as a participant in dialogue and the more formal "Thou" was appropriate. Kaufmann argued that this translation worked against Buber's contention that one could have a familiar, even intimate relationship with God. Thus, he translated "Du" as "You."

Buber (1970) proposed two types of relation in *I and You*: the I-You and the I-It. He described these two types of interaction as the two "basic words" of life. An "I-It" relationship is composed of internal experience. It is a contemplative, intrapsychic exploration of an *object* rather than a connective relationship. He proposed that such objects may be past, present, or future. The "I-You" relationship occurs only in the present. Buber believed that an I-You relationship was not spoken intellectually — distant from a partner in the relationship — but with all of one's essence. The basic word, I-You, requires the dyadic partner to also seek real connection with her whole being. It is in this immersion in each other that the "I" and the "You" are formed.

Buber's work was one of the first statements of an interpersonal perspective, though it broadly encompassed the spiritual realm. It was of great interest to most of the faculty at the Washington School of Psychiatry. On a personal level, Martin Buber was especially important to Erich Fromm and Frieda Fromm-Reichmann. Both counted Buber as a friend and colleague.

## Martin Buber at the Washington School of Psychiatry

During the White lectures, Buber (1999) introduced his Washington audience to the realm of the "interhuman." The interpersonal and the interhuman share some characteristics, but Buber emphasized that the latter requires a relational quality — participants in the interhuman are not merely objects to each other.

A second concept developed during the lectures concerned two types of relation; the first, which Buber (1999) described as "seeming" and the second, "being." Seeming is a form of relationship in which one or both participants relate as who they wish to be, rather than as they are. Being is a relationship in which both parties commit the essential truth of themselves. Buber (1999) wrote that "truth … in the interhuman realm … means that men communicate themselves to one another as what they are" (p. 77).

Finally, Buber (1999) continued to develop his ideas regarding "dialogue." These ideas criticized the psychoanalytic approach to psychotherapy. He believed that exploration of the unconscious partializes the patient rather than encountering her as a complete person. Genuine dialogue requires both therapist and patient to commit their entire being to the effort. Finally, he criticized free association as not falling in the realm of dialogue, which requires of both participants to speak from their being and say only what they need to say as fully human.

## Buber at Chestnut Lodge

One part of Buber's Washington visit was to lead a case discussion at Chestnut Lodge concerning a patient. There was a hope that Buber could illustrate his precepts by a detailed case discussion. The patient was chosen because of her interest in poetry and mysticism and was presented by her therapist, a man of Hasidic lineage. The therapist and patient were believed by the staff to be ideal for interesting Buber. Buber listened to the long (perhaps too long) presentation and frustrated many in attendance by offering only that he discerned no direction in the therapy (Friedman, 1991). While Buber believed that contact could be made with schizophrenic people, he apparently did not sense contact that day at Chestnut Lodge (Buber, 1999).

While at the Lodge, he met with the despairing Frieda Fromm-Reichmann. The meeting was private, but, no doubt, he listened attentively to her desperation and despair. Her loneliness must have been palpable. Yet, their time together brought her little relief. As described above, she died later that year (Friedman, 1991; Hornstein, 2000).

Patrick Will remembered Buber coming to the Will home after the discussion at Chestnut Lodge. He described him as: "A strange looking fellow with lots of hair and a beard." He must have seemed somewhat like Santa Claus. Though very young, Patrick believed that his father and Buber talked about the schizophrenic in an "I-You" relationship (personal communication, February 26, 2011). Though the interview that day was frustrating, neither man would give up on contact between two human beings, no matter how flawed either was.

A few years after Buber's presentation, Margaret Rioch (1960) wrote a paper entitled: "The Meaning of Martin Buber's 'Elements of the

Interhuman' for the Practice of Psychotherapy," published in *Psychiatry*. This paper together with Farber's (1956) serve as excellent bookends to Buber's contributions. In Rioch's paper, she proposed that psychotherapy would be practiced more effectively if viewed as "education," rather than a form of healing. Rioch also argued against the notion of anonymity in psychotherapy: "the more the therapist makes his assumptions and values explicit, the more the patient can find his own way with them or against them" (p. 139). In this statement, she captures an important dimension not only of Buber's thought, but also of Otto's.

---

In 1959, Otto's mother came to live with the family in Bethesda, Maryland. She was 73 and had been ill for several months (the exact nature of the illness is not clear). In January 1960, she died at their home. Otto recalled feeding her and holding her in his arms when she died. She had been a figure of such ambivalence in his life that grieving her must have been difficult. After she died, he cried, which surprised Gwen. He conveyed a sense of having had too little time with her after she began to improve psychologically.

Otto related that both of his parents were cremated. After his father died in 1958, his mother kept his ashes. After her death, he took both sets to Colorado and hiked up a small trail in the mountains. He put their ashes in the snow beneath a small tree. "As I walked down the trail it was dark, and I fell down a steep hill. [I was] shaken up a bit." After finishing his descent down the trail, he called Gwen. He told her that he had fallen.

She asked, "Were you hurt?"

"No, I'm all right."

"Well," Gwen responded, "she didn't get you after all."

## An Hour with Your Father

In 1959, Otto and Gwen's daughter, Deirdre, was born. Patrick was around three and, no doubt, Gwen was very busy with two young children. Otto was always preoccupied with work. Both Patrick and Deirdre remember their parents often in consultation, with Otto receiving ideas about his patients from Gwen. Both remember often feeling that they did not get enough interaction with their parents — especially their father who worked long hours throughout the week. Deirdre recalled that her father: "worked all the time. He wasn't there a lot — his work was his life" (personal communication, January 29, 2011). Patrick remembered an unsatisfying rationalization that Gwen offered in this regard: "An hour with your father is worth a week with any other parent" (personal communication, December 29, 2010). This reassurance did not, however, make up for the time missed with a real father.

Deirdre became interested in music and sports. In one of Otto's letters to Patrick, he described a desire to hike the Ice Glen Trail (a scenic 1.4 mile trail near Stockbridge, Massachusetts) with Deirdre when she was about 12. In another missive written around the same time he noted: "Deirdre is complaining — half bitterly and half humorously — about being goalie on the hockey team. We were kidding her a lot last night about her objections, and I gather they are not very serious." Also, he described attending a concert at which she performed at Simon's Rock, Massachusetts.

Yet, there is also a tentativeness in these letters. He closes a 1971 letter to Patrick about an upcoming visit with a note about his availability: "I shall be working this weekend on some writing that I must do, but I certainly shall have *some* time to be with you" (emphasis added). In a sense, Otto may have characterized his involvement as a father in a 1971 letter to his son:

> I did enjoy the shopping on Saturday afternoon. I was troubled at one point when we had to go back to the first record shop. At that time you said that you thought that you were being something of a pain to me, and I told you that was not the case. I have not had a great deal of time during these years of your rapid growing up, and I value what little time I do have with you, although I often am not very verbal about the matter. I am not a very good talker in a casual way, but I guess you can accept me as I am.

At moments, Otto seems tone deaf to what he is communicating. In a 1977 letter, he informs Patrick that he is planning a teaching trip to Chicago — where Patrick was attending college. While expressing a desire to see Patrick, he asks his son not to delay returning home for vacation just to be available to see him in Chicago. "It is important that you have time here and that mother and Deirdre get to see you as much as possible." Otto then informs his son that, after his visit to Chicago, he will fly to San Francisco to follow up on possible job leads. This trip, though, will last "only a couple of days." He reassured Patrick that "the trip will not cost much as it is tax deductible."

In a February 1978 letter, Otto wrote to Patrick:

> As you probably know, I have many requests to take part in conferences and so on. It would help a good deal if you could find out the date of your graduation ceremony. I know that we should all like to be there, and I do not want to schedule something and find that I cannot come to graduation.

Otto seems to be communicating his priorities in this letter, work is privileged over Patrick's graduation. Otto could also be manipulative with his children. This is not unheard of, nor even unusual, in parent-child relations, but for a man who valued clear, direct communication, it is noteworthy. In the following letter from 1976, he responds to Patrick's interest in enrolling in the Berklee College of Music:

> Mother tells me you are very pleased with the program at Berklee, and I do not want you to feel that I am opposed to that school; I am not. I do very much want you to give time to looking around when you make the change into music. I want you to get the best education in this field that you can qualify for and which we can provide. I also want you to go to a place from which you can move on to graduate work — if that is your desire. I also will thoroughly back up your working, if that is what you wish to do. It is possible that some months of work at a good job in the music field may be an excellent preparation for later study. It is also possible that you may like the work itself so much that you continue in that particular field. Should that be the case, I trust you know that I shall fully support you in your choice.

The suggestions for modifications in Patrick's plans are many and couched as random thoughts but it seems clear that he had reservations about those plans.

The overall picture of Otto Will as a father is characterized by reticence and self-absorption. One of the key elements of his idea of emotional intimacy was learning deeply about another person and allowing that person to know you. Otto seems not to have been an emotionally intimate father. Nevertheless, his children learned ways to live with satisfaction from him. Deirdre related having developed a love of the outdoors from her father, as well as a love of books, learning, and ideas. She became a writer and a writing educator. Reflecting upon her family situation growing up, she also made a deliberate effort toward creating a more child-focused family (personal communication, January 29, 2011). Patrick suggested that his father "was not a warm father because he hadn't had a warm father" (personal communication, May 21, 2011).

## Helping Others to See What *Is*

Otto's work was increasingly recognized, and, as he reminded Patrick, he was often invited to present at conferences and universities, often in the latter case to students intending to become psychiatrists. He told Kim Chernin that he had lectured at over 50 universities during his career; this number did not include lectures at professional conferences or at institutions such as the Menninger Clinic, where he was often invited.

Patrick Will remembered watching his father participate in a panel presentation with Buckminster Fuller, the architect, philosopher, and systems theorist, and Marshall McLuhan, the Canadian philosopher and media theorist. He told me that both Fuller and McLuhan exceeded the time allowed for their presentations. Otto, who followed them, found his own time significantly limited. His presentation was a contrast to theirs in that he spoke in a low voice and communicated great humility. As the formal proceedings broke up and audience members rushed to talk with their favorite speaker, Otto far outdrew Fuller and McLuhan, particularly in women. "He was mobbed by women, excited by his ideas and way of presenting them" (personal communication, May 21, 2011).

Otto also held an array of faculty appointments. Between 1950 and 1967 he was a faculty member at the Washington School of Psychiatry. He often led seminars with Frieda Fromm-Reichmann which were highly popular. Between 1953 and 1967, he was also on the faculty of the Washington-Baltimore Psychoanalytic Institute. He became a training analyst there in 1958. From 1956 to 1964, he served as an associate clinical professor at the University of Maryland School of Medicine. He was promoted to clinical professor in 1964 and remained on that faculty until 1967. Between 1962 and 1967, he was a lecturer at Johns Hopkins medical school. Irvin Yalom (2017) met and studied with Will there and described him as a "world-class storyteller" and as one of his "first models for the practice (and narration) of psychotherapy" (p. 95).

During the 1963-1964 academic year, Otto was a visiting professor of psychiatry at the University of Chicago. Carl Rogers had been professor of psychology there between 1945 and 1957. Bruno Bettelheim was professor of psychiatry and director of the Sonia Shankman Orthogenic School. Heinz Kohut, "Mr. Psychoanalysis," was on the faculty of the Chicago Institute of Psychoanalysis. Otto's time at one of the greatest universities in the world offered him the opportunity to implement his ideas about teaching as being rather than doing.

Though I could find little information about his time in Chicago, I surmise that much of his time was given over to lecturing. Yet, he would have had opportunities to develop relationships with residents, psychoanalytic candidates, and young clinicians. As Scott (1987) points out, it is these relationships that encourage attachment. Identification then becomes an important aspect of learning (Eiseley, 2012; Will, 1962).

After leaving Chestnut Lodge in 1967 and becoming medical director at the Austen Riggs Center, Otto held the following academic positions: clinical professor of psychiatry at Cornell University between 1967 and 1975; visiting professor of psychiatry at the University of Cincinnati for the academic year 1972-1973; and lecturer at the University of Massachusetts, Amherst between 1976 and 1978 ("Prabook: Otto Allen Will," n.d.).

In 1983, Otto was invited to spend part of the summer at Naropa University in Boulder, Colorado. He felt that the approach to psychotherapy taught there was similar to his own. He was presented with an acknowledgement, "Gift to Otto Will, June 1983, calligraphy by the Venerable Chögyam Trungpa Rimpoche." Trungpa was one of the first of the Buddhist teachers to bring Tibetan Buddhism to the West. He founded Naropa in 1974 (Chögyam Trungpa Biography, 2025). Written in a Tibetic dialect, it was roughly translated to Otto as:

> "The Great Eastern Sun,
> The quality of mind that can be glimpsed
> in an instant, which is clear,
> far outgoing like the sunrise, and completely free
> from preoccupation of oneself."

Throughout his career, Otto was a clinical resource for other therapists who found themselves struggling with a patient. He (1965) described his approach to consultation as focused on the person of the therapist, fostering acceptance of uncertainty, a willingness to allow others to grow in unconventional ways; a freedom from the competitive need to prove that hers is the *right* way. He did not discount compassion and kindness, and emphasized curiosity about the therapist as a person, hoping to understand her worldview.

He wished to enhance the therapist's ability to see beyond "right" and "wrong" to what *is* — an understanding of what is happening, rather than what *should* be happening. It is only an understanding of what *is* occurring that the patient can use to grow. He (1965) described a lack of emphasis on technique and emphasized growth of the capacity to observe and reflect on what occurs between patient and therapist.

## Leaving Chestnut Lodge

In 1967 Otto left Chestnut Lodge, his professional home for two decades. Why he left is unclear. He told Kim Chernin that he had established a reputation which interested other facilities, such as the Menninger Clinic in Topeka, Kansas. Patrick, who was 11, remembered that Otto considered both Menninger and Austen Riggs; Roy Menninger, the president of the Menninger Foundation, confirmed to me that the Clinic was interested in having Otto as a member of the staff (personal communication, April 8, 2011). In 1965, the Menninger organization had undergone a power struggle ultimately involving Karl and Will Menninger, the brothers who founded the clinic and foundation. Karl Menninger was stripped of his role as chief of staff and effectively exiled from the organization (Friedman, 1990). Reverberations from this conflict would continue for years and this, no doubt, was a consideration for Otto.

Robert Knight, medical director of Austen Riggs since 1947 died in 1966 of lung cancer. After his death, Austen Riggs was seeking a medical director and chief executive officer. Like all moves, the relocation to either institution involved a geographical change, and geography often represents highly emotional memories. For Otto, the geographical choice was stark. It was between Topeka, a flat Kansas town less than two hundred miles from where his life began — and where he experienced his first trauma — and Stockbridge, Massachusetts, in the Berkshire Mountains. The mountains had always been his sanctuary. It was the Austen Riggs Center that won out.

# Chapter Twenty-One: A Time of Great Pain

## The Austen Riggs Center

The Austen Riggs Center is located on a hill overlooking Main Street in the sleepy hamlet of Stockbridge, in the Southwestern part of Massachusetts. In 1970, Stockbridge had a population of just over 2,000 people (U.S. Census Bureau, 1970). During Otto's time there, it was like other small towns with a lunch counter at one of the two small local markets where Austen Riggs patients met for meals and a drugstore that served ice cream sundaes (Gordon, 2000; P. Will, personal communication, June 2, 2025). It is technically a part of the Pittsfield, Massachusetts metropolitan area which had a population of just over 57,000 in 1970 (U.S. Census Bureau, 1970).

In 1967, there was a dramatic contrast between Stockbridge and the rest of the United States. While Stockbridge was a peaceful and largely homogenous community, the rest of the country was in upheaval. The struggle for civil rights for African Americans that began in the 1950s continued. The struggle grew in intensity when right-wing government functionaries like J. Edgar Hoover, director of the Federal Bureau of Investigation, portrayed the movement as a front for communism (Gage 2022). The escalation of the war in Vietnam and the associated backlash had begun. By January 1969, when Richard Nixon was inaugurated President of the United States, American armed forces personnel in Vietnam numbered 540,000, most having been drafted (Kastenberg, 2019). In 1966, the year before Otto assumed the directorship at Austen Riggs, the U.S. Army had a desertion rate of 14 out of every 1000 soldiers. By 1970, that figure reached 70 per 1000 soldiers (Kastenberg, 2019). In 1962, African Americans accounted for six percent of all service personnel, by 1970, that figure had doubled to 12 percent (Kastenberg, 2019). Such struggles rent America and created bitter animosity between Americans, especially in urban areas. 1968 would also see the assassinations of two visionary leaders, Dr. Martin Luther King Jr. and Senator Robert F. Kennedy.

In Stockbridge, the Austen Riggs Center gracefully dominated — and still dominates — the landscape surrounding it. Its buildings are a mix of 1890s estate and modern architecture. The town could be part of a Norman Rockwell painting; Rockwell, in fact, lived on South Street in Stockbridge for the last 25 years of his life. Indeed, Rockwell was connected to Austen Riggs in various ways, the most personal being through his analysis with Erik Erikson, probably around 1953 (Capps, 2008). He also drew portraits of luminaries at the facility. According to Deirdre Vinyard, the Wills bought a home in the village for about $75,000 (over $700,000 in 2025 dollars) (Measuring Worth, 2025). While opulent, the house was not in the style that Gwen most appreciated. It was new and very formal, but she made no substantial changes. In this regard, Deirdre informed me that her mother "was a practical person as well as a brilliant one." She settled into a more domestic role than had been the case in Maryland (personal communications, January 29, 2011; June 2, 2025).

The Austen Riggs center began in 1913 as the Stockbridge Institute for the Study and Treatment of Psychoneuroses. It was founded by the physician, Austen Fox Riggs. He was tall, charismatic, and had intense brown eyes. Born in Germany to American parents (while his father was studying medicine), Riggs was educated at Harvard, where he studied with the influential pioneer William James, and the Columbia College of Physicians and Surgeons. He began his career as an ambitious New York internist and seemed destined to achieve great success in medicine. He was the attending physician at one of New York City's Houses of Rest for Consumptives. There were a number of such homes, designed primarily for patients with tuberculosis too advanced to be cared for in a general hospital. In the course of these duties, he fell ill and was diagnosed with tuberculosis (Peattie, 1941).

On learning of his illness, Riggs moved his family to a farm in Stockbridge, Massachusetts where his wife's extended family resided. He was briefly a semi-invalid and while recuperating became interested in psychiatry. During this period, he considered the role that perspective plays in one's adaptation to life. He chose to reject the life of an invalid and, in contrast to Otto's father, chose to embrace a life of service. When he founded the Stockbridge Institute for the Study and Treatment of Psychoneuroses its primary goal was to treat the indigent burdened with neuroses. Familiar with the ideas of Jean-Martin Charcot and Freud, Riggs developed a theory of neurosis that involved the patient's unwillingness to accept emotions and thus an unwillingness to accept reality. Like Freud, Riggs's theory developed from deep introspection. He had an authoritarian bent to his personality that stemmed from a certainty of purpose and a certainty about the correctness of that purpose (Millet, 1969). Much of his success resulted from the strength of his personality. Some of his patients spoke of him "as if he had been God" (Peattie 1941, p. 200).

In 1919, Riggs incorporated his Institute as the Austen Riggs Foundation. Fully twenty-five percent of his patients were treated free of charge with some receiving financial aid for other life expenses (Peattie, 1941). Riggs created an early prototype of the therapeutic community and activity therapy (Millet, 1969). His psychotherapy, which he called "reeducation," incorporated aspects of what is now called cognitive behavioral therapy and mindfulness training. "The method of treatment evolved by Riggs is one of frank discussion with the patient, the doctor seeking to understand the patient's life and personality and to bring him to self-understanding and self-help" (Peattie, 1941, p. 205). Also, according to Peattie (1941), Riggs's treatment rested on four pillars: a life of balanced work, play, and rest; living in the present; acceptance of reality; and the employment of one's energies in a "useful purpose," (i.e. being of service). Finally, he sought to impart that while human beings are not responsible for their emotions, they are responsible for *how* emotions are expressed. Otto shared with Riggs the belief that dysfunctional behavior was learned.

One important aspect of his reeducation model was helping his patients develop a wider perspective on their lives. Walt Whitman captured an aspect of such a perspective after being at the front in Fredericksburg during the Civil War. He wrote to his sister-in-law, Martha Mitchell Whitman ("Mattie"), that, "since I have spent a week in camp … and seen what well men and sick men, and mangled men endure — it seems to me … I can be satisfied and happy henceforth if I can get one meal a day" (Loving, 1999, p. 17). H.P. Lovecraft wrote to one of his many correspondents that

> Half our misery — perhaps more — comes from our mistaken notion that we ought to be happy … that we … "deserve" or "have a right to" acute happiness, whereas happiness [is] a transient, ephemeral thing. The best one [can] reasonably hope for [is] the lack of acute suffering (p. 402).

Both of these examples were derived from traumatic events in life and could easily lead to a nihilistic stoic philosophy, but they suggest the process of expanding one's perspective.

Having led the foundation for over 20 years, Riggs died in 1940. He was briefly succeeded by his assistant medical director, Horace K. Richardson. Richardson (1935) who maintained an interest in educating general practitioners about handling neurotic patients, resigned, though, after only a short time as director of the foundation. He, in turn, was succeeded by a psychoanalyst named Charles H. Kimberly ("Dr. Kimberly gets foundation post …," 1940). Kimberly, who had been educated at Williams College and the Harvard Medical School, joined the Riggs Foundation staff in 1934, following study in both England and Germany ("Dr. Kimberly named V.C. Psychiatrist; Succeeds Dr. Riggs," 1940). Kimberly (1936) integrated Riggs's reeducation approach with the psychoanalytic ego psychology emerging at the time.

In 1946, Kimberly stepped down as medical director. The Foundation had grown into an internationally renowned treatment center and the trustees began the search for a medical director of equal stature, for the first time, seeking a candidate outside the current staff. Fairly rapidly, a potential new medical director was identified — Robert Palmer Knight, Chief of Staff at the Menninger Clinic. Knight was 43 and had already held the presidency of both the American Psychoanalytic Association and the American Psychiatric Association from 1945 until 1946. Counting Anna Freud among his friends, Knight was a leading figure in American psychoanalysis ("Robert Knight of Riggs Center," 1966).

In 1946, Knight resigned from the Menninger Clinic to assume leadership at Austen Riggs. During his years at Menninger, he had overseen the development of a world-class research department which included David Rapaport, the Hungarian psychologist, psychoanalyst, and poet; Merton Gill, who was trained as both a psychiatrist and psychologist; and Margaret Brenman-Gibson, the first woman psychologist to complete psychoanalytic training approved by the American Psychoanalytic Association (Friedman, 1990). Knight attracted brilliant young professionals like Roy Schafer who joined the staff in 1947, even before earning his doctorate in psychology (Michels, 2019). Erik Erikson joined Riggs in 1951. For nearly two decades, Knight's leadership style and ego psychology dominated Riggs. Otto's successor, Daniel Schwartz, told the *Berkshire Eagle* that the era when Knight and Erikson worked together were the halcyon days at the Center ("A clear look at Austen Riggs," 1980). Indeed, it had been a productive period but the innovations that Otto brought to Austen Riggs were both underestimated and undervalued.

In 1966, Knight died of lung cancer. The search for a new medical director and chief executive officer began. The search committee, composed of Trust and staff members, interviewed 11 candidates before Otto applied. Margaret Brenman-Gibson was on the search committee and was impressed with Otto. She had a close collegial relationship with Erikson and wrote (2009) that none of the candidates interviewed before Otto knew much about Erikson or his work. This seems to have been an exaggeration, however, because Lars Lofgren, one of those candidates, had been analyzed by Erikson between 1958 and 1960 ("Lofgren, Lars Borje, M.D.," 2010).

Trained by Anna Freud, Erikson was both a profound thinker and psychoanalytic clinician. His psychosocial conception of development was an important innovation in psychoanalysis to many, though not to Anna Freud, who dismissed it as a popularization of her father's ideas (Brenman-Gibson, 1997; Friedman, 1999). Brenman-Gibson was protective of Erikson and was shocked at what she perceived as the ignorance of the other candidates (Brenman-Gibson, 2009).

Otto made a favorable impression on Brenman-Gibson. First, he knew of Erikson and his work. Second, he was open and funny. Brenman-Gibson (2009) wrote that Otto was "an original and open thinker." Others she experienced as burdened by dogma. Otto responded to the search committee's questions with candor. He surprised the group by saying, "My analyst [Sullivan] was probably the only analyst in the world who was simultaneously schizophrenic and alcoholic; that sounds like he would be a terrible analyst — but he was wonderful!" His colleagues at Chestnut Lodge recommended him as a brilliant clinician. His published papers were known to committee members who found them interesting and original. Brenman-Gibson (2009) became an advocate for Otto, though later, she regretted it deeply.

Otto was, in due course, offered the medical director's position. Initially, he accepted it. However, he quickly reversed himself and declined it. Patrick Will remembered that his father "had a hard time making a decision" about the position (personal communication, February 26, 2011). After this sequence of events, some at the Riggs Center joked that "Otto Will, Otto won't" (G. Fromm, personal communication, August 22, 2007). In the end, Otto accepted the position and began work in June 1967. He brought patients that he was treating at the Lodge.

## An Inpatient Psychotherapy Center

After assuming the leadership at Riggs, Otto (1968a) described the need for what he termed "inpatient psychotherapeutic centers," emphasizing that there were few hospitals in the world that provided psychotherapy (and even fewer now). He believed that psychotherapy should be one of the central pillars of such an institution. He also broadly outlined changes that might enhance therapeutic effectiveness: one therapist working with each patient throughout that patient's stay and specific training for each psychotherapist focused on implementing this training in accord with the therapist's own personality dynamics.

During a conference soon after Otto assumed the medical directorship, Barton Evans, a student of Sullivan's thought and a close colleague of Margaret Rioch at the Washington School of Psychiatry, presented a paper questioning the employment of psychoanalytic psychotherapy in an inpatient setting. This was, of course, in direct opposition to Otto's stance. In addition to his considered position on the topic, there was a covert, personal aspect to his opposition. Evans had supported another candidate, Lars B. Lofgren, for the medical directorship. A Swedish psychiatrist, Lofgren had been an admired supervisor of Evans. In addition to his analysis with Erikson, he had experience working at Riggs, having been on the staff between 1964 and 1969. Evans told me that he initially had "a chip on his shoulder" with Otto. However, after his presentation:

> Otto invited me to his office and for over an hour we first shared much about our mutual friends and colleagues from the Washington School of Psychiatry. He was very warm and inviting and was openly and non-defensively interested in my further thoughts about intensive inpatient psychotherapy, even though I was quite young (28) and a newly minted Ph.D. Of course he was Otto Will, one of the giants in the world of Sullivan and interpersonal psychotherapy. I remember and still feel his warmth, openness and presence now nearly 50 years later. (personal communication, February 4, 2025).

However, Otto could be critical of ideas with which he disagreed, as well. Stephen Schlein recalled that during his first group meeting with Otto, "he [Otto] was putting down family therapy — he was furious with Donald Bloch" (personal communication, August 19, 2007). Bloch was director of research at Riggs and, after leaving there, became director of the Ackerman Family Institute in New York City (Guerin, 1976). Margaret Brenman-Gibson wrote that she found Otto highly competitive; he was intolerant of ideas concerning therapy different from his own, often labeling them "bad."

Margaret Brenman-Gibson was considered by some to be something of a grande dame at Austen Riggs. Her marriage to the playwright William Gibson, whose work included *The Miracle Worker* and *Two for the See-Saw*, added to her stature (Belfer, et al., 2006). She wrote that, with each passing month, she became more disappointed in Otto's leadership. Otto, in turn, found her "airs" irritating. He recalled a discussion of a patient who sat on the floor during sessions, while Otto sat in a chair. Brenman-Gibson offered "that she would've asked the patient, 'Why don't you come up to my level?'" Otto then suggested, "The proper answer the patient should give: 'I don't, because there's no oxygen up there and I can't breathe.'"

## Envy?

The relationship between Otto and Erik Erikson was often tense. Both were ambitious men, though also humble in appreciative contexts. In 1969, Erikson was awarded the Pulitzer Prize and featured on the cover of *Time* magazine (Goldberger, 2021). In 1970, he received the National Book Award (Friedman, 1999). Otto was successful but could not match these achievements. Stephen Schlein, Erikson's last supervisee at Riggs, recalled that Erikson felt patronized by Otto and that, "Erikson didn't feel respected by Will" (personal communication, August 19, 2007). Gerard Fromm remembered, "Erikson once said to Otto, 'You award the diagnosis of schizophrenia like a merit badge.' There was tension between their viewpoints." However, to Fromm, "It didn't seem that either worried about what the other thought — both had made their names" (personal communication, August 22, 2007). Patrick Will confirmed that there was little warmth between his father and Erikson (personal communication, January 16, 2011). Yet, he also described some playful interactions between himself, his sister, and the psychoanalyst with the white mane. On occasion, the Wills would host small gatherings of the Riggs' staff and trustees at their home. According to Patrick, Erikson would often depart the company of the adults and seek out the children, explaining that "he was bored with all the talk." On one of these occasions, Patrick remembers placing a "Whoopie cushion" beneath Erikson's seat. "He sat on it with the expected result." He remembered his father being angry with him but that Erikson "laughed and laughed" (personal communication, May 31, 2025).

Such light moments aside, the tension between the two men created a rift in the staff, some of whom felt they needed to take sides. Institutional politics were pervasive and destructive. Otto told Kim Chernin that he quickly began to feel isolated.

Perhaps to ease his isolation, in 1968, Otto invited former colleagues from Chestnut Lodge to join him at Austen Riggs. One was Martin Cooperman, the clinical director at the Lodge, who was offered the same position at Riggs. He would be promoted to associate medical director and spent twenty years at the center.

Cooperman was pursuing his second career; prior to becoming a psychiatrist and psychoanalyst, he had been a U.S. Navy flight surgeon. Like Otto, he served in the Second World War on the aircraft carrier U.S.S. *Wasp* which was sunk by a Japanese submarine. In 1955, after twenty years in the navy, he decided to pursue training as a psychiatrist, followed by training as a psychoanalyst. Cooperman graduated from both the Washington School of Psychiatry and the Washington-Baltimore Psychoanalytic Institute ("Martin Cooperman Obituary," 2006).

Cooperman was one of those rare human beings who could separate useful ideas from the frustrating personality of the originator of those ideas. While he described Harry Stack Sullivan as "a son of a bitch" he found his ideas full of potential (Pepper, 2019, p. 106). Along with Otto, Cooperman represented what Christopher Bollas (2025) described as the "unique American 'school' of psychoanalysis (the 'aw shucks what do I know?')" perspective at Riggs (p. xx).

Though not a theorist or writer by nature, Cooperman's (1983) writing was required reading in many psychiatry programs, particularly his assertion that patients must give up symptoms and therapists technique to actually meet as people. Another important contribution was his description of the "defeating process" in psychotherapy during which a patient may destroy her own therapy in retaliation for an injury by her therapist (Fromm, 2011; Pepper, 2019).

Otto also brought Leslie Farber, the director of psychotherapy at the Lodge, to be director of psychotherapy at Riggs. Later, along with Rollo May, Farber was an important figure in existential psychoanalysis (Beira & Hassan, 2005). Otto promised Farber time to write, but this never materialized. Farber grew increasingly disenchanted with Riggs and Stockbridge and became "weary of maple sugar and Norman Rockwell and power struggles within the hospital administration" (Gordon, 2019). Farber was probably the most controversial of the talented, but sometimes eccentric, clinicians at Austen Riggs. Examining remembrances of Farber by his patients, Emily Fox Gordon and Katharine Graham, Barbara Moore (1999) relates that Graham described his work as "bizarre, sloppy or selfish" while Gordon viewed the same qualities as "thoughtful, humane and devoted" (p. 256). Farber left for private practice in Manhattan in 1969 (Clark, 1981).

It is interesting that Erikson and Otto had difficulty finding common ground. Edward Hall (1992) wrote that, "Otto had long been preoccupied with envy" believing it to be highly destructive in relationships (p. 238). While in the Washington area, Otto formed a group to study the phenomenon of envy. According to Hall, who participated in the group, there was no significant progress made in understanding it conceptually. One question that presents itself is what, if any, role did envy play in the relationship between Otto and Erikson.

Courtesy of Patrick Will

Otto

Circa 1970

Otto was medical director of the Austen Riggs Center from 1967-1978. This was a period of deep pain for him. His second marriage ended, his drinking increased, and he was often in conflict with other staff members. However, he was a popular teacher and speaker who presented his ideas quietly and modestly. In this photo, he is speaking to a professional audience perhaps at the Menninger Clinic.

Courtesy of Jon Erikson & Science Source

Erik H. Erikson (1902-1994)
circa 1970

Erikson returned to the Austen Riggs Center after teaching at Harvard and being awarded both the Pulitzer Prize and the National Book Award. Otto and Erikson maintained a tense relationship.

Erikson was interested in Sullivan's work. Brenman-Gibson (1997) wrote about a conversation in which she took part with Erikson and David Rapaport. She described Erikson as highly interested in Sullivan's concept of the Self as more in keeping with the identity that Erikson wanted to conceptualize. Patrick Will remembered that his father found Erikson's clinical style "too touchy-feely" (personal communication, February 26, 2011). Yet, like Otto, Erikson did what he thought the patient needed and this included: going to patient's homes, dining with their families, and inviting patients to his home to meet his family (Friedman, 1999; Schlein, 2016). Erikson also believed that it was the relationship between therapist and patient that functioned as the active ingredient in change (Schlein, 2016).

In addition to a new perspective, Otto also brought other changes to Riggs. When he began as medical director, approximately 30 percent of the center's patients were discharged within 30 days. He created a new policy requiring a commitment that patients stay at least twelve months (Thompson & Thompson, 1998; Will, 1977c). When Otto became medical director, the median patient age was 26; in 1977 it had decreased to 21. Forty-one of these patients were housed at "The [Red Lion] Inn" and eight patients resided at "The Elms," a halfway house (Will, 1977c). Otto described Austen Riggs as what he (1968a) had termed earlier, a psychotherapeutic center. For him that meant that, "the essential ingredient of the work is the use of the human relationship" (Will, 1977c, p. 368).

## Analytic Niceties

Otto was familiar with a system of psychoanalytic training foreign to that at Riggs. At Chestnut Lodge, the senior staff analyzed the junior staff (as Fromm-Reichmann had analyzed him). At Riggs, the psychoanalytic training program was centered at Yale University. Otto changed this arrangement with the Western New England Psychoanalytic Institute and Western New England Psychoanalytic Society, which had been in place since 1951 (Carlson, 2003). He recreated the system at Chestnut Lodge (Thompson & Thompson, 1998). Further, Otto's conception of psychoanalytic development was focused on education and not rote training. He objected to purveying received knowledge and focused instead on assisting psychotherapists in learning to become themselves. As noted above, he (1962) found too much about institute-based training authoritarian. He (1977c) described the third- and fourth-year residency and postdoctoral fellowships in psychology as consisting of: a personal analysis, weekly individual clinical supervision, bi-weekly clinical staff conferences, seminars on theory and technique held twice or thrice weekly, and training in group dynamics and psychotherapy.

Brenman-Gibson may have resisted Otto's changes to the psychoanalytic training at Riggs because of the difficulty she had previously experienced in such a system. The Menninger Clinic had a training program very much like that at Chestnut Lodge. The senior staff provided training analyses for the junior staff. Robert Knight, Chief of Staff of the Menninger Clinic, was considered the most skilled analyst at the clinic and was sought after for training by the younger staff. He, therefore, had his pick of candidates for analysis. Among those for whom he provided training analyses were the brightest — Merton Gill, David Rapaport, and Margaret Brenman-Gibson.

As they were all close colleagues, these analyses presented complications to their work together. Brenman-Gibson described the situation as "incestuous" (Friedman, 1990, p. 249). This was not ameliorated by Knight's decision to invite all three to join him at Austen Riggs in 1947. Though the history of psychoanalysis is replete with such incestuous arrangements — certainly not least Freud's analysis of his daughter, Anna — there were hazards involved. Despite these hazards, Knight recruited the psychologist, Roy Schafer, to join the Riggs' staff who then began a training analysis with Knight. It may have seemed to Otto and others that Brenman-Gibson was resistant to anything Otto suggested, her resistance to this change, however, may have reflected her own experience with such a training arrangement.

Few of Will's changes were popular with the entrenched ego psychologists. No doubt it was of little help that, as Deirdre Will Vinyard told me about her father, "He was very passionate about his views. He didn't compromise" (personal communication, January 8, 2011). Gradually, though, Otto's ideas began to take hold. In an interesting study comparing the emphases of psychological testing at Austen Riggs under its various medical directors, Ridenour and Zimmerman (2017), psychologists at Riggs, noted that psychological testing at Riggs was less concerned with diagnosis during Otto's administration and personality disorders were less frequently noted. "Schizophrenia" was given as a diagnosis more often. The stance of the testing psychologist vis à vis the patient evolved: "from an objective observer to an empathic, therapeutic participant" (p. 6). Psychologists often included subjective reactions in reports. The authors offer this example: "One knows this patient is hurting, but it is very hard to feel it. It is easy to become very bored with him" (p. 6). Ultimately, Ridenour and Zimmerman assert that, "The language of developmental psychology and object relations gradually replaced Erikson's life cycle stages of development" (p. 6).

Otto's drinking also created situations in which he undermined himself (Brenman, 2009). James Gorney (2021) offered an example of such a situation. He remembered Otto arriving, already intoxicated, at an annual cocktail party for the medical staff and trustees. Gorney writes that he had recently been passed over for a position at Riggs and was disappointed and angry about that. Otto approached Gorney at the party, physically grabbed him, and repeatedly demanded that Gorney acknowledge his desire to murder him.

Otto began corresponding with the Scottish analyst, R.D. Laing, in April 1973. They exchanged at least two letters, reflecting a relationship of mutual interest and respect. Between April and October 1973, they met at Riggs and Laing arranged for his time with the Riggs staff to be filmed. Apparently, Otto was concerned that the filming would inhibit discussion but assured Laing in an October 23 letter that "I very much enjoyed meeting with the members of the camera crew and did not feel that they interfered at all with our discussions." A copy of this film is housed in The Special Collections Department (R.D. Laing Archive) of the University of Glasgow Library in Scotland.

Otto and Laing held very similar views on psychotherapy generally and the treatment of schizophrenia specifically. According to Michael Guy Thompson, who knew both men, Otto and Laing shared a willingness to accept other points of view, even if they did not fully understand them. Both believed that what Otto called "analytic niceties" sometimes interfered in responding effectively to patients. Neither was afraid to hold a patient if that seemed indicated. Both believed that patients had a right to "keep things to themselves;" that was a freedom to which all patients were entitled. Both accepted the patient's "truth" based on their experiences, even if it was not verifiable. Thompson related that, "Nobody's personal narrative is without contradictions and how we react to these contradictions is part of our personal truth" (personal communication, July 6, 2007).

In a May 29 letter, Laing expressed much interest in meeting Dr. Robert Bergman who was chief of the mental health program for the Navajo Nation and chief of national mental health programs for the Indian Health Service ("Robert Bergman, MD," n.d.). Bergman had been a resident at the University of Chicago while Otto was a visiting faculty member. Otto praised the young psychiatrist's ongoing attempts to combine traditional Navajo medicine (which included the use of peyote) with psychoanalysis and other modern medical practices (see Bergman, 1971) and agreed to facilitate a meeting. Of course, Otto did not miss the opportunity to share his love for the southwest with the Scottish analyst.

Otto's relationship with Laing also provided an opportunity for Otto and Patrick to bond, as Patrick was interested in Laing's ideas. He told me that he was also a fan of the musical group Gentle Giant, a progressive British band popular between 1970 and 1980. Some of their lyrics were inspired by Laing's philosophy and his idiosyncratic book of poetry, *Knots* (1970) (P. Will, personal communication, May 21, 2011).

It is not clear when it began, but Otto was involved in an affair with a staff member at Austen Riggs. She had previously worked at Chestnut Lodge. This affair exacerbated conflicts both in his family and among the Riggs staff, and some viewed it as an indication of Otto's professional inadequacy. Unfortunately, it did represent a lapse in Otto's management of professional boundaries. It was also quite distressing to Gwen as she had been betrayed by both her husband and a woman that she had previously considered a friend (P. Will, personal communication, May 25, 2025).

Gwen discovered the affair, and this knowledge made its way to Patrick and Deirdre. Deirdre remembered that her parents' relationship began to show signs of strain in 1969. In 1972, they separated, and Otto moved out of the family home. For a time, he lived on the campus of the center. The next year, Gwen accepted the position as director of community care at the Berkshire Mental Health Center in Pittsfield (Sullivan, 2007). Otto and Gwen remained separated until their marriage ended in 1980. During the separation, Otto remained financially responsible for the family, structuring a trust for their use. During this period, Otto's drinking intensified. After twenty-seven years of marriage, Gwen and Otto were divorced by a decree from the Dominican Republic. Deirdre remembered her parents remaining friends and after her father married Beulah Parker, Gwen developed a friendship with her, as well (personal communications, January 8, 2011; January 29, 2011, May 30, 2025).

What happened at Austen Riggs? According to Deirdre Vinyard, her mother had questioned Otto's abilities as an administrator. He was passionate and often provocative. "My dad ran hot and cold with a lot of people. He wasn't a peacemaker" (personal communication, January 29, 2011). In the end, Patrick Will described Austen Riggs as "a huge detriment to him" and a place that "really took his soul!" (personal communication, January 16, 2011).

## Leaving Austen Riggs

In March 1977 Otto began searching for a position in the California Bay Area. He recalled having fond memories of his years there. On April 28, 1977, Otto wrote to his old friend, Hilde Bruch. He was not retiring, he assured her, though he was planning to leave his position as medical director at Riggs. He wrote that he hoped to continue working as a psychotherapist and teacher. On July 31, 1978, the official announcement of his departure was released. His resignation had actually been effective July 1. The announcement stated that he had accepted the position as director of adolescent and young adult psychiatric services at Mount Zion Hospital (now Mount Zion Medical Center), a renowned psychoanalytic hospital. He would begin work September 1, 1978 ("Dr. Otto Will leaves as director at Riggs," 1978).

Otto remained on the Austen Riggs board until his death in 1993. He also remained a polarizing figure. When the *Berkshire Eagle* newspaper published Otto's obituary, associates were asked about his impact on the fields of psychiatry and psychoanalysis. One characterization was that he had not been a leader in those fields but was a master craftsman in the application of extant knowledge. This drew a concerned letter to the editor, entitled "The Strengths of Dr. Will" by a former Riggs employee who wrote, "What stood out for me about Otto Will was his deep respect for his patients and his remarkable openness about his life and experiences" (Mooney, 1993, p. 10).

This letter seems almost beside the point but certainly is not. Otto did not hold himself out as a master theorist and would not have recognized himself in such a description. Psychoanalysis has always had more theorists than master practitioners. Otto was among the very few of the latter.

# Chapter Twenty-Two: Clinical Studies from Austen Riggs

Though Otto's tenure at Austen Riggs was one of administrative difficulties — perhaps failure — he continued to be the consummate psychotherapist. His clinical work there has been lauded by Christopher Bollas (2015), Gerard Fromm (2004), James Gorney (2021), and Eric Plakun (2021). As he had at Chestnut Lodge, he worked with schizophrenic, schizoid, and borderline patients without ever prescribing medication or, to borrow Leslie Farber's (2000) colorful phrase, "with his bare hands" (p. 66).

That Otto did not prescribe medications in what was an increasingly medication-oriented profession is noteworthy. It was a part of his faith in the human relationship as the medium for healing. When one of his patients experienced a crisis or regression, he "rode it out" with them, making the time necessary to do so (Bollas, 2004). Bollas (2013) also recalled that after Otto left the medical directorship at Austen Riggs, he returned for extended visits. Bollas described Otto as attending to his former patients if there was a decompensation. He would go and sit with the patient — "in it together" with her. Bollas (2004) contends that addressing a crisis in this way reduces the anxiety of both patient and therapist. Otto's willingness to avoid medication and swim against the current of the psychiatric profession also speaks to an oppositional aspect of his personality (Hirsch, 1998).

It is unfortunate that Otto never discussed patients at Austen Riggs with Kim Chernin and because of the need to protect patient privacy, all that can be drawn from are the published records he left. It is noteworthy that his writing from these years contains fewer vignettes and those contain less information. I will summarize some of his clinical work during this period in the vignettes below.

## "Miss C": The Therapist's Responsibility

In Chapter Eighteen, "Miss A" was discussed. Otto (1970b, 1972) also gave this designation to a patient at Austen Riggs, so I have modified the pseudonym to avoid confusion.

Otto met 20-year-old Miss C after she was hospitalized during her freshman year of college. She had given up on her classes and withdrawn from her friends. She stayed secluded in her room and was on the verge of failing in her studies. She had unsuccessfully been treated with insulin coma and ECT at another hospital and had worked with two therapists prior to seeing Otto.

Miss C felt alienated from her family. As a child she withdrew into music and church-related activities. Primarily, though, she fantasized about relationships. She was confused about why she had none that were close and gradually developed the theory that she was somehow unworthy of others' care and regard. Even this theory, however, was better to her than chaotic questions.

From the beginning, Miss C was suspicious and harshly critical of Otto, often suggesting that he was a cold and unfeeling phony. He described responding with appreciation for her willingness to speak openly about her feelings rather than hide them. As their acquaintance grew, he began asking her which of his actions formed the basis of her assessments. He would confirm her accurate perceptions. Otto wrote that relationships had previously been a source of pain for Miss C, and, as their relationship developed, she feared that he was leading her into danger.

At times during his work with Miss C, he felt unappreciated and fantasized about withdrawing from their relationship. However, he held to the belief that the psychotherapeutic relationship cannot be abandoned because the therapist experiences anxiety. Still involved in Miss C's therapy at the time of writing the vignette, Otto ended it by noting that he and Miss C would experience the ending of their relationship and the grief that accompanies it.

In closing, he (1970b) emphasized the importance of the therapist not hiding behind a façade of neutrality or impersonality. To be fully engaged and available as a real human being will invariably result in embarrassing and painful moments; indeed, "they are inevitable in this work and give some hint of what we ask the patient to experience" (p. 24).

## "Kay": Connecting the Parts

Otto (1972) wrote that he first met seventeen-year-old Kay during a consultation on a general medical ward. Her parents were concerned about a change in her affect. She seemed "depressed" and began to withdraw from the world. She met with a guidance counselor at school briefly. After her fourth visit, she became mute and immobile. She kept her eyes closed and Otto noted that she drooled. A neurological work-up suggested no physical abnormalities.

In his first two-hour meeting with her, Otto introduced himself and told her a little about why he was there. He described asking her, "Who are you?" to which she replied "I don't know" (p. 30).

Kay's image of herself was something like that of a jukebox. She contained "records" of how to interact with specific family members (e.g., how to speak with father, how to speak with mother, etc.). Corresponding to these records were different selves, again defined by who she was interacting with and what function was being served (e.g., she had an emotional self, an intellectual self, and so on). The different records and selves had begun to overwhelm her with their complexity, and withdrawal seemed her only recourse.

Otto and Kay determined that her catatonic behavior had developed from the feeling that she was, at least partially, "evil." Her actions, focused on exact specifications, allowed her to maintain a semblance of relationships while preventing others from seeing what she thought of as her evil qualities. It was a compromise that allowed her to avoid complete rejection. Otto described this not as "crazy," but as having a problem-solving quality. He hypothesized that during infancy she had received contradictory messages about her value and which behaviors would get her needs met by mother.

According to Otto, Kay was hospitalized at Riggs for two years, followed by five months of outpatient treatment. During this period, Otto and Kay met for 550 sessions; these sessions occurred five days a week for a minimum of 55 minutes. The location of sessions varied with some in his office, some in her room, and some outdoors while walking on the campus. Otto noted that the location at which a session occurred was dictated by the intensity of her anxiety.

During the first seven months of Kay's hospitalization, she was self-mutilative of her face and extremities by burning, biting, and cutting; she also attempted suicide. During her fourth month of hospitalization, a nurse asked Otto to come from home to see Kay, who was described as "unresponsive." Otto related that he sat beside her, gently touching her hand, and shared with her his confusion about the reason for her withdrawal. He specifically noted that he offered no interpretations but simply shared his lack of understanding about what had occurred in their relationship to trigger a catatonic response.

After the resolution of this catatonic episode, she was plagued by nightmares and frightened to go to sleep. At times, Otto would sit with her until she fell asleep (at other times a nurse would sit with her). Otto ultimately considered her withdrawal to be a form of reorganization that allowed her to integrate her many "selves" without the pressure and complexity of meeting others' expectations. The "records" she described initially seemed to be ways of simplifying her experience with stereotypy. Her withdrawal also included fantasies of being more competent and accepted by other people. In the security of her attachment to Otto she could risk revealing all of herself without the disaster of rejection.

After her treatment ended, Kay enrolled in college. She was successful in her studies and graduated. Otto attended Kay's graduation ceremony and Deirdre accompanied him (D. Vinyard, personal communication, January 29, 2011). Describing his approach to psychotherapy with Kay, Otto (1972) wrote that he had employed: "a quiet, patient, tolerant attitude — combined with a bit of confidence, humor, and endurance," he had also been "interested in observing and learning" (p. 56). As in all psychotherapy, the primary work involved reestablishing hope and trust.

## "Miss D": Psychotherapy & Friendship

On October 16, 1969, Otto presented a case to the Topeka Psychoanalytic Society, which was recorded (in writing) by Ann Appelbaum (Will, 1970a). He described a young woman whose age was not specified. She apparently reacted with destructive anxiety to any attempts that he made at interpretation. He related that he held interpretive work in abeyance and instead focused on decreasing her anxiety by careful attention to the environment of their relationship.

Miss D was often late for sessions with Otto, sometimes missing them altogether. He developed a schedule in which he had two-and-a-half hours available daily for her. She could arrive at any time within that period. Aside from questions she posed, she revealed little about herself. Otto noted that he responded to her questions with honesty and simplicity.

Since she would not talk about herself, Otto began to fill the silence in their sessions by sharing aspects of his life, about which she would also ask questions and to which he would reply honestly. He told the group that he was attempting to model the self-revelation inherent in intimate relationships.

At some point in their work together, he invited Miss D to go on a Will "family outing." After this experience, she began to share a little during sessions. Specifically, she disclosed her fear of saying too much and being rejected as "crazy." After this tentative movement toward Otto, Miss D described thoughts about suicide. He told her that he would miss her, and she assured him that she would not kill herself. After this interaction, she began to talk about the relationship that she had with Otto, and he believed her to be moving toward recovery.

Otto stressed the following points in his presentation: 1. the creation of a reliable environment in which psychotherapy can take place; 2. the therapist listening and accepting before attempting change; 3. that sharing a space and making sounds with each other, even if such sounds are not words is helpful; 4. the therapist focusing on current interactions, rather than searching the past; and 5. when offering an interpretive remark, doing so with possibilities potentially more acceptable to the patient. Apparently, someone attending asked Otto how he differentiated the psychotherapeutic relationship from friendship. He described these relationships as related in many ways but stressed that the goal of friendship is to remain in relationship while the goal of psychotherapy is growth and separation.

This last point is an interesting one. Throughout his writings, Otto emphasizes the need for termination but as discussed in previous chapters, he had great difficulty tolerating separation. There is evidence that the boundaries of his separations from former patients were permeable, and contact was maintained after psychotherapy ended (see Will, 1971b).

———

The experience at Riggs and the end of his marriage to Gwen seem to have left Otto emotionally fatigued and battered, prompting him to question fundamental aspects of himself. He (1979) wrote, "There is not in me, I often think, the ability to form an enduring relationship of love. There always looms the separation which repeatedly I, myself, seem to provoke, even against my known desires" (p. 575). He had, however, not given up on love completely, and his time in California would offer another opportunity for it.

After leaving Riggs, Otto's clinical work was directed toward the growth of patients not burdened by such catastrophic problems in living as schizophrenia. His published work focused on a variety of broader areas which require no vignettes for explication. These topics included: the future of psychotherapy (1977a), the professional life of the psychotherapist (1979), the role of values for the therapist (1981), and shame in psychosis (1987b).

# Chapter Twenty-Three: The Psychoanalytic Outsider

## "A Troubled Girl"

In the early fall of 1978, Otto returned to the West Coast, making his home near San Francisco. He met Beulah Parker, a psychiatrist and psychoanalyst interested in psychotherapy with schizophrenics. She was interested in how family organization affects a child's development and had been a guest speaker at Austen Riggs; she was also an educator at Mount Zion Medical Center. Beulah (1987) described interacting with Otto "from time to time" at professional events (p. 155). She respected his professional stature and enjoyed his sense of humor.

She was a handsome, intelligent, and professionally accomplished 66-year-old widow. Her first husband, Leland "Punk" Vaughn, was head of the landscape architecture program at the University of California, Berkely and died in 1974.

In addition to her professional interests, she was also a writer. By the time she met Otto, she had written one book (1962) and was finishing another (1978). Both were mixtures of the scholarly and the creative. The first, entitled *My Language is Myself* (1962), concerned psychotherapy with a deeply troubled boy. She clearly had the gift for touching the isolated and lonely. The second, *A Mingled Yarn* (1978), was a portrait of her family — though highly disguised. Her family had experienced schizophrenia and suicide — terrible levels of madness that she wanted to understand with more clarity. Both books were written for a lay audience, but psychoanalysis was an important part of the fabric.

Otto was impressed with her courage and resiliency. Besides overcoming familial trauma, she had pursued a medical, psychiatric, and psychoanalytic education when all three fields were dominated by men. He encouraged her to write a memoir, *The Evolution of a Psychiatrist* (1987), which she dedicated to him. It begins: "This is the story of a troubled girl from a troubled family who, by slow and painful steps, became a woman, a doctor, a psychiatrist and a psychoanalyst" (p. ix). A smaller work than her previous books, it has a quaint, old-world modesty. She also explains concepts in plain language, and there is virtually no use of jargon. Her perspective is open and enlightened. For example, she wrote that: "The person who carries out major bodily care of an infant becomes that child's psychological mother, whether that person is female or male" (p. 16).

Beulah and Otto shared traumatic experiences involving attachment. Beulah's mother was distant and wanted her children (Beulah had a brother five years her senior) raised by a nanny. A professionally trained German nurse was hired for this purpose. "Fraulein," as she was called, became Beulah's psychological mother. However, as the bond between them grew, Beulah's biological mother became jealous. When Beulah was five, Fraulein was summarily dismissed. Like Otto, she had experienced a serious abandonment, though somewhat further along in her development.

Beulah received an Ivy League education, undergraduate at Bryn Mawr, and then her medical studies at the Columbia School of Medicine and Surgery. She found courses in psychiatry to be, at best, irrelevant to the study of people and, at worst, confirmatory of the deprecating jokes made about psychiatrists (Parker, 1987).

One medical specialty in which women were more accepted than in others was pediatrics. Like Hilde Bruch, this is where she began her medical work. In 1943, having just graduated from medical school, Beulah was accepted at Babies Hospital in New York. This was, she knew, unheard of, but because of a shortage of physicians due to the war, she thankfully began her studies there. She remained for two years, until 1945 when, along with her best friend — another woman pediatrician — she moved to California to complete her residency at the University of California Hospital in San Francisco. Again, because of the Second World War, the final "year" of residency was reduced to nine months and residents rotated among three specialty areas. For Beulah, her first rotation was in psychiatry at the Langley Porter Institute, which was then under the leadership of Karl Murdock Bowman (Solomon, 1946).

Bowman was president of the American Psychiatric Association and had three primary interests: schizophrenia, alcoholism, and homosexuality. He was known as a compassionate and caring physician, a benign presence in the lives of his students and faculty members (Bowman, 1969; Solomon, 1946). While this seems to have been true, in his early studies of homosexuality he suggested that castration might be one potential treatment for male homosexuals. By 1961, however, he was arguing that homosexuality was not a mental disorder and should be decriminalized (Largent, 2011).

Erik Erikson would also play a key role in Beulah's life. In late 1939, Erikson left Yale University's Institute for Human Relations. This was the environment in which he was no doubt exposed to the ideas of Harry Stack Sullivan through Edward Sapir, head of the Yale Anthropology Department in which he studied the impact of culture on personality (Darnell, 1990). The tall, blond Danish child psychoanalyst had been recruited from the Harvard Psychological Clinic in 1936 with the promise of a major research project. By 1938, he was disappointed that such a project had not developed. He was offered the opportunity to work with researchers at the University of California's Institute of Child Welfare on a longitudinal study of child development. He also taught in the psychiatry program at the University of California and the San Francisco Psychoanalytic Institute. He began a private practice in San Francisco specializing in training analyses (Friedman, 1999; Parker, 1987).

In her rotation in the psychiatry department, Beulah was assigned a patient that she called "Gordon." After three sessions with this eight-year-old, she was sure she wanted to be a psychiatrist and subsequently changed her course of study. Beulah was also prone to anxiety and depressive periods, and a desire to understand herself more fully also played a part in this change (Parker, 1987).

After completing her residency, Beulah became involved in the founding of a counseling clinic focused on developing brief dynamic approaches to psychotherapy. In 1946, she approached Erikson for psychoanalysis, and he agreed to see her if she applied and was accepted for formal psychoanalytic training. She was. For the next 40 years, she worked in private practice (Parker, 1987).

Beulah (1987) wrote that in 1950 she met Leland "Punk" Vaughn. Leland Vaughn had been called "That Little Punk" by an older brother throughout his childhood and the name "Punk" stuck. When she met him, she described "Punk" as "charming," "quiet," "loyal," "reliable," and "absolutely honest." "He was both an artist and a practical man" (p. 139). She admired and fell in love with him. They were married over 20 years until his death in 1974.

Over the years, Otto and Beulah became acquainted at professional events. She found him "brilliant," and "playful." She admired his diverse interests; she also acknowledged that he could be "impulsive," "moody," and "unpredictable" (p. 155). When Otto moved from Massachusetts to California, they began living together in Beulah's home in Point Richmond, sometimes referred to as "the Point," in Contra Costa County. Situated across the bay from Marin County, Point Richmond was a fashionable neighborhood. They married in 1982 ("Beulah Parker Obituary," 2007). According to Beulah (1987), she and Otto enjoyed their life together until his death in 1993.

## Not a Psychoanalyst

In talking with Kim Chernin, Otto recalled that Harry Stack Sullivan had once advised him to avoid mentioning the name "Sullivan" in psychoanalytic circles. In San Francisco Otto found out why.

Otto spent about a year at Mount Zion. As an analyst he found himself once again on the outside. As is always the case in interpersonal relationships and group dynamics, there were overt and covert agendas in operation. Otto was not readily accepted by the psychoanalytic establishment in San Francisco because of his loyalty to Sullivan and his interest in psychosis. He was, like Erikson had once been, designated a "psychotherapist" rather than a "psychoanalyst." The infinitesimal difference between these two terms is meant to carry an insult. Otto felt the slight (Benveniste, 2006). He did not become officially involved with the San Francisco Center for Psychoanalysis (M. Thompson, personal communication, June 22, 2007). Yet, he developed a private practice in which he supervised seasoned psychoanalysts and psychotherapists. Kim Chernin was referred by her analyst, a man of some stature within the object relations tradition, to Otto for clinical supervision. She (2017) described running into "many people from the psychoanalytic institute, candidates and practicing analysts, looking sheepish and exposed as they went up and down the steps to Will's office" She believed that,"They had come to learn a different way to listen, to become engaged with their patient[s], and to be themselves" (p. xiii).

Once again, Erik Erikson turned up in his life. Several years after Erikson had retired to San Francisco, he proposed to a small group of older analysts that they meet weekly to discuss old files of patients diagnosed as schizophrenic. The group gathered on Thursday evenings at the home of Robert Rubenstein, the director of inpatient psychiatry at Mount Zion Medical Center and former co-director of the Yale Psychiatric Institute. Rubenstein would retire from psychiatry around 1991 to become a painter. Regular participants included Erik's wife, Joan, Otto, and Beulah (DeFao, 2001; Friedman, 1999).

One of the analysts who sought Otto out was Michael Guy Thompson. Thompson had undergone psychoanalytic training at the Philadelphia Association in England, which was founded by R.D. Laing. Thompson had been supervised by Laing. After completing this training, he returned to the Bay Area in 1980. Thompson told me, "I was always struck by how much Otto's way of doing things was like Laing's" (personal communication, June 29, 2007). Thompson found that his views of psychoanalytic process were compatible with Otto's. As Otto had learned from Sullivan and Thompson from Laing, they agreed that "It is much more important to hear yourself say something new than to hear the analyst say it" while recognizing that not all patients can achieve this observational position (M. Thompson, personal communication, July 6, 2007).

Otto held the view that psychoanalysis had developed a bureaucracy that interfered with effective psychoanalytic education. He believed in helping people, and often the traditions and "rules" of institutional psychoanalysis thwarted those efforts to help (M. Thompson, personal communication, June 29, 2007). In 1988, Thompson began an educational program that he named Free Association and invited Otto and Beulah to be on the faculty. Both readily agreed.

Thompson told me that Free Association was meant to, "capture an earlier era of openness, especially in terms of the therapeutic relationship." He also related that there was a good-natured joke about the program that "no one on the faculty was under the age of 70" (personal communication, June 23, 2007). Currently, the Free Association program offers a certificate in existential psychoanalysis. The program strives to develop what Thompson (2025) describes as an "existential sensibility." Such a sensibility is not technique driven but emphasizes conversation between two human beings searching for authenticity. Thompson lists Otto as demonstrating this sensibility.

By 1989, Otto felt that he had no clear professional identity. He (1989b) wrote: "I am not a physician in the traditional sense of the term, or in the modern sense either ... I am a psychiatrist and a psychoanalyst, but I am not in the mainstream of either of these activities" (p. 8).

## Final Years

During the last two years of Otto's life, he suffered from congestive heart failure. He continued to consult, supervise, and work with patients until a few months before his death. In the last year of his life, Otto experienced a cognitive decline. Patrick Will remembered that his father told Beulah he was going to Berkeley — a short trip of nine or ten miles. However, sometime later, she received a phone call from Cloverdale, California — about ninety miles north of their home. Otto having had trouble with his car, called from a farmhouse, mildly disoriented (personal communication, May 21, 2011). His physician was convinced that he had suffered a stroke and urged him to stop drinking. Patrick also remembered his father began to withdraw after this incident. He died on November 17, 1993. According to Patrick, Beulah described his last moments. He was sitting in his favorite chair and asking her for a cup of tea. She asked him if he was alright and he replied, "I am just trying to survive" and was gone (personal communication, May 29, 2025). His Death Certificate lists the immediate cause of death as acute cardiac arrhythmia due to ischemic congestive cardiomyopathy and atherosclerosis.

# Part Three: Hard Work & Common Sense

§

"In brief, psychotherapy requires hard work and a bit of common sense"

Otto Allen Will

# Chapter Twenty-Four: Becoming

One of the longstanding difficulties in the field of mental healthcare has been the conceptualization of "normal" human functioning from what may be regarded as "dysfunctional" or "pathological." The study of aberrations in human mental functioning is probably as old as humanity itself. One traditional view, as has been discussed, is that psychological dysfunction is the result of physiological defect(s). With the advent of psychoanalysis, the human environment in which a child is cared for (or otherwise) has been increasingly emphasized. Most theorists currently believe that both physiology and the human environment play significant roles in both normative and aberrant development. However, there remain competing views of human development and the nature of the human mind. Though theorists and clinicians hold loyalties to one view or another, a thoughtful appreciation of the state of our knowledge suggests that we have no definitive understanding of mental health or mental illness (Foehl, 2008; Gay, 2001; Levenson, 2018).

Otto had a view of human development to which he subscribed, though he did not enshrine it as indisputable truth. It began with the ideas of Harry Stack Sullivan but diverged in important ways. Its most basic constituent element concerns the nature of "mind." I find it helpful to consider Sullivan's view in comparison to that of Sigmund Freud (Cornett, 2017b).

## Freud & Sullivan

Freud was trained in the traditions of the nineteenth century physician and scientist. Within that historical context, he held the view that all phenomena were explainable by recourse to the precepts of energy and its disposition — particularly its discharge — and that human actions are focused on the gratification of physiological needs (Bowlby, 1987; Gill, 1987). Merton Gill (1987) held that Freud developed a psychology of energy discharge rather than that of the person.

Freud and the early psychoanalysts considered the essence of the human mind to be autonomous from the surrounding interpersonal environment (i.e., a closed system), mechanistic and potentially perfectible (Levenson, 2017). The brain was complete at birth, "with all the raw materials and potential for becoming an adult individual present" (Coltart, 2011, pp. 281-282). "Reality" was both identifiable and definable by an objective observer (i.e., the analyst, though not necessarily the patient) — an aspect of what is now considered a "one-person psychology" (Coltart, 2011; Hirsch, 2015). "Classical" analysts believed that repression was the primary defense mechanism (Cortina, 2020; A. Freud, 1966).

Certain assumptions were held to be universally valid: conflict was inherent in human instincts and drives, psychosexuality was the primary motivation from birth, and the Oedipal conflict shaped personality. The father was assumed to be the most psychologically important of the child's caregivers. It was also assumed that the successfully or completely analyzed psychotherapist could differentiate healthy from unhealthy psychological functioning (one of the authoritarian dichotomies to which Martin Buber objected).

In contrast, Sullivan maintained that "the mind" was an open system, constantly interacting with the surrounding environment, and that experience from interaction with others (beginning at birth) shaped it. He viewed the mind and "reality" as social constructions (though he did believe that a version of reality could be *consensually validated* between two or more people). Sullivan challenged "the traditional European-Platonic notion that reality was observed as a shadow on a wall, and what was behind it all was some real, arcane force, like instinct or drive" (Feiner, 2005, p. 678).

Freud hypothesized five *psychosexual* developmental stages focused on the body's erogenous zones: the oral, anal, phallic (during which the

Oedipal conflict occurs), latency, and genital (Elkatawneh, 2013). The foundation of Freud's developmental theory is physiological.

The developmental theorist, Erik Erikson, expanded Freud's psychosexual stages with his eight *psychosocial* stages of development, each characterized by a particular crisis with the potential for two outcomes — 1) the development of a basic strength, and 2) a core deficit that may result in psychopathology (Erikson, 1950). Erikson's wife, Joan suggested a ninth stage. These nine stages are as follows:

> Birth to age one year: Basic Trust versus Basic Mistrust;
> One to three years: Autonomy versus Shame and Doubt;
> Three to six years: Initiative versus Guilt;
> Six to twelve Years: Industry versus Inferiority;
> Twelve to eighteen Years: Identity versus Identity Confusion;
> Nineteen to forty years: Intimacy versus Isolation;
> Forty to sixty-five years: Generativity versus Stagnation;
> Sixty-five to eighty years: Integrity versus Despair
> Eighty years to death: Transcendence Versus Withdrawal
> (Erikson & Erikson, 1997)

The foundation of Erikson's developmental theory is broadly social. Unfortunately, Erikson tied himself to Freud's psychosexual model, rather than declaring a new paradigm (Erikson & Erikson, 1997).

Sullivan's theory of development is based not on the individual but on the person in an interpersonal field. A friend and colleague of Otto's, Martin Cooperman (1987), suggested the emphasis of Sullivan's developmental hypotheses, "Although the basic unit of biological functioning is the individual, the basic unit of psychological functioning seems always to be a twosome" (p. 22). Sullivan's developmental stages or epochs are: Infancy, Childhood, the Juvenile period, Preadolescence, Early Adolescence, Late Adolescence, and Adulthood (Evans, 2024). Otto employed this model — integrated with the insights of attachment theory —in considering human development.

## Developmental Epochs

The following periods of development do not correspond to specific ages but represent critical periods for the acquisition of particular interpersonal skills. A critical period may be thought of as an interval during which physical maturation and previous skill acquisition coalesce to offer the best chance of success in the introduction of the organism to a new situation. For the human organism the timing of such critical periods is not rigid and is contextualized by the skills needed to further the realization of dormant potentialities (Will, 1963a, 1971b).

## Infancy

Of the developmental stages originally envisioned by Sullivan, Otto believed that the foundation of schizophrenia is laid in infancy (Will, 1972). Infancy is the critical period for attachment and the development of a cohesive self-concept. However, before describing this developmental schema, it must be noted that elements of it are based on inferences which cannot be confirmed or disconfirmed. Otto remained aware of that.

## Complete Dependence: The First Six Months

Infancy encompasses roughly the period between birth and 18 months. *Functionally, Infancy is the period of absolute dependence, ending with the development of rudimentary expressive speech.* Otto (1971b) suggested that what might be called "interpersonal" in later life periods is more accurately termed "interhuman" in infancy due to the lack of a fully developed personality.

Human beings are born with a variety of needs that create physiological tensions which cannot be satisfied without the cooperation of a caregiver. This cooperation Sullivan (1953b) called *tenderness*. The infant must be fed and hydrated; caregivers must ensure a survivable temperature, must protect the infant from danger, and must clean the infant to prevent both discomfort and infection.

Otto (1963a) defined *need* as a requirement of the organism, "which prompts to action" (p. 1). Without symbolic, expressive speech, the infant has multiple needs but a limited repertoire of actions with which to engage the caregiver. Therefore, to satisfy a need or reduce the tension of it, the infant *acts* to engage the caregiver in addressing, and hopefully satisfying, the need. Such engagement involves vocalizations (e.g., screaming), affective displays (e.g., crying), and body movements (e.g., facial expressions). Caregiver empathy is necessary to establish successful patterns of tenderness.

During Infancy, the reliability of caregiver responsiveness forms the rudimentary elements of a *worldview*. A sense of reliability or lack thereof in meeting her needs predisposes the infant to view the world as *satisfying* or *frustrating*. This view is very similar to Erik Erikson's (Erikson & Erikson, 1997) conception of the psychosocial crisis "Basic Trust vs. Basic Mistrust." When a view of the world as unsafe or frustrating is developed and then strengthened by subsequent experiences, one of the primary goals of psychotherapy is providing a relationship that is safe for dependence; Otto (1975) emphasized that dependency coupled with security is the foundation for the development of independence.

## Six to 18 Months: Differentiation & Origins of the Self

Around six months, the infant develops — in rudimentary form — an awareness of being separate from the primary caregiver. Sullivan (1953a) proposed that the infant's differentiation of herself from the primary caregiver (mother) begins with the infant's realization that the nipple is not always immediately responsive to her need. The infant becomes aware that the primary caregiver's body is not her own body (Sullivan, 1953b). The infant develops a rudimentary understanding that the nipple is not a part of her but is *more or less* responsive to her needs. This understanding then expands into the recognition that her actions play a role in the satisfaction of her needs.

With the understanding that her actions determine, to some extent, the availability of the nipple, *personifications of the nipple are gradually transformed into personifications of the self.* John Bowlby (1987) suggested that the infant begins to form an internal representation of who and what mother is (i.e., an internal object). Sullivan's model describes a tripartite structure of the self: *Good Me, Bad Me, and Not-Me. Good Me* is composed of those actions which result in need satisfaction and approval from caregivers; *Bad Me* is the personification composed of those actions which elicit disapproval from caregiver(s). In this process of the development of Good Me and Bad Me, appears the earliest form of what can be referred to as *splitting*. As the infant grows, she attempts to hide Bad Me from herself and others. Splitting is one of the precursors to selective inattention (which is mastered in the juvenile developmental period).

The final component of the self, developed through what Sullivan called *foresight* (learning the often-predictable consequences of one's actions on others), is *Not-Me*. Not-Me is created as the infant's actions call forth overwhelming anxiety in the caregiver(s). Anxiety is experienced as destructive and potentially threatening to existence itself. Any actions calling forth such anxiety must be disavowed *as if* they do not exist. They are then dissociated. Dissociation can be thought of as keeping from awareness anxiety-provoking perceptions; it is akin to denial. However, these perceptions return in instances of deep anxiety, when we act or speak in ways we think ourselves incapable of, confusing and disorienting ourselves and those around us.

Otto did not write about personifications, though he was interested in dissociation. He preferred Bowlby's idea of the "internal working model" in which internal objects become the basis for what can be expected in relationships (see Bretherton & Munholland, 2008). The internal working model operates both in awareness and outside of it (i.e., covertly). A similar process occurs with socialization into the family as the infant is taught values — how the world *should* be (Will, 1964, 1981b).

The infant gradually acquires the physical capacity for basic speech. She also begins to notice which of her behaviors elicit need satisfaction and which bring frustration. From the latter, and through "contagion" from the mother, the infant experiences anxiety (see below). Based on interactions that bring about satisfaction or anxiety, the infant begins to develop an internalized representation of herself (Will, 1960).

There is no physical escape from a malignant environment. The infant's responses to anxiety are limited to sleep, withdrawal, and dissociation (Will, 1960, 1971b). In combination with dissociation, she may employ distorted perceptions of herself and others to mitigate anxiety (a form of psychic escape). If the human environment cannot satisfy the infant's needs and she must cope with chronic anxiety, she will resort to dissociation to manage it and will enter the next phase of development with deficits that, if not corrected, will become cumulative (Will, 1971b).

In infancy, both mother and infant learn from each other. In partnership with an adequate mother, the infant learns how to engage her in responding to specific needs. Mother learns which actions and vocalizations approximate requests for the satisfaction of particular needs (Will, 1964). If this occurs erratically, or not at all, the infant will begin to develop a view of the world as arbitrary and confusing.

## Childhood

As the capability for speech matures, the infant enters the developmental period of childhood. Childhood encompasses approximately ages two to four. It begins with the use of expressive speech and continues until the development of the skills and abilities to deal with children outside the family (Will, 1960). Effective speech requires the organization and use of symbols. The most important skill developed in childhood is the manipulation of symbols involved in communicative speech. One of the most basic aspects of schizophrenia involves the ineffective use of symbols and, therefore, of communicative speech.

Symbols that are communicative within the family may or may not be generalizable outside of that context. If the family employs idiosyncratic symbols in communication, the child may face difficulties in making her desires and needs — in short, herself — known to others. One result of this may be isolation (Will, 1964). Another is that the cultural nuances of communication may be highly confusing. Otto (1968b) described a patient confused about her grandmother's death when described as her grandmother being "gone." Typically, other children may help in the acquisition of more effective verbal communication and help clear up confusion about nuance.

Another important aspect of childhood is the ability to differentiate fantasy from reality. David Rioch (1985) described an interesting anecdote about Sullivan in this regard. As a lonely and isolated child, Sullivan began to make up tales that he thought would interest and impress other children. They often involved exciting and adventurous trips that his family was supposed to have taken. His family, however, was not affluent enough to take such trips. Over time these stories became grander and more detailed. Finally, Sullivan related that when he was about 12, "I suddenly realized I was beginning to believe them myself! So I stopped making them up" (p. 153). While concocting stories from imagination to share with peers is not unusual, to be potentially confused about their origin until the age of twelve is. This is an anecdote about a potentially dangerous process from childhood that was corrected in a later developmental period.

## The Juvenile Period

The Juvenile period, beginning around age four, is concerned with the development of peer-related social skills. The juvenile is sensitive about being accepted by her peer group and the potential for rejection arouses anxiety. As she observes and interacts with peers' families, particularly with their parents, her views of her parents will be modified, generally becoming more "realistic" — becoming increasingly aware of their inconsistencies and contradictions (Will, 1960). This latter accomplishment may be hindered, though, by parents who must be viewed in a particular way (Bowlby, 1987). Some parents, denying aspects of themselves, demand that their children do so as well, sometimes even when such aspects are evident to all. This is a precursor to "mystification."

Joakim Garff (2005) documents an example of such an occurrence in his biography of Søren Kierkegaard. One evening, the young Kierkegaard knocked over a saltcellar at the dinner table. His father, a hosier and autodidact, became enraged and said "frightful things" to his son (p. 11). Søren protested that his sister, a few years older, had broken a very valuable tureen at the table and nothing had been said to her. His father responded that her awareness of the tureen's value was reproach enough. Though confused, the boy accepted his father's explanation. It was only as an adult that Kierkegaard understood that he had not incurred his father's rage because of clumsiness or poor manners, but because his father, a wealthy businessman, subscribed to a superstition that scattering salt portended a loss of money. Portraying himself as an enlightened man, though, he could not reveal this — perhaps even to himself. Otto (1971a) understood that parents who teach their children that their own perceptions are not trustworthy are sowing destructive seeds.

The juvenile period is concerned with being a part of groups. To be part of a group, one must view others as not part of that group. A group cannot exist without the rejection of some who are deemed as inappropriate to belong. The process of stereotyping, often grounded in family stereotypes, emerges.

It is during the juvenile epoch that we begin to imagine and create the "Other." The process begins with noticing that some with whom we interact are physically different from us. They look different, they sound different. As we interact a little more closely, we begin to notice that some experience the world differently. Perhaps they enjoy foods that we do not or aesthetically enjoy what we do not (e.g., music, art, and so on). Perhaps they do not attach the same importance to sports that we do. They may worship a deity that we both agree exists but worship differently. The process of differentiating ourselves from them then assumes a life of its own. "People have always tended to like and to trust most those most like themselves" (de Camp, 1996, p. 91). Difference becomes different and the different become strange. Those who are strange become strangers and strangers are owed no consideration. In fact, strangers may signify that there is more than a single way — our way — to be in the world. Their existence may thus begin to disturb us (Vanier, 1998). Disturbance requires action to alleviate — minimally that we create distance from the source of the disturbance. Distance from others intrinsically creates a level of isolation and "the relative isolation of our lives can make us less aware of others and of the spaces we share" (Cusk, 2019, p. 4). In a stepwise process, then, fellow human beings can become something other than ourselves. This something cannot be superior as that would make us inferior — so they must be inferior. In this way, deprecating stereotypes are formed.

Obviously, stereotypes are overly simplified ways of evaluating others. However, stereotypes can become extremely rigid and develop into what Otto (1961a) termed "the paranoid solution to living." People and the world generally are perceived in stark absolutes. Shading does not develop, and everything becomes black or white, good or bad, and right or wrong. In the fullest expression, the paranoid solution to living results in relegating some people to the realm of sub-human and provides a rationalization for cruelty. Future developmental periods can correct such an approach to the world, but correction is hindered by the human tendency to maintain relations almost exclusively with those sharing our values. Ralph Waldo Emerson wrote in *Circles* (1844/2009a) that: "A man's growth is seen in the successive choirs of his friends" (p. 126). Often, one sign that psychotherapy is working is the development of friendships with people who are more affirming and capable of greater intimacy with a wider group.

Among the social skills developed during the juvenile epoch are the capacities for cooperation and negotiation, the latter including the ability to compromise. These skills are requisite to remain part of any group. They can be sorely tested, though, by another development in this period — that of competition. While competition can offer a way of demonstrating physical and mental skill sets, thus increasing confidence and self-esteem, it may have the opposite outcome as well (Will, 1960).

## Preadolescence

The next developmental period, preadolescence, begins just before the onset of puberty and continues until puberty's full physical and emotional eruption. This period's primary challenge is the establishment of an emotionally intimate relationship with a peer. This is often a child of the same gender but is not required to be so. In Sullivan's day, such a friend was known as "a chum," but each new generation uses their own nomenclature (Will, 1960). The experiences involved in this process will serve as a model for later attempts to develop emotional intimacy.

Intimacy requires that we allow another to know us. It is, of course, anxiety-provoking to share aspects of ourselves of which we are not proud or even ashamed. It is in the acceptance of us by another that we may modify an overly harsh self-concept and increase self-esteem and confidence. If we receive condemnation or another form of rejection upon revealing ourselves, then intimacy may be considered dangerous and a source of overwhelming anxiety.

Intimacy also requires the attempt to know and accept our partner in the relationship. Effective listening skills are needed as is patience. These are learned within the family from the experience of being listened to. Louise Glück (1994) described growing up in a family in which she was seldom allowed to express a thought or feeling without interruption.

What she attempted to say was often dismembered and became what another family member wished her to say; her words were "transformed not paraphrased" (p. 5). Such is not an environment which fosters the skills needed for intimacy.

The development of this intimate relationship may also involve sexual exploration. To be successful the relationship, however, must involve emotional and communicative intimacy in which the participants share ideas and emotions. Often one or both youngsters have kept troubling aspects of their families to themselves. In the preadolescent relationship, such "secrets" may be aired; one's friend may then confirm that what has been shared is a common concern or may offer feedback that aids the other in viewing it. This friendship can thus provide an experience that corrects distortions in perception. In a newspaper article, Otto explains that a single friendship may mean the difference between mental illness — including schizophrenia — or health. A friendship can open the door to other relationships and confound isolation ("Much Truth in Old Saw," 1962, p. 8). One may note that the therapeutic relationship shares elements with this preadolescent era friendship (Will, 1960).

Another characteristic of the juvenile and preadolescent periods involves the increased importance of "we" in the youngster's developing identity. Prior to this epoch, "I" is dominant, with the unrealistic grandiosity and crippling sense of responsibility that accompany it. "We" offers the potential for facing challenges with greater success and puts into perspective the limitations of one alone. The responsibility for "getting it right" becomes more diffuse for a group; the capacity to share triumph or failure reinforces the need for others in life (Will, 1960).

This period continues the development and refinement of values begun in childhood. Those values imparted by the family may continue to be compared with those of other families. Some of these values may be discarded, some reinforced, others retained but not spoken of (Will, 1981b).

## Adolescence

Adolescence is an era of profound physical changes. Hormones hitherto latent or released minimally are greatly increased in the system and prompt the development of secondary sexual characteristics. The developing intimacy of preadolescence is integrated with what Sullivan (1953a) termed *lust* — sexual expression. Under the best of circumstances, adolescence is a time of confusing change. The adolescent attempts integration of sexual desire into her self-image. Emotions may become more labile, challenging what may have seemed a stable view of herself (Will, 1960).

As intimacy and lust become integrated, there begins a search for a partner with whom both may be expressed (Will, 1960). Of course, 1960s America believed that such a partner should be of the opposite sex. Since the mid-1940s, the United States had been in a "Lavendar Scare," promulgated by those, often gay themselves, who told Americans that national security could be compromised by the vulnerability of homosexuals to blackmail. Thousands of government employees were fired during the 1950s for being homosexual or allegedly homosexual — more, in fact, than were dismissed for having communist ties (Gage, 2022). The promulgators of the Lavendar Scare, figures like J. Edgar Hoover and Roy Cohn, were aided by conservative psychiatrists and analysts who argued that homosexuality was "a sexual perversion." Otto's stance on homosexuality seems to have been ambivalent. According to their daughter, Otto and Gwen were accepting of gay men and lesbians (though Deirdre perceived her mother to be the more progressive). They asked a close friend of Gwen's, who they knew was gay, to be Deirdre's godfather (D. Vinyard, personal communication, June 2, 2025). Otto did not refer to homosexuality often in his published work but did note that the homosexual patient of one discussion paper had directed his sexual strivings toward "an inappropriate object," another young man (Will, 1966, p. 17). He declined to discuss "The *problem* of the patient's homosexuality" (Will, 1966, p. 19, emphasis added).

In the search for a partner, one must deal with new forms of rejection, and these exact a toll on self-esteem. Ultimately, however, an initial — if only temporary — partner is found, and love may develop. In love, the adolescent learns that her needs can include the satisfaction of her partner's needs (Will, 1960).

Adolescence generally involves exposure to new experiences, new people (who may, initially, seem Other), and new values. Exposure to new cultural mores and traditions, encourage the adolescent to examine those of her own culture and, at times, reject what has been held as sacred in this regard. The evaluation of what the adolescent has been taught and its relevance for her life often involve conflict with parents and other family members. Rejection for this reevaluation can assume many guises. The English essayist, Rachel Cusk (2019), in an amusing, but ultimately tragic essay, describes the tendency of her parents to respond to challenges to their worldview with the "silent treatment," called in her family "being sent to Coventry" (pp. 24-25). Cusk describes the imaginary banishment to Coventry as encouraging consideration of the world without her in it. The most damaging aspect of this exile is that there are no words of explanation or clarification as to why the world would be better without her. Such a parental strategy impedes or derails the central task of adolescence — answering the question "Who am I?" (Will, 1960, 1981b).

## Late Adolescence & Adulthood

In more affluent societies, like the United States, adolescence is often extended into the mid-20s, with opportunities to continue education in college and beyond. However, even in affluent nations, not all its young people desire, or can afford, an extended adolescence. Whatever the opportunities or limitations of opportunity, a central task of late adolescence and adulthood is twofold: establishing an intimate relationship — a primary attachment figure (R. Bowlby, 2004) — and committing to an activity to which one dedicates a significant portion of life. Often, this is a vocation — whether as an artist, manual laborer, writer, or cleric. It is not so much what one does as it is the fact that *something* serves to anchor life. Without a focus, one can be cast adrift and, thus, isolated. Owen Renik illustrated this, describing a moving case discussion concerning a late adolescent hospitalized at Mount Zion Hospital in San Francisco. "Otto emphasized the need to *tactfully* convey to the patient that he had to develop a work ethic in order to get better" (personal communication, May 14, 2007, emphasis added).

During Otto's lifetime, one was expected to engage in a profession or to have some form of employment. At present, this expectation still exists but opportunities are less available. For over two centuries from the advent of the industrial revolution, human beings have been forced to compete with automation. Machines have increasingly brought obsolescence to work that once required human beings and are doing so at an accelerating rate. There may be a time when the opportunity to dedicate oneself to a vocational calling becomes the province of a small self-defined "elite."

---

There are multiple models of human development in the field of psychotherapy. None is intrinsically better than another. To be useful, any model of development must be helpful to the person employing it to understand her fellow creatures. It must also allow for the development of the human being *throughout* life. *The experience of a long career in psychotherapy teaches that a human being is always becoming and never beyond new learning.*

# Chapter Twenty-Five: Madness

Problems in living are ubiquitous. In the *Berkshire Eagle* newspaper, Otto proposed that, "To some extent, despair, loneliness, uncertainty and a sense of madness are part of the existence of every man" ("Quotes," 1971, p. 25). These qualities ultimately develop from experiences in relationships. Edgar Levenson (2018) proposes that, "The patient is a patient because his/her life has been characterized by a loss of authenticity, by being used by other people for their own ends" (p. 36). The poet, Thomas Lynch (2020), similarly notes, "Who among us is not withered and weighed down by the accrual of actual or imagined slights, betrayals, resentments, estrangements and wrongdoings done unto us most often by someone we've loved" (p. 299). For all the psychoanalytic theorizing about unconscious conflicts, drives, and fixations, problems in living are created by our interactions with other people.

Patients seek out psychotherapists to help with a variety of diverse and complex difficulties, often involving a sense of meaninglessness, emptiness, despair, shame and loneliness. Like the constant drip of water on a stone, patients are often worn down, fearing psychological disintegration. They often appear with the confusing, complex, and terrible question, "Who am I?" (Will, 1972, 1981b, 1987b). However, Otto (1987b), also challenged the reductive nature of efforts to portray fellow human beings as Other: "there is no escape from the human condition by resort to such concepts as being bestial, inhuman, or saintly" (p. 317; see also Will, 1987a).

## The Interpersonal Context

With a few exceptions (e.g., tumors, endocrinological dysfunction), problems in living, what is also called "psychopathology," are problems of relationships. Otto (1960, 1961b, 1965) believed that problems in living are *learned interpersonal actions that interfere in developing and sustaining relationships, particularly intimate relationships*. Yet, they are also goal-directed and represent an attempt to maintain some form, however tenuous, of interpersonal connection (1987a). Though there are a myriad of ways that problems in living may be displayed, they are often most evident in anxiety, restrictions in awareness, and ineffective communication.

Problems in living can arise in any developmental period, but they will likely be related to patterns originating in infancy, the first developmental period. Though symptoms may erupt in adolescence or early adulthood, the most deeply troubling symptoms arise from experiences in the first year and a half of life and are the most difficult to ameliorate. Certainly, Otto (1959a, 1960, 1964, 1971a, 1972, 1973, 1974, 1987a-b) believed that schizophrenia was an outcome of serious problems encountered in infancy and uncorrected in subsequent development. He suggested that the essential problems of human life are those of attachment, regression, and separation. These problem areas are particularly pronounced in schizophrenia (Alanen, Silver & de Chávez, 2006).

Human beings are mammals born without instincts and completely dependent on caregivers for survival (Sullivan, 1953b). Because we have no independent survival skills, we form an attachment to a caregiver almost immediately; however, the process requires a reciprocal attachment from the primary caregiver whom I will call the mother. If such an attachment does not occur, in extreme cases, the infant may die but certainly will develop serious problems in relationships.

The quality of attachment is determined by the mother's ability to satisfy the infant's physiological tensions — thirst, hunger, temperature regulation, and physical touch. The more reliably such tensions are satisfied, the more likely the infant will develop an early sense of the world as trustworthy. The more erratically or unreliably satisfaction occurs, the less stable the infant's feeling of trust will be (Will, 1975).

For a variety of reasons, the infant may have difficulty engaging the mother in addressing her needs. Caregivers may be misattuned, distracted, or otherwise unable to decipher the infant's signals.

## Misattunement

*Misattunement* is the process in which the infant's signals for need satisfaction are misunderstood by the mother. The infant is hungry, but the mother responds as if the infant is signaling fatigue. An infant may need physical touch, but the mother perceives her to be hungry. While the process of feeding will meet the infant's need for touch, there is an extra element that is unneeded. This may create anxiety. Misattunement confuses the infant, and, if chronic, the infant may become misattuned to herself. Additionally, if the infant senses no correlation between her actions and the responses of caregivers, she may attempt novel actions (e.g., frowning rather than smiling). These actions may either be more communicative to caregivers (i.e., growth) or more confusing (i.e., an impediment to attunement). Especially after the development of speech, idiosyncratic communication that was understandable in the family may be a detriment outside the family.

Misattunement may also involve reaction to an affective state as if it were a different affective state. For instance, the caregiver responds to the infant's cries of anger as if they communicate sadness. Misattunement occurs most often when caregivers employ selective inattention in dealing with anxiety. If an infant's particular feeling arouses anxiety for a caregiver, that feeling will not be perceived and will either elicit no reaction or be perceived as a more "acceptable" feeling and responded to as such. The ambiance thus created does not confirm the infant's actual feeling — encouraging the infant to avoid experiencing it or, over time, to confuse one emotion with another.

Lawrence Friedman (1990) describes misattunement between Florence (Flo) Menninger and her son, the future psychoanalyst, Karl. As her first child, she was unsure of the "right" way to respond to him. She acknowledged, "I think he often feels just the opposite of what I would have him … Because Flo felt inadequate to the task, she encouraged Karl to nap" (p. 12).

Misattunement generally leads to misattribution. R.D. Laing (1969) maintained that human beings learn many of their views of the world and how they fit into that world, through direct attributions. This, of course, is directly applicable to our personal worth and lovability. If one or both parents consistently describe a child negatively, such as "worthless," "stupid," or "a failure," then these become powerful "reflected appraisals" composing the self (Sullivan, 1953a). Such attributions or appraisals can have a devastating effect on the developing person's self-esteem. Attribution may also be more insidious.

Francis King (1976) offers an example of such an insidious attribution in a discussion of the life of novelist and biographer, Daphne du Maurier. According to King, du Maurier's father, the actor, Gerald du Maurier, routinely (perhaps obsessively) told her that he would have preferred her to be male. Even as a youngster, Daphne du Maurier developed the idea that she was, in fact, a male trapped inside a female body. Similarly, the writer, H.P. Lovecraft, endured his mother's relentless demands that he be female; as a young child, he maintained that "I'm a little girl" (de Camp, 1975, p. 3). I would quickly add that I have no expertise in the transexual experience and that du Maurier *may have been* a man trapped by physiology. After childhood, Lovecraft did not assert that he was female. I offer these examples of attribution to suggest that it potentially has powerful consequences.

To consider oneself as "worthless" is a debilitating and painful form of existence — yet it provides a coherent view of the self, which can be tested against other appraisals in the interpersonal environment. Although the parents' attributions are always the most durable of others' appraisals, relationships with other valued people can challenge and modify them — for example, when a spouse clearly values someone who considers herself to be "worthless." Challenging such a perspective about the self is also a principal function of the therapeutic relationship.

What if, however, there is little coherence in the self? Such a situation represents even earlier (usually before the infant's development of expressive verbal communication) confusion. *Misattribution* is generally the process that serves as the origin of a noncohesive and incoherent development of the self. Chronic misattribution can lead the infant to perceive herself as unknowable and, is hypothesized to be a factor in schizophrenia (Will, 1968b).

## Anxiety

*Anxiety* is the central phenomenon behind all interferences in interpersonal functioning. *The infant learns to seek security when afflicted by anxiety*. Without language, anxiety is difficult to communicate to caregiver(s) because it does not involve a material element. The infant may try to reduce anxiety by using behaviors that have resulted in satisfaction previously, such as sucking at the breast, when not hungry. However, such behaviors may confuse the mother. Restoring a sense of security (a state characterized by the absence of anxiety) to the infant requires that mother (or father, in some instances) have a close enough emotional connection to the infant that the need for soothing is recognized. A process like that in psychotherapy can occur in which mother recognizes anxiety in the environment (perhaps, including her own) and intuitively comforts her child. Such a response becomes much more difficult if the anxiety of mother and infant form a pattern in which the anxiety of one increases the anxiety of the other.

The need for security in moments of anxiety is lifelong. If caregivers are reliable *enough* in soothing the infant's anxiety, she is believed to experience what later can be called self-esteem and personal agency. If a pattern of unreliable responses to her anxiety develops, then such anxiety may begin to be unrecognized (e.g., experienced as anger), unattended to (e.g., dissociated), and confused with somatic processes (e.g., hunger).

Thus, early experiences of anxiety create an early warning system that detects potential situations involving anxiety and keeping potential threats out of awareness through *selective inattention*. Selective inattention is not intrapsychic, but interpersonal in nature. Edgar Levenson (2018) contrasts the interpersonal from the Freudian position by asserting that the interpersonal is founded upon *omission*, not *repression*. Repression describes an intrapsychic or intrapersonal process, whereas omission refers to a situation in which "something is left-out in a discourse between people" (p. 57). Psychotherapy focuses on expanding the boundaries of awareness to free-up problem-solving capabilities.

## Restrictions in Awareness

Restrictions in awareness are the result of what Sullivan called security operations, of which the self-system is composed. Security operations begin in infancy as an exquisite awareness of what may elicit disapproval from parents; these operations serve to maintain the infant's sense of well-being (i.e., lack of anxiety) in the face of potentially injurious situations to her self-esteem (Sullivan, 1954). In its most basic expression, the self-system employs selective inattention, "… the process of shifting awareness away from anxiety-laden interpersonal situations as if they did not exist" (Evans, 2024, p. 101). Otto (1971b) also described selective inattention as "the complicated device of carefully noticing what not to notice" (p. 25).

In a 1987 paper presented as part of a celebration of Otto Will's life, John Bowlby, a pioneer in the exploration of attachment, described restrictions in awareness with concepts from cognitive psychology. He (1987) noted that human beings are constantly excluding information that is not useful to them in their present situation. This is an automatic process that operates outside of awareness. It is not consciously considered. However, it is not unconscious, a concept employed by Freud to describe experiences, fantasies, and feelings that are made unavailable to conscious awareness by repression.

Otto (1962) expanded a concept originally introduced by Sullivan who proposed that elements of experience may be "dissociated." Dissociated material is experience that is unformulated or that may be termed "subsymbolic" (Cortina, 2020). It cannot generally be formulated and expressed in language. For this reason, it remains unintegrated into the self (Breger, 2000). Edgar Levenson (2017) likens the experience of dissociation (and selective attention more generally) to "a vague sense of knowing there is something he/she does not know; … [or] like remembering vaguely that there is something one has forgotten to do" (p. 47). Dissociated experience often persists as sensations in the body remaining outside of conscious awareness (Breger, 2000, p. 17).

The restriction of awareness is largely why a troubled human being often employs *unclear communication*. William Alanson White (1938), Sullivan's most important psychiatric influence, wrote, "I have always said that clear thinking involved the capacity of clear expression, that if a person could not tell a thing so that someone else could understand it, it was because he did not understand it himself" (p. 176). Unclear communication may stem from an incomplete or disorganized understanding of the topic, particularly when it appears around emotions, memories, or descriptions of interpersonal events.

During development, after the acquisition of expressive speech, selective inattention is expressed through communication with discontinuities that are glossed over and that create misunderstanding with others (Sullivan, 1954). Such "misunderstandings" often involve people "talking past each other," introducing highly ambiguous abstractions, and changing the subject — strategies that help the patient maintain a seemingly coherent narrative that avoids vulnerability, but leaves the listener disconnected.

Otto (1954) observed that language (symbolic communication) is often employed defensively, to protect self-esteem by maintaining distance from others. An observant therapist can gauge the level of anxiety in the room by noting the prevalence of abstraction and ambiguity in the conversation. *Clear communication is a goal of psychotherapy because obscurity and opacity prevent connection.*

## Mystification

As the infant develops the capacity for expressive verbal communication and enters childhood, misattribution often becomes *mystification*, which is "the teaching of the child to disbelieve his own perceptions" (Will, 1972, p. 86). It is the difference between the spoken and the demonstrated (Levenson, 2018). Laura Walls (2017), Henry David Thoreau's biographer, offers a simple example, "You all know the lecturer who speaks against money is being paid for his words — and *that's* the lesson you remember" (p. 169, emphasis in the original). As adults, we often dismiss such performances as "hypocritical," but children do not have that luxury, especially when parents are involved. The child still needs parents for the satisfaction of needs. Parental actions that could compromise the meeting of such needs "must be ignored (dissociated), or 'explained away'" (Will, 1972, p. 208). Bowlby (1987) wrote that:

> Children not infrequently observe scenes that parents would prefer they did not observe; they form impressions that parents would prefer they did not form; and they have experiences that parents would like to believe they have not had. Evidence shows that many of these children, aware of how their parents feel, proceed then to conform to their parents' wishes by excluding from further processing such information as they already have; and that, having done so, they cease consciously to be aware that they have ever observed such scenes, formed such impressions, or had such experiences (pp. 74-75).

Otto (1972) asserts that a child may become aware that a parent's public and private behavior is fundamentally different. In that situation, the child may ignore part of what she perceives about the parent or decide that she "is a bad and unappreciative child, or … somehow crazy" (Will, 1972, p. 209; Laing, 1969).

Erwin Singer (2014) viewed mystification as "the very nucleus of *all* psychopathology" (p. 68, emphasis in the original). It represents the loss of a fundamental human ability "to hear what can be heard, to see what can be seen, to grasp what can be grasped" (p. 68).

Sustained misattribution and mystification are often involved with caregiver psychopathology (especially selective inattention). Steven Mitchell (1988/2017) suggested that "The interpersonal tradition … teaches one to listen and 'think parental character'" (p. 233).

One example of mystification comes from the childhood of the American poet, Robert Frost. Will Frost, Robbie's (as he was called as a child) father, was a heavy drinker (today he would probably be diagnosed as an alcoholic) and paid scant attention to his health. According to Parini (1999), in 1876, about two years after Robbie's birth in 1874, he was hospitalized with the primary symptoms of tuberculosis — weight loss, a "gaunt and jaundiced" appearance and coughing blood (p. 11). He denied that he was seriously ill and continued his reckless, alcohol-driven lifestyle. Will Frost denied the seriousness of TB and combatted his awareness of it with increased drinking. Though his children — both Robbie and his younger sister, Jeanie, born in 1876, witnessed him coughing up blood into a handkerchief and hurriedly hiding it in his pocket — both he and his wife, Belle, told the children that he was suffering from the flu. Robbie developed "stomach pains" that in 1880 forced him to drop out of the first grade. In 1885, as Will Frost's physical decline reached its nadir, he was too weak to leave the family apartment on some days (Parini, 1999). Will Frost died in 1885 at the age of 34. In 1888, Robbie began to "hear voices and experience a touch of clairvoyance" (Parini, 1999, p. 15). Rather than feeling concern about Robbie's mental health, his mother, who believed herself to be clairvoyant, described this development as "a gift" (p. 15).

In his description of the outcome of such experiences of mystification, Bowlby (1987) described patients whose "problems included chronic distrust of other people, inhibition of their curiosity, distrust of their own senses, and a tendency to find everything unreal" (p. 76). These symptoms certainly describe aspects of Robert Frost's life.

Robert D. Richardson Jr. (1995), in his biography of Ralph Waldo Emerson, relates that Emerson's father, William Emerson, was a "'somewhat social gentleman' who was severe with children" (p. 20). He set out to "teach" Waldo to swim. Forty years after the event, Emerson could still "recall the fright" [and] "mortal terror" [of his father] "forcing … [him] into the salt water off some wharf or bathing house" (p. 20). William Emerson was a clergyman who treated adults with respect — perhaps even empathy — but terrified his son with a brutal method of teaching him to survive in an alien and dangerous environment.

Bram Stoker's biographer, David Skal (2016), describes a similar incident in which Stoker threw his son, Noel, into the ocean off Whitby, determined that he would learn to swim. According to Skal, "The only lesson he learned was the terror of parental abandonment and threat of infanticide …. According to Noel's daughter, he never did learn how to swim" (p. 214). In addition to the aspects of mystification suggested by these anecdotes, one, following Steven Mitchell's reasoning, might hypothesize that both William Emerson and Bram Stoker had sadistic qualities among the many others comprising their personalities.

Finally, it is worth noting that Sigmund Freud may have experienced both attachment difficulties and mystification during his childhood. The former may have involved a mother who was distracted by pregnancy and childbirth for most of his first decade of life and therefore not fully available to him. The behavior of his mother, Amalia, may also have been mystifying. Potential evidence of this comes from Freud's son, Martin. He remembered his grandmother as having a strong and domineering personality; "She was charming and smiling when strangers were about, but I, at least always felt that with familiars she was a tyrant, and a selfish one" (Breger, 2000, p. 29). Under such circumstances, children are faced with a difficult question: are strangers more lovable than I or am I imagining something that is not there?

## Loneliness

During the process involved in creating the self, the infant experiences a sense of separateness and distance. This is the beginning of loneliness and is an essential part of human nature (Vanier, 1998). *Adjusting to at least transient loneliness is a lifetime task and many find themselves defeated in their attempts at this adjustment.* Chronic loneliness is a potentially devastating emotional experience. Bertrand Russell (2002), one of the great humanists of the twentieth century, described his experience of observing a friend who experienced a deeply painful heart attack which seemed to separate her from all those around her by "walls of agony" (p. 15). As he reflected on this later, he wrote, "the loneliness of the human soul is unendurable." (Russell, 2002, p. 15).

After Sullivan's death, Otto (1949a) wrote a memorial article in the *Washington Post*, praising his mentor as a theoretician and clinician. No doubt thinking of Sullivan, but perhaps about himself, as well, he wrote that: "Psychiatry might be defined in part as the study of human loneliness and isolation" (p. B5).

Loneliness can be transformed into a sense of non-existence or a sense of being viewed with indifference. Some symptoms that develop from the fear of non-existence and perceived indifference can mimic the delusions of schizophrenia (and may account for some aspects of this disorder). Otto suggested to Kim Chernin that symptoms which might be considered paranoid — "Everyone hates me," "I'm always rejected" — also serve the purpose of confirming that other people think about me and that the world is not completely indifferent to me.

Neville Symington (2006) wrote, "A patient said to me: 'I think Descartes had it wrong. It is not 'I think therefore I am' but '*You* think therefore I am'" (p. 3, emphasis in the original). We exist — sometimes only in the thoughts of someone else.

# Chapter Twenty-Six: Unending Curiosity

Novice psychotherapists are usually anxious about being with patients and want to know *what to do* with them. Educators often respond to such anxiety by offering prescriptions about how to work with patients. The result generally seems to be a diminution of the student's anxiety about not knowing what to do balanced by increased anxiety about satisfactorily implementing what she has been told "should" or "will" work. Since the proposed technique is often so generalized that it may be employed by "anybody," the novice therapist must discover on her own how to employ it within the context of her own personality interacting in the unique circumstances with each patient. It could be said that the novice therapist is back where she started from in terms of her anxiety, but the situation may be even more anxiety-provoking because she now must decide how to represent what she does with patients to a clinical supervisor. Hopefully, the supervisor creates a safe enough environment that the therapist can discuss her attempts to personalize what she has been taught. I believe this set of circumstances has led many master therapists to suggest that suspending what one has been taught — particularly about theory — is the first step toward mature psychotherapy (see Binder, 2004; Binder & Betan, 2013; Bruch, 1974; Budd, 2011; Coles, 2010; Foehl, 2008; Frankl, 2000; Guntrip, 1971; Havens, 1989; Horney, 1987; Levenson, 2017; Lurie, 2008; Renik, 2006; Rudnytsky, 2011; Rubin, 2014; Sutherland, 1989; Symington, 2006; Yalom, 2017). The second step is to learn theory and technique from each patient.

Otto (1970b) seems to have been guided by these fundamental ideas and a few other principles, rather than the dictates of any particular theory. The cardinal principle was a conviction that *certainty* does not exist. While he understood the desire to seek certainty as a form of anxiety management, he believed that the search for it interfered in psychotherapy; and, as such, represented a form of countertransference. As the poet, Wendy Bourgeois (2018), has suggested, theory functions as a sort of anesthetic to aid in the management of anxiety (see also Lurie, 2008). Beyond this use as a form of insulation against anxiety, Otto (1970b) viewed the prescriptions and proscriptions developed from theory as suspect.

## One: The Need for Relationships

Otto assumed that human beings have an inherent need for relationships. He (1963a) believed that the full development of our humanity requires relationships with others of our kind. Interpersonal relationships initially provide for our physical survival. Throughout life they provide emotional sustenance, intimacy, and the context for genital sexual expression (Will, 1971b, 1979, 1981a). Emotional survival throughout life depends on the ability to elude loneliness, even if the capacity for intimacy and sexual expression is inhibited or absent.

Otto (1960, 1970c, 1971b) wrote that the relationship between therapist and patient provides the potential for growth. It must be remembered, though, that the power of the relationship may also result in harm to the patient, if not monitored carefully (1970c). The relationship can provide the basis for an attachment when the patient's earliest attachment was characterized by destructive anxiety (1973). The relationship provides a context in which previous interpersonal experience may be studied and clarified (1960, 1961a).

## Two: Finding the Person in the Patient

Otto (1966, 1972) encouraged the psychotherapist to invest enough time in the person with whom she is working to allow that patient to become a fellow person. The more the therapist comes to know a patient, the less she will seem like a disease or disorder (Will, 1960, 2021). She will then take the form of an unhappy, despairing, and discouraged person confused by her relationships with others. Human beings defy categorization and simplification (Will, 1987a).

There are no *psychotics* or *neurotics* or any other groups that are not ultimately one version of the human condition, separated from other versions only in degree; diagnostic labels only distance us from actions of the patient that frighten or repulse us (Will, 1970b).

To find the person with whom one is working, Otto stressed that the therapist must be a real person. She cannot hide behind the armor of her theory or technique. She must risk being seen as imperfect, ignorant, and fallible with her own problems in living (1961a, 1964, 1970c, 1975).

## Three: "Nothing Human is Alien to me"

The Roman playwright, Terence, asserted, "I am a human being, I consider nothing human alien to me." Harry Stack Sullivan called this the "One Genus Theorem." All human beings are more alike than different. Put simply, it means that I could be the savage murderer, the pedophile, the physically abusive parent, the sadist, and the schizophrenic; the potential for the actions ever taken by a human being are also within me, and, given the appropriate circumstances, I would also carry out those actions. All feelings and thoughts that have ever motivated a human being are within each of us.

This principle encourages one to forgo the easy dismissal of humanity in any of its complicated forms. Perhaps, we can only tolerate in others the level of humanity that we can tolerate in ourselves. For the psychotherapist, the ultimate question becomes, "Can I see myself in this other person — can I see the humanity that we share?"

Otto's (1975) writing demonstrates that he maintained no illusions that he was somehow different from those who sought his help or that he knew how life *should* be lived. His willingness to face his own humanity allowed him to aid others in facing theirs. He helped each patient shoulder the burden of living, while, together, they clarified how she had learned the patterns that kept her interpersonal relationships troubled and unsatisfying.

## Four: We Learn to be Who We Are

Within the limits set by genetics, what we become as human beings is primarily learned through interpersonal experiences (Will, 1970b, 1971a, 1975, 1987b). We are not bound by instincts or drives as traditionally defined (Will, 1987a). Much of our learning occurs during our earliest years, before the development of speech. Therefore, we cannot always describe what we have learned in words. New learning is more deeply dependent on experience than on words (Benjamin, 2014; Levenson, 2018). New learning that leads to change is possible throughout life (Will, 1963a, 1970b, 1981, 1987a).

## Five: Accepting Ambivalence & Uncertainty

Otto (1970a, 1971a) wrote that the ability to avoid the oversimplification of other's motivations and actions into certainties (e.g., Black/White, Good/Bad, and so on) was a sign of maturity. As Doris Lessing (1987) maintained, "Adults who hold on to all kinds of cozy illusions and comforting notions remain immature" (p. 19). Closely related to the ability to tolerate ambiguity is the capacity to tolerate uncertainty. We need not worship uncertainty, but we serve ourselves and our patients best if we tolerate it — because, despite illusions, uncertainty is the essence of life.

## Six: Past, Present & Future

For Otto, understanding another person requires curiosity about not only her past and present but also about her expectations for the future (Will, 1961a, 1968b, 1970b, 1973). These three elements form a gestalt, which cannot be understood by a focus on any individual element.

Toward the end of the twentieth century, psychoanalysts became interested in defining *the self*. Although Freud's mechanistic understanding of the human being did not accommodate what could be considered the foundation or essence of a person, it became evident to many clinicians that the concept of self would advance our understanding of human development (Guntrip, 1971). Though the name most associated with the idea of the self is Heinz Kohut (1971, 1977), Otto (1961b) developed a construct of the self — a decade before Kohut. Like Sullivan (1953a), Otto proposed that the self is composed of "reflected appraisals" from the person's matrix of interpersonal relations. Additionally, however, he moved away from the idea of the self as a structure. In a paper entitled, "Paranoid Development and the Concept of the Self" (1961a), Otto first proposed that the self was less precisely definable than the ego, yet it encompassed both past and present experience and a future dimension — ultimately unknowable and, in the present, made up of only expectations of future experiences — which nevertheless completes the person's view of self. By the end of his career, Otto (1989a) suggested that the self is a process, always grounded in interpersonal relations but having a sense of familiarity, or the quality of "me," woven through. This is also the view of the self in object relations theory (Sutherland, 1989).

## Seven: Curiosity is More Helpful than Theory

The poet, Emily Ogden (2022) has asserted that understanding another person in a theoretical sense may interfere with change because change must then conform to the predictions of theory. Otto (1961a) acknowledged that every clinician has a theory, though she may not always be aware of all its aspects. However, theory must not assert hegemony over the therapist's mindset. He suggested that the psychotherapist be concerned with the aspects of the patient that are "… unique and unpredictable, and which elude conformity and rule" (p. 223). Otto (1968b) approached theories by viewing them as "… symbolic representations of events that could, perhaps be symbolized in other and more meaningful ways" (p. 553). He (1971b) suggested that we be prepared to modify our theories or let them go when they are contradicted by emerging data.

Rather than reliance on theory, Otto (Will & Cohen, 1947) suggested that the psychotherapist is served well by "an unending curiosity" about people — including herself (p. 281). Marianne Horney Eckardt held that "… we learn by open minded listening. Our "wisdom" is good listening and reflecting on what we think we hear. Our understanding is always limited" (Rubin, 2014, p. 117). Like Louise Glück (1994), Otto seemed to "dislike the idea that a single mind, or even a collective bound together by common theory, should determine what is called best" (p. 96). Ultimately, he (1989b) maintained, "there is no belief that is not enriched by doubt and question" (p. 139).

## Eight: Simply Being with a Patient is Helpful

The act of being with and available to a patient encourages her growth. The therapist is not required to understand everything about the patient's life (and, in fact, such a comprehensive understanding cannot be attained). She is not required to be infallible. The aspiration to attain infallibility may cause her to pressure the patient to conform to her beliefs (Will, 1960).

Otto believed that words had their place, but not everything had to be explained. The patient could have an experience that supported growth without it being fully understood by either member of the relationship. Indeed, he believed that the therapist's attempts to bring about change, especially if introduced too early, could hinder the process of growth. Like Emerson, Otto "would always prize knowing over knowledge, process over product, activity over object" (Richardson, 1995, p. 104).

Otto (1979) demonstrated a commitment to the relationship with a patient. That commitment included the hard times, the times *when neither therapist nor patient knew what to do* and the times when both were anxious, perhaps even desperate.

## Nine: Reconsidering "The Frame"

Gerard Fromm told me that one of the distinctive features of Otto's work was his ability to work "outside the frame." Though he respected that ability, he found that he could not effectively emulate it (personal communication, August 22, 2007). While I did not ask for clarity as to what "the frame" meant to him, I assumed it to be what is considered a "holding environment," characterized by dependable qualities that offer safety to the patient. Such qualities include: a set number of sessions each week, each session having a set duration, a generally fixed location for sessions, a set fee (including some arrangement concerning missed sessions), and an agreement as to whether a patient will sit or recline during sessions. Limits to destructive actions are initially imposed by the therapist but are open to negotiation as the relationship develops.

Otto negotiated a frame for work with each patient, but it was generally more relaxed. When working with an inpatient, he often met with her in her room. Sometimes sessions took place on the campus grounds, and at other times, as in the case of "Professor M," they took place off campus at various sites around Washington. In his practice in California, he described walking with patients. He shared meals with patients. Sometimes they met Gwen or other family members (Will, 1971b). Deirdre Vinyard remembered attending the graduation of the patient he called "Kay" with Otto (personal communication, January 29, 2011). Patrick Will remembers his father's patients occasionally having meals with the family and, at least on one occasion, one of his patients stayed overnight in their guest bedroom (personal communication, May 31, 2025). In psychoanalytic practice, touch, except in the case of a handshake, is generally refrained from, yet Otto bathed Miss M, perhaps a turning point in her progress. In terms of fees, his were generally lower than other practitioners with his experience. On an outpatient basis, he charged $35 a session, while the standard was $50 (D. Vinyard, personal communication, January 29, 2011). According to Michael Guy Thompson, a colleague in San Francisco, he sometimes charged nothing (personal communication, June 29, 2007). The length of his sessions was a minimum of fifty-five minutes and often much longer.

Of most importance to Otto was that therapy arrangements were simple, minimizing anxiety and confusion. He attempted to maintain congruity between the physical environment and the communication of respect to the patient. His goal was also a congruity between what he said and his other actions. He had no requirement of "free association," whether the patient was hospitalized or an analytic candidate; instead, he asked patients to listen to what they said. Like himself, he encouraged them to be participant observers (Will, 1964, 1968b, 1973).

## Ten: There is More to Life than Transference

Otto believed that transference was ubiquitous to all human interactions. After childhood, it is not created — it simply exists. Clinical research confirms this (Høglend, 2014). Otto, however, expanded the time frame in which transference exists to match his understanding of the self. It is not simply the transfer of past to present. He (1989b) maintained that transference from past to present always exists within a projected view of the future. Transference is composed of learned patterns of responding to anxiety in interpersonal situations. It is communicated through words and actions. Otto deemphasized transference interpretation as the central focus in psychotherapy. He believed that therapist congruence and self-disclosure were more effective in addressing transference phenomena than interpretation. His work in this area is compatible with what Leston Havens (1976, 1979) described as counter-projective interventions. Such interventions comprise: what the therapist says or does in a natural, uncontrived way, that disconfirms the patient's expectations (Havens, 1989).

## Eleven: The Uses of Countertransference

Otto (1961a) offered one of the simplest, yet most comprehensive, statements ever made about countertransference: "It strikes me quite frequently that I as a therapist may engage in evasive operations to avoid dealing with something in the immediate interpersonal field" (p. 159). Just as transference can be defined as learned ways of dealing with anxiety in interpersonal situations, countertransference is simply this definition applied to the therapist. It is a reciprocal process arising from the fact that both therapy participants are under observation (Hirsch, 2015).

Attention to countertransference may be helpful in multiple ways. If therapist and patient are at an impasse, an examination of countertransference may suggest how and why the impasse was reached. Sharing one's discoveries with the patient may move the work past the impasse. The therapist's exploration of her feelings may aid in understanding what the patient may be feeling. Attunement to potential countertransference reactions models for the patient the important function of self-observation in interpersonal interactions.

## A Synopsis of Otto's Clinical Approach

Though the foundation of Otto's clinical perspective is found in the principles described above, these principles must find expression in the therapist's attitude and actions to be of benefit to the patient. Otto described those attitudes and actions, as well. They include the following.

One: The Therapeutic Instrument

Otto recognized that the only instrument available to the therapist is herself. The therapist accepts that the following qualities will probably characterize her relationship with the patient: 1) as she explores the patient's personality, the patient will explore hers, as well; 2) feelings common to relationships — affection, friendship, love, anger — will develop; 3) the patient will come to identify with the therapist; and 4) the patient will have expectations of the therapist, based on past experience (i.e., transference) (Will, 1964, 1968b, 1970a, 1971b, 2021).

Two: Presence

The therapist must be prepared to be physically and emotionally present with the patient, particularly when being present is most difficult (Will, 1964, 1968b, 1989b).

Three: Boundaries

The therapist and patient must establish a set of simple and clear boundaries for their work together. Such boundaries may be similar with each patient, but some aspects will be unique, as well (Will, 1959a, 1960, 1961a).

Four: An Orientation for the Patient

The therapist shares something of her background and experience as a psychotherapist. She offers a tentative definition of psychotherapy (Will, 1964, 1975).

Five: Managing Anxiety

The therapist initially focuses on listening, understanding, and accepting. Being aware that both participants will be anxious at points throughout their relationship, but most acutely as they begin their work, the therapist focuses on managing the anxiety in the room to facilitate communication (Will, 1964, 1965, 1968b, 1970b).

Six: Clear Communication

The therapist speaks in a clear and direct manner, avoiding abstractions. She is honest, particularly about feelings that she experiences (Will, 1954, 1964, 1968b, 1981b).

Seven: Congruence

The therapist avoids hiding behind a professional façade, instead seeking to be authentic — congruent in what she says and does — and consistent over time (Will, 1970b, 1970c, 1971b).

Eight: The Here-and-Now

The therapist observes both verbal and nonverbal aspects of the patient's communication and offers comments about these observations to the patient in the here-and-now. She refers to current interactions between them rather than historic behaviors or situations (Will, 1959b, 1960, 1964, 1970b, 1970c, 1971b).

Nine: Clarifying Transference

The therapist addresses transference phenomena when doing so will aid the patient in integrating disassociated aspects of the self. Interpretive clarifications may be helpful in this regard; most effective, however, may be confirmation of the patient's accurate perceptions of the therapist and disconfirmation of inaccurate perceptions by acknowledging what the therapist is experiencing and feeling (Will, 1961b, 1964).

Ten: Monitoring Countertransference

The therapist monitors her own countertransference reactions, which often include: a desire to flee the relationship entirely or to withdraw emotionally; a desire to hide behind a façade; an expectation of personal perfection; a tendency to judge the patient based on the therapist's values; attempts to "convert" the patient to the therapist's worldview; an expectation for the patient to make "progress" — however that term is defined (Will, 1965, 1970b, 1970c, 1973). For a similar perspective, see Bion (1965/2018).

Eleven: Termination

The therapist and patient end psychotherapy and mourn it as a loss, both similar and dissimilar to other losses in life (Will, 1959a, 1968b, 1971b, 1971c). Perhaps successful psychotherapy does not end in termination, but in the transition from the therapist as an external object to an internal one.

## "Cure?"

What is "cure" and is it a valid concept? It is helpful to remember that what constitutes cure is based on the therapist's theoretical biases, particularly her values concerning "health." "Health" is often interchangeable with "good." When parents describe a child as "good," they generally mean compliant, not requiring an inconvenient amount of time or effort (Will, 1949b). Without being aware of it, therapists often equate health with acceptance of their values and ideology (Phillips, 2021, p. 147). It can be the adult version of "good."

Otto believed (1970c, 1979) that "cure" cannot be directly applied to the outcome of psychotherapy. Instead, he proposed that therapists offer their patients a new experience in a relationship from which they may learn more about themselves and other people. They may also learn how to deal more effectively with anxiety. He (1973) also stressed that the psychotherapeutic relationship offers the potential for increased awareness of one's feelings. A successful therapeutic experience also offers the potential to face the ambiguity and uncertainty that characterizes life (Will, 1975). As the poet, Greg Teicher (2018), suggests of poetry, "This is medicine that doesn't pretend to cure, but that helps one to live nonetheless" (p. 158).

As Adam Phillips (2021) suggests, "Psychoanalytic treatment is an antidote to indoctrination; it is an enquiry into how people influence each other, into the individual's history of living in other people's regimes" (p. 163). This, of course, is the ideal and our work sometimes falls seriously short of it. Sometimes, it is gratifying enough to observe our patient and, as the poet, Vrest Orton (1979), suggests, acknowledge that, "he no longer exists, he lives" (p. 10).

# Chapter Twenty-Seven: A Good Man

It seems to me that, if we live long enough, we consider what legacy we will leave behind when we are no more. This is not so much the preoccupation of the young who are busy building their lives. They are shaping their legacy, and as Emerson (1841/2009a) wrote in *Circles*, "The field cannot be well seen from within the field" (p. 128). It is rather a potential source of reflection for those of us who are both lucky and sturdy enough to reach an age when the shadow of non-being is identifiable. There is a German idiom, *torschlusspanik*, that is variously translated as "panic at the closing of the gate" or "panic that the door will soon close;" it suggests that the process of reviewing our lives is not a casual activity but instead an emotional imperative. We take stock of what has been and tentatively plan for what still can be.

Introspection suggests that the initial — though not necessarily the most profound — consideration of my legacy involves a determination of whether I have lived my life well. Despite mistakes in judgement and responding from angry, petty, vindictive, or envious motivations, will I, on balance, leave the world a better place?

There is little doubt that Otto was reflecting upon this in his last months. During one conversation with Kim Chernin in March 1992, about twenty months before his death, Otto described saying to Beulah, "I think I'm a pretty good man, by God, and I've come to accept it." He related that he arrived at that conclusion because she loved him, and she was a competent, productive person. This assertion seems a bit childlike for a man in his eighties, perhaps, but it represents one of life's earliest questions: "Am I deserving of love?" I do not think that question was answered for Otto at its developmentally appropriate time. Both Guntrip (1971) and Sutherland (1989) pointed out that the experience of being loved simply for being who one is and being allowed to give love are the qualities upon which our view of ourselves is constructed. Reflecting on Otto's early life, it is not at all clear that his family environment was one that supplied these qualities. This is not meant to imply that others in his life — Adeline, Gwen, Patrick, Deirdre, and many others — did not love him or that their love was unimportant; instead, I think that Otto was not capable of feeling it throughout his being. Perhaps he finally did.

This is, perhaps, what made Otto the clinical genius that he was. He understood that patients damaged in the first year(s) of life need a loving relationship to develop a sense of themselves and their place in the world. But how could he give such a relationship to others when his earliest development did not include such a loving and tender relationship? Perhaps, he offered patients intuitively what he desperately wanted. To quote Emerson (1844/2009b), again from his essay, *Compensation*: "Our strength grows out of our weakness" (p. 144). I think that his realization also reflects a quality of the human condition that Otto trusted and relied on — we learn from relationships throughout life. Returning briefly to the poetic, I believe that the essence of psychoanalysis and psychotherapy are captured by the poet, Carl Phillips (2022), who writes: "I hope to learn from those who love me — to be nurtured toward my best self, who I *am* and *can* be, not pressured by expectation into what others have decided I *should* be" (p. 76, emphasis in the original). Otto understood that a psychotherapist's work is like that of Donald Hall's (1992) description of the poet's: "We work in the dark — we do what we can — we give what we have" (p. 12).

While Otto was often not available to his family — which was particularly painful to his children — Patrick recognizes that "the work he did for others was good, honorable, and loving" (personal communication, May 31, 2025). Perhaps not a fair exchange for them — but fully human.

In these pages I have attempted to capture something of the story of a man. Bruce Murphy (2003) notes in his comprehensive biography of the late Supreme Court Justice, William O. Douglas, that such figures as Douglas can easily become legends, rather than human beings with complicated life histories. In some ways, we may prefer them as legends.

They can then be great and good or infamous and malignant. Otto Will may be such a figure — more easily viewed as a legend than a human being. Yet, that would distort the emotional legacy of his life.

For psychotherapists, the qualities that Patrick describes his father displaying with patients — the attempt to be good, honorable, and loving — are a priceless legacy. This legacy requires no superhuman or legendary qualities. Instead, it requires that we approach our patients with the poet's sensibility and that we acknowledge our humanity and respond to others in distress as fellow human beings.

# Acknowledgements

For me, it has always been one of the most enjoyable parts of a book to gratefully acknowledge those people who made its completion possible. As this has been my most ambitious book, it is especially a joy to do so now.

First, it is to my partner of over thirty years that I feel my warmest gratitude. He has read, reread, corrected, then corrected again and always been patiently available to help with the text. He suggested words and phrases, questioned my inferences, and knew to offer reassurance just when I most needed it. He has always been my most supportive editor.

Patrick Will and Deirdre Will Vinyard, Otto Will's now middle-aged children, have given me access to their memories, their collected memorabilia and facilitated the collection of relevant materials held by others. Their father had many imperfections; yet, if he had any responsibility for inspiring the unfailing generosity of spirit that both have demonstrated, then he accomplished something important.

Charles (Chuck) Knight has been a splendid copyeditor. He employed something of a Socratic method in editing the book. He suggested possibilities and asked questions in drawing my attention to areas that could be improved. These questions were always thoughtful and pertinent, having qualities that parallel those of an attentive and focused psychotherapist.

My publisher, Mary Catharine Nelson, offered guidance on what to put in and what to leave out and oversaw the publication process from layout to printing. She did so with a sense of humor. Her commitment to publishing works that may not have a large audience is an admirable rarity in the current publishing climate.

In the Reference section, I have listed several individuals that offered their memories and insights about Otto Will. They stimulated my thinking, often encouraging me to question my conclusions.

Acknowledgements

Since this book has been in creation for many years, and has evolved from previous writings, I wish to thank those I acknowledged in my 2017 book, *Being with Patients*. These include: The staff of the Annette and Irwin Eskind Biomedical Library at Vanderbilt University; Pamela R. Cornell, M. Ed., and Elizabeth Borst White of the John P. McGovern Historical Collections and Research Center, Houston Academy of Medicine-Texas Medical Library (Hilde Bruch, M.D. Archives); William Wears, formerly assistant director for academic affairs at the now defunct Washington School of Psychiatry, Washington, DC; Marisa Shaari, MA, MLIS, archivist at the The Dorothy Blitsten Papers, The Oskar Diethelm Library, DeWitt Wallace Institute for the History of Psychiatry, Weill Cornell Medical College, New York, NY; Ms. Sarah Hepworth, Senior Assistant Librarian in The Special Collections Department (R.D. Laing Archive) of the University of Glasgow Library, Scotland; Nancy Pickard, Executive Director and Miriam Bunow, Ph.D., Education & Outreach Manager of Peerless Rockville, MD.

Though all the people I have mentioned were instrumental in providing information for this book, I, alone, am responsible for any errors — whether of fact or interpretation.

# Appendix One
# Important Terms in Otto Will's Writing

Often, terms intended to convey precise concepts may have various meanings among those who employ them. It is helpful to define terms that are likely to have such diverse meanings (Will, 1954, 1960).

### *Anxiety*

An interpersonal phenomenon in which one feels the potential for, or actual experience of, disapproval by another and rejection because of that disapproval (Will, 1959a, 1960).

### *Automatism*

A behavior or set of behaviors that seem to be automatic, unrelated to other people, but are actually symbolic actions involved with past, present, or anticipated future experiences (Will, 1972).

### *Behavior*

Ways of relating to and interacting with other people (Will, 1972).

### *Belief*

The disposition of placing trust in a principle, perspective, or practice, which is often not demonstrable and therefore very difficult to modify. (Will, 1981b).

### *Catatonia*

A stuporous condition with unusual muscular rigidity or pliability; extreme excitement or overactivity (Will, 1972).

### *Chronic Mental Disorder*

Rigid behavioral patterns, resistant to change, that impede need satisfaction and interpersonal relatedness and often involve a sense of hopelessness (Will, 1960).

***Coercion***

The act of compelling or restraining the action of another through threat or promise of benefit, often based on a belief or value that is not shared by both parties (Will, 1968/1987).

***Control***

The guidance or restraint of the actions of another to achieve desired ends (Will, 1968/1987).

***Countertransference***

The therapist's use of selective inattention or another means of controlling awareness to avoid recognition of, or acting upon something in the interpersonal field with the patient (Will, 1961a).

***Covert***

Actions or ideas that operate outside a person's awareness.

***Critical Period***

An epoch during which physical maturation and previous skill acquisition coalesce to offer the best chance of success in the introduction of the organism to a new situation (Will, 1963a, 1971b).

***Cure***

The nature of "cure" is simply unclear at present, but an approximate definition is as follows: the patient's understanding of herself as more aligned with how others perceive her to be (Will, 1961a).

***Depression***

An unpleasant, painful, and undesirable affect involving both an ambiguous self-concept and an inhibition of self-esteem that interfere with actions in the interpersonal field to confirm self-worth; depression is often highly resistant to hope and change (Will, 1966).

***Desire***

Movement toward a person or experience which will likely result in satisfaction when attained (Will, 1963b).

***Despair***

The result of anxiety disorganizing perception of past and current experience so that expectations of the future reflect an absence of hope (Will, 1959a).

***Dissociation***

Related to denial — the avoidance of awareness to maintain a precarious hold on one's self-esteem; an unformulated experience (Will, 1970a, 1971b).

***Education***

A process during which latent abilities and unformulated information are brought to a more complete realization (Will, 1962).

***Foresight***

Anticipation of the future based on previous experience which can be used in predicting future experience; the development of pattern recognition (Will, 1961a).

***Internal Working Model***

A concept developed by John Bowlby, involving the infant's formation of internal objects into a broad expectation for all relationships (Bowlby, 1987).

***Knowledge***

An organization of facts gathered by observation and evaluation which allows inferences to be made (Will, 1962).

***Loneliness***

A feeling of isolation ubiquitous to the human condition. The experience of anxiety is preferable to the state of loneliness. Loneliness seems to arise with the awareness that we cannot be entirely known by another person and cannot fully know another person. It is the awareness that we live generally unknown to other people (Will, 1961a, 1968b, 1989b).

### *Love*

Within a loving relationship, the abiding regard for another in which the satisfaction of the needs of the other person is *almost* as important as the satisfaction of our own needs (Will, 1981a).

### *Maturity*

The state in which the natural behavior of the human organism is expressed in an integration with its natural biological, social, and interpersonal environment (Will, 1964)

### *Mental Disorders (Psychiatric Disorders, Problems in Living)*

The formation of destructive and overly complex ways of relating to others which provide a tenuous relation; they are not intrapsychic diseases but arise from anxious experiences during which self-esteem is protected by distortions in perception, including perceptual distortions of the self. It is characteristic of mental disorders that they restrict freedom, interfere with learning, and reduce the possibility of self-realization (Will, 1959a, 1960, 1965).

### *The Mind*

A process, rather than a physical entity, of interactions between the person and her environment, based on previous experience, current perception and foresight of future involvement, particularly with the person's interpersonal environment. This does not obviate the brain but puts it in a different context, as part of the overall functioning of the human being. (Will, 1959b, 1960).

### *Mystification*

An interpersonal interaction in which one party manipulates the perceptions of another to avoid the anxiety that would arise without such manipulation. Often employed in connection with denial, it can also involve coercing a child to disbelieve her or his own perceptions (Will, 1971a).

### *Need*

A prompt to action in satisfying an organismic deficit, such as to drink when thirsty (Will, 1963a).

***Neutrality***

The chimeric idea that a psychotherapist may avoid influencing a patient by what is done or not done. All actions or inactions have consequences, which often cannot be predicted (Will, 1968b).

***One Genus Theorem***

The idea, according to Sullivan (1953a) that, "We are all much more simply human than otherwise ..." (p. 16). All human beings share the essential qualities of the human condition; there is no one who is either more or less human (Will, 1989b).

***Panic***

The desperate feeling that occurs when an important interpersonal relationship is threatened (Will, 1961a).

***Paranoid Solution to Living***

An oversimplified approach to people, ideas, and behavior as either "Good" or "Bad" without any acknowledgement of ambiguity (Will, 1961b).

***Personality***

The constant interaction of the biological substratum (e.g., heredity, physical developmental delays) with all the interpersonal fields of a person's life (Will, 1971a).

***Professionalism***

Knowledge tempered by an awareness of its limitations without surrendering to despair (Will, 1970a).

***Psychotherapy***

A special instance of a human relationship in which resolution of the problems in living of one person (and growth in the other) is sought (Will, 1973, 1977a).

***Relatedness/Relation***

The interaction between people in social fields composed of past and present experience and expectations of the future; the ties between people that result from their similarities as human beings (Will, 1959a).

***Regression***

A return to an era of interpersonal living recalled as being more satisfactory than the present in an attempt to decrease anxiety and increase security (Will, 1961b).

***Resistance***

The general reluctance — brought about by anxiety — to make changes in one's life (Will, 1972).

***Schizophrenia***

An attempt (accompanied by either overly complicated or overly simplified thought and action) to relate to other human beings when faced with panic or severe anxiety (Will, 1971b).

***Security***

A state characterized by the absence of anxiety (Will, 1961b).

***Self***

The being of a person reflecting her past and present experience and expectations for the future, which can only be understood as an irreducible whole and generally only through inference (Will, 1961b).

***Selective Inattention***

Careful, covert attention to avoiding anxiety by failing to notice facets of the interpersonal environment that arouse anxiety (Sullivan, 1954).

***Sentiment***

A complex organization of emotions and ideas that purport to explain the life experience of a human being (Will, 1961c, 1963a).

### Shame

A painful emotion developed from what is perceived as wrong-doing, impropriety, or moral failing with regard to what is acceptable to a particular group (Will, 1987b).

### System

Complicated patterns of behavior developed to deal with interpersonal relationships that may or may not be readily available to awareness (Will, 1963b, 1964).

### Teacher

One who imparts information through didactic instruction, but also experientially through availability for identification (Will, 1962).

### Transference *("Parataxic Distortion")*

An experience of other people in what Sullivan termed the parataxic mode, thought processes which are poorly organized in terms of cause and effect and therefore of dubious predictive power, often developing from experiences that aroused anxiety and were poorly understood. Transference is ubiquitous to all interpersonal situations and represents the experience of the present as a repetition of the past. (Will, 1961a, 1977a, 1989b).

### Values

Fixed beliefs developed early in life within the family about "right" and "wrong" not necessarily related to rational thought; convictions about "just how things are;" seldom questioned or challenged these convictions are considered part of the self (Will, 1968b, 1981b).

### Wisdom

A combination of judgment, experience, learning and understanding that transcends information in approaching practical life and philosophical thought (Will, 1962, 1968a).

# Appendix Two
# The Wit & Wisdom of Otto Will
## As recorded by Kim Chernin

"I think a little humanity can do a lot of good."

"If I were in that person's position, I might do thus and so, but I'm not in that person's position, which is why I never tell anybody to get a divorce."

"Sometimes a person will say to me, 'I feel worse with you.' I say, 'Well it really isn't necessary for you to like coming to see me — let's just get on with the work and *listen*.'"

"The attachment to an unpleasant situation or dominating person is commonly a very strong one. What would life be like if you weren't governed, controlled, and all that sort of thing? You might feel very lonely."

"Depression obscures anger and the patient is often afraid of what might happen if that anger showed — that people won't have anything to do with them or they might hurt somebody, or God knows what. You get into this business of the person feeling that they are kind of dangerous to others and to themselves. I'm interested to know where they got that idea..."

"If you agree with somebody you may lose yourself — that is, you're not distinct — there isn't any *you*. In an intimate relationship there may be a struggle going on to maintain a feeling of independence."

"One of my more burdensome patients kept saying, 'Oh, I just love coming to see you.' I thought, 'Oh for Christ's sake, I have to hear this once more.'"

"Free association:
Doctor: 'What's on your mind?'
Patient: 'Frankly doctor, not one fucking thing.'"

"Getting 'better' can be terribly threatening."

"People often think, 'I want to live with people, but the trouble is I can't stand them.'"

"Sometimes people complain in a way that conceals what there really is to complain about."

"Help isn't just giving something; it's an opportunity to learn."

"I like the phrase, 'He who loves gives hostages to fate,' because you always lose what you love, one way or another."

"Somebody asked me, 'What is a training analyst?' I said, 'Well, when they [patients] come to see you, they have to lie down.'"

"Always remember that if therapy works, it carries the risk that you will have more contact with people. You will have to make more adjustments, decisions about whether they're friendly or not, trustworthy or not, and so on."

"I knew a lot about my therapists, Sullivan and Fromm-Reichmann. I like to think there's a lot more to life than transference."

"Too much of a fear about [losing others] is loneliness and unrelatedness."

"I raise the question [with patients] every once in a while: 'Doing therapy is, we guess, to bring about changes — what would actually happen to you [if you changed]?'"

"There is a certain attractiveness for some people to a person being dependent and then working, usually unsuccessfully, to save them."

"I think sometimes patients don't really connect with the idea that the therapist has to earn a living."

"I remember a patient came in, I'd been seeing at the time, a young woman.

She said, 'You don't look very well today.'

'I'm fine.'

'I think you're sick.'

'No, I'm not, I'm not sick.'

'Have you got cancer?'

'No, I don't have cancer. There's nothing the matter with me as far as I know.'

'You're going to kill yourself.'

'No, I don't intend to kill myself.'

'I think you will, and then, you son of a bitch, you'll leave me!'"

"Love — it's one of the most dangerous words in the language."

"Analysis is something you can do in many ways. The patient can lie down, sit down, stand up or lie on the floor."

"I remember a man I saw many years ago. For some time, he stood in the corner with his back turned. I thought, 'That's great; I wish they would all do that — I could just sit here and do anything I want.'"

"Sometimes, a patient says she feels a lot worse after seeing me than before.

I say, 'That's why that old saying sticks with us — ignorance is bliss.'"

"I see this one patient who's a pretty disturbed person. If I cross my legs he asks, 'Why do you do that?'

I say, 'Because I want to.'

He asks, 'Just what does it mean?'

'It means I was a little uncomfortable.'

'Well, am I making you uncomfortable?'

'No more than usual.'"

"Absence may not make the heart grow fonder, but it tends to loosen the tongue."

"I think, for some people, abusiveness becomes related to relationships."

"No one's life is quite like another person's life — that would be too boring."

"I'm not kicking you out, I'm just opening the door for you."

"Sometimes I say to a patient, 'You don't trust me, huh? Okay, simplifies things, does it?'"

"In a situation of dependence, there is power. One has to take a real look at whether one has the need to have this power and keep the other person dependent. That certainly would be a very unfortunate trait in a parent."

"Some analytic institutes say it's hard to find somebody well enough to be a patient."

"I don't try to hold on to such elusive things as the truth."

# References

Unless attributed otherwise, all quotes from Otto Allen Will come from conversations recorded by Kim Chernin, Ph.D. between May 15, 1991, and August 16, 1993.

**Interviews & Correspondence**

The following individuals were kind enough to give interviews and/or furnish material that has been used for the completion of this book. Their assistance is greatly appreciated.

Sue Erikson Bloland, M.S.W.
Kim Chernin, Ph.D.*
Robert A. Cohen, M.D., Ph.D.*
F. Barton Evans, III, Ph.D.
Anne Farber*
M. Gerard Fromm, Ph.D.
Robert W. Gibson, M.D.*
John S. Kafka, M.D.*
Beatrice Liebenberg, M.S.W.*
Leon M. Lurie, M.S.*
Roy W. Menninger, M.D.*
Morris B. Parloff, Ph.D.*
Owen Renik, M.D.
Stephen Schlein, Ph.D.
Clarence G. Schulz, M.D.*
Michael Guy Thompson, Ph.D.
Jerome Styrt, M.D.*
Mary Styrt*
Deirdre Will Vinyard, Ph.D.
Patrick Will

*Deceased

## General & Documentary References


155 pass state test for medical licenses. (1940, August 15). *The San Francisco Examiner*, 8.

A clear look at Austen Riggs. (1980, October 22). *Berkshire Eagle*, 19.

Abbott, C., Leonard, S.J., & Noel, T.J. (2013). *Colorado: A history of the centennial state* (5th ed.) University Press of Colorado.

Abrahams, J. (2007). *A passionate psychoanalyst: Poems and dreams*. Xlibris.

Abzug, R.H. (2021). *Psyche and soul in America: The spiritual odyssey of Rollo May*. Oxford University Press.

Agassi, J.B. (1999). Preface. In J.B. Agassi (Ed.). *Martin Buber on psychology and psychotherapy*. Syracuse University Press.

Alanen, Y.O., Silver, A.S. & de Chávez, M.G. (2006). *Fifty years of humanistic treatment of psychoses: In honour of the history of the International Society for the Psychological*

*Treatments of the Schizophrenias and Other Psychoses, 1956 - 2006*. Fundación para la Investigación y Tratamiento de la Esquizofrenia y otras Psicosis.

Albom, M. (2002). *Tuesdays with Morrie: An old Man, a young man, and life's greatest lessons*. Broadway Books.

Alexander, I.E. (1990). *Personology: Method and content in personality assessment and psychobiography*. Duke University Press.

Alexander, K. (2022). John Chisum — cattle baron on the Pecos. *Legends of America*. https://www.legendsofamerica.com/we-johnchisum.

Alexander, K. (2023). Caldwell, Kansas — the wicked border queen. *Legends of America*. https://www.legendsofamerica.com/ks-caldwell.

Allen, J.B. (2016). The man who came to dinner and stayed a year. *Skiing History*. https://skimuseum.ca/wp-content/uploads/2022/01/Albizzi-Nov-Dec-2016.pdf.

Allen, J.G. (2018). The person of the therapist and the liberation of the patient. *Psychiatry, 81*(4), 330-336.

Allen, M.S. (1995). Sullivan's closet: A reappraisal of Harry Stack Sullivan's life and his pioneering role in American psychiatry. *Journal of Homosexuality, 29*(1), 1-18.

American Foreign Service. (1949). Report of the Death of an American Citizen. https://www.ancestry.com/search/collections/1616/records/125845.

Applegate, D. (2006). *The most famous man in America: The biography of Henry Ward Beecher*. Doubleday.

Barberis, I., Bragazzi, N.L., Galluzzo, L., & Martini, M. (2017). The history of tuberculosis: from the first historical records to the isolation of Koch's bacillus. *Journal of Preventive Medicine and Hygiene*, *58*(1), E9-E12.

Barker, K. (1972, July 16). 5 days inside St. Elizabeths: anguish, boredom, despair. *Washington Post*, A1.

Baxter, W.E. (1986). John C. Whitehorn (1894-1973) papers: archives finding aid. Melvin Sabshin, M.D. Library & Archives, American Psychiatric Association Foundation. https://www.apaf.org/getmedia/c883f5a0-3ea7-4c05-b199-0d8678d25010/John-Whitehorn.pdf.

Bazerman, C. (2005). Practically human: the pragmatist project of the interdisciplinary journal *Psychiatry*. *Linguistics and the Human Sciences*, *1*(1), 15-38.

Beira, M.L. & Hassan, S.E. (2005). On Heidegger to Lacan: An interview with William J. Richardson, S.J., Ph.D. *Acheronta*, *22*. https://www.acheronta.org/reportajes/richardson-en.htm.

Belfer, M.L., et.al. (2006, April 20). Margaret Brenman-Gibson. *The Harvard Gazette*. https://news.harvard.edu/gazette/story/2006/04/margaret-brenman-gibson.

Benét, S.V. (1936). *The Devil and Daniel Webster and other writings*. Penguin Classics.

Benjamin, L.S. (2014). Insight about insight. *Psychiatry*, *77*(3), 236-238.

Benveniste, D. (2006). The early history of psychoanalysis in San Francisco. *Psychoanalysis and History*, *8*, 195-233.

Bergman, R.L. (1971). Navajo peyote use: Its apparent safety. *American Journal of Psychiatry*, *128*(6), 695-699.

Beulah Parker Obituary. (2007, February 11). *East Bay Times*, San Francisco, CA. Retrieved from https://www.eastbaytimes.com/obituaries/beulah-parker.

Bever, C. T. (1993). *Ernest E. Hadley, M.D., 1894-1954: Washington promoter of psychoanalysis* [Unpublished master's thesis]. University of Maryland.

Binder, J.L. (2004). *Key competencies in brief dynamic psychotherapy: Clinical practice beyond the manual.* Guilford Press.

Binder, J.L. & Betan, E.J. (2013). *Core competencies in brief dynamic psychotherapy*. Routledge.

Bion, W.R. (1965/2018). Memory and desire. In C. Mawson (Ed.). *Three papers of W.R. Bion* (pp. 1-10). New York, NY: Routledge.

Blackbourn, D. (2003). *History of Germany 1780-1918,* (Second ed.). Blackwell Publishing.

Blackburn laboratory. (n.d.). DC Historic Sites. https://historicsites.dcpreservation.org/items/show/986.

Blanke, R. (2014). *Orphans of Versailles: The Germans in Western Poland 1918-1939*. University Press of Kentucky.

Bloland, S.E. (2005). *In the shadow of fame*. Viking Press.

Bly, N. (2019). *Ten days in a mad-house*. Dover. (Original work published 1887)

Bollas, C. (2004, October 2). *The Christopher Bollas Conference on Free Association*, (L. Lucas, Recorder). Toronto Psychoanalytic Association, Mount Sinai Auditorium. https://ctp.net/PDFs/CBOLLAS.pdf.

Bollas, C. (2015). *When the sun bursts: The enigma of schizophrenia*. Yale University Press.

Bollas, C. (2013). *Catch them before they fall: The psychoanalysis of breakdown*. Routledge.

Bollas, C. (2025). *Streams of consciousness: Notebooks 1974-1990*. Karnac Books.

Bosworth, R.J. (2002). *Mussolini*. Hodder House.

Bought home here. (1901, October 19). *Wichita Eagle*, 6.

Bourgeois, W. (2018). *The Devil says maybe I like it*. Propeller Books.

Bowlby, R. (2004). *Fifty years of attachment theory*. Karnac Books.

Bowlby, J. (1987). Defensive processes in the light of attachment theory. In J. Sacksteder, D. Schwartz, & Y. Akabane (Eds.), *Attachment and the Therapeutic Process: Essays in Honor of Otto Allen Will, Jr.* (pp. 63-79). International Universities Press.

Bowman, K.M. (1969). *My years in psychiatry, 1915-1968: an interview with Karl M. Bowman, M.D., San Francisco, February 27 and 28, 1968*. California State Department of Mental Hygiene. Sacramento: State of California, 1969. OCLC 58860757

Breger, L. (2000). *Freud: Darkness in the midst of vision*. John Wiley & Sons.

Brenman, M. (2009). It's not a layer cake. *The Third Table.* https://thethirdtable.wordpress.com/chapters/5-dr-margaret-brenman.

Brenman-Gibson, M. (1997). The legacy of Erik Homburger Erikson. *The Psychoanalytic Review, 84*(3), 329-335.

Bretherton, I., & Munholland, K. A. (2008). Internal working models in attachment relationships: Elaborating a central construct in attachment theory. In J. Cassidy & P. R. Shaver (Eds.), *Handbook of attachment: Theory, research, and clinical applications* (2nd ed., pp. 102 —127). The Guilford Press.

Brininstool, E.A. (1935, January 10). Strategic return of the Dull Knife band of Cheyenne Indians which resulted in their death in 1879. *Northwest Nebraska News*, 8.

Brown, M.W. (1942). *The runaway bunny.* Harpers.

Bruch, H. (1974). *Learning psychotherapy: Rationale and ground rules.* Harvard University Press.

Bruch, H. (1978). *The golden cage: The enigma of anorexia nervosa.* Harvard University Press.

Bruch, H. (1987). The changing picture of an illness: Anorexia Nervosa. In In J. Sacksteder, D. Schwartz, & Y. Akabane (Eds.), *Attachment and the Therapeutic Process: Essays in Honor of Otto Allen Will, Jr.* (pp. 205-222). International Universities Press.

Bruch, J.H. (1996). *Unlocking the Golden Cage: An Intimate Biography of Hilde Bruch, M.D.* Gurze Books.

Buber, M.M. (1970). *I and Thou* (W. Kaufmann, Trans.). Simon & Schuster.

Buber, M.M. (1999). *Martin Buber on psychology and psychotherapy: Essays, letters, and dialogues* (J.B. Agassi, Ed.). Syracuse University Press.

Budd, S. (2011). Nina-isms. In P.L. Rudnytsky, & G. Preston (Eds.). *Her hour come round at last: A garland for Nina Coltart* (pp. 3-9). Karnac Books.

Bullard, D.M. (1939). The application of psychoanalytic psychiatry to the psychoses. *The Psychoanalytic Review, 26,* 526-534.

Bullard, D.M. (1956). Foreword. In H.S. Sullivan, *Clinical studies in psychiatry.* Norton.

Bullard, D.M. (1959). Editor's preface. In D.M. Bullard (Ed.), *Psychoanalysis and psychotherapy: Selected papers of Frieda Fromm-Reichmann* (pp. xi-xii). University of Chicago Press.

Bullard, D.M. (1961). Introduction. In *Chestnut Lodge symposium: Papers presented on the fiftieth anniversary, 1910-1960* (pp. v-vi). The William Alanson White Psychiatric Foundation, Inc.

Burnham, D. L. (1978). Orthodoxy and eclecticism in psychoanalysis: the Washington-Baltimore experience. In J.M. Quen, E.T. Carlson, and A. Meyer (Eds.). *American psychoanalysis, origins and development: The Adolf Meyer seminars* (pp. 87-108). Brunner/Mazel.

Business Records. (1932, February 27). *New York Times*, 22.

California Voter Registrations, Santa Clara County. (1936), p. 401. https://www.ancestry.com/imageviewer/collections/61066/images/santaclaracounty_9-00224a?pId=6471971.

Callaway, E. (2007). *Asylum: A mid-century madhouse and its lessons about our mentally ill today*. Praeger.

Capps, D. (2008). Erik H. Erikson, Norman Rockwell, and the therapeutic functions of a questionable painting. *American Imago*, *65*(2), 191-228.

Carlson, D. (2003). A brief history of the Western New England Psychoanalytic Society (WNEPS). https://static1.1.sqspcdn.com/static/f/584938/27540643/1493300114543/A+Brief+History+of+WNEPSFeb10b.pdf.

Carlson, P. (2019). The nut house. *Contemporary Psychoanalysis*, *55*(1-2), 73-85.

Carmosino, J. (2013). Cleveland State Hospital exposed. *Cleveland Historical*. https://clevelandhistorical.org/items/show/574.

Caruso, J.P. & Sheehan, J.P. (2017). Psychosurgery, ethics, and media: a history of Walter Freeman and the lobotomy. *Journal of Neurosurgery*, *43*(3), 1-8.

Chapman, A. H. (1976). *Harry Stack Sullivan: The man and his work*. G.P. Putnam's Sons.

Chernin, K. (1995). *A different kind of listening*. HarperCollins.

Chernin, K. (2017). Foreword. In C. Cornett, *Being with patients: An introduction to the psychotherapy of Harry Stack Sullivan, M.D. and Otto Allen Will, Jr., M.D.*, Westview Press.

Chögyam Trungpa Biography. (2025). Chögyam Trungpa Institute. https://chogyamtrungpa.com/about/chogyam-trungpa-biography.

Chuang, H.T. & Addington, D. (1988). Homosexual panic: a review of its concept. *Canadian Journal of Psychiatry*, *33*, 613-617.

Christ, G.H., Bonanno, G., Malkinson, R., & S. Rubin. (2003). Appendix E: Bereavement experiences after the death of a child. In Institute of Medicine (US) Committee on Palliative and End-of-Life Care for Children and Their Families. Field, M.J. & Behrman, R.E. (Eds.) *When children die: Improving palliative and end-of-life care for children and their Families*. National Academies Press.

Christy, T.E. (1969). *Cornerstone for nursing education; a history of the division of nursing education of Teachers College, Columbia University, 1899-1947*. Teachers College Press.

Clark, A.E. (1981, March 27). Dr. Leslie Farber, 68, leading theoretician of psychiatric school. *New York Times*

Clark, C. (2003). The famed green dragons. Turner Publishing.

Clark, C. (2009). *Kaiser Wilhelm II: A life in power*. Penguin Books.

CMEA Hall of Fame. (n.d.). Colorado Music Educators Association. https://cmeaonline.org/about/cmea-hall-of-fame.

Cohen, R.A. (2010). Notes on the life and work of Frieda Fromm-Reichmann. *Psychiatry*, *73*, 209-218.

Coke, T.S. (2005). Gunfighters and lawmen. *Wild West*, *17*(5), 14-16, 70-71.

Coles, R. (2010). *Handing one another along: Literature and social reflection*; Hall, T., & Kennedy, V. (Eds.). Random House.

Coltart, N. (2011). Self-regarding. In P.L. Rudnytsky, & G. Preston (Eds.). *Her hour come round at last: A garland for Nina Coltart* (pp. 279-282). Karnac Books.

Cooperman, M. (1983). Some observations regarding psychoanalytic psychotherapy in a hospital setting. *The Psychiatric Hospital*, *14*(1), 21-28.

Cornett, C. (2008). Of molehills and mountains: Harry Stack Sullivan and the malevolent transformation of personality. *American Imago*, *65*(2), 261-289.

Cornett, C. (2017a). *Being with patients: An introduction to the psychotherapy of Harry Stack Sullivan, M.D. and Otto Allen Will Jr., M.D.* Westview.

Cornett, C. (2017b). Interpersonal theory. In A. Wenzel (Ed). *SAGE encyclopedia of abnormal and clinical psychology* (p. 1885). Sage Press.

Cortina, M. (2020). Harry Stack Sullivan and interpersonal theory: a flawed genius. *Psychiatry*, *83*(1), 103-109.

Crowley, R.M. (1977). Sullivan, Harry Stack (1892-1949). *International encyclopedia of psychiatry, psychology, psychoanalysis, and neurology*. Aesculapius.

Cunningham, V. (1980). *The Penguin book of Spanish Civil War verse*. Penguin.

Cusk, R. (2019). *Coventry: Essays.* Farrar, Straus and Giroux.

D'Amore, A. R. (1976a). Introduction. In A. R. D'Amore (Ed.) *William Alanson White: The Washington years, 1903-1937* (pp. 1-12). DHEW Publication No. ADM 76-298, U.S. Government Printing Office.

D'Amore, A. R. (1976b). William Alanson White — pioneer psychoanalyst. In A. R. D'Amore (Ed.) *William Alanson White: The Washington years, 1903-1937* (pp. 69-91). DHEW Publication No. ADM 76-298, U.S. Government Printing Office.

Daniel, T.M. (2006). The history of tuberculosis. *Respiratory Medicine*, *100*(11), 1862-1870.

Darnell, R. (1990). *Edward Sapir: Linguist, anthropologist, humanist.* University of California Press.

Davis, C. (2023). *God's scrivener: The madness & meaning of Jones Very*. University of Chicago Press.

Dawidziak, M. (2023). *A Mystery of mysteries: The death and life of Edgar Allan Poe*. St. Martin's.

De Camp, L.S. (1996). *H.P. Lovecraft: A biography*. Barnes & Noble Books.

DeFao, J. (2001, December 18). Dr. Robert Rubenstein. *SFGATE (San Francisco Chronicle)*. https://www.sfgate.com/news/article/Dr-Robert-Rubenstein-2838059.php.

de la Bédoyère, G. (2017). *Praetorian: The rise and fall of Rome's imperial bodyguard.* Yale University Press.

Decuers, L. (2020). WWII post-traumatic stress. *The National WWII Museum.* https://www.nationalww2museum.org/war/articles/wwii-post-traumatic-stress.

Delbanco, A. (2005). *Melville: His world and work.* Alfred A. Knopf.

Di Donna, L. (2011). Oral history: the life and work of Robert S. Wallerstein, a conversation. *American Imago*, *67*(4), 617-658.

Dr. Kimberly gets foundation post; Psychiatrist Named Medical Director of Austen Riggs, Massachusetts Institution. (1940, August 30). *The New York Times*. https://www.nytimes.com/1940/08/30/archives/dr-kimberly-gets-foundation-post-psychiatrist-named-medical.html.

Dr. Kimberly named V.C. Psychiatrist; Succeeds Dr. Riggs. (1940, October 9). *Vassar Miscellany News*, p. 3. https://newspaperarchives.vassar.edu/?a=d&d=miscellany19401009-01.2.14.

Dr. Otto Will leaves as director at Riggs. (1978, July 31). *The Berkshire Eagle*, 13.

Eagle, M.N. (2013). *Attachment and psychoanalysis: Theory, research, and clinical implications*. Guilford Press.

Eiseley, L.C. (2012). *Mind as nature*. Harper & Row.

El-Hai, J. (2007). *The lobotomist*. John Wiley & Sons.

Elkind, D. (1972, September 24). 'Good Me' or 'Bad Me' — The Sullivan approach to personality, *New York Times*, Section SM, page 18.

Elkatawneh, H. (2013). Freud's psycho-sexual stages of development. https://ssrn.com/abstract=2364215 or http://dx.doi.org/10.2139/ssrn.2364215.

Emerson, R.W. (1993). Self-reliance. In *Self-Reliance and other essays* (pp. 19-38). Dover Press. (Original work published 1841)

Emerson, R.W. (1993). Experience. In *Self-Reliance and other essays* (pp. 83-101). Dover Press. (Original work published 1844)

Emerson, R.W. (2009a). Circles. In *Nature and other essays* (pp. 123-132). Dover Press. (Original work published 1844)

Emerson, R.W. (2009b). Compensation. In *Nature and other essays* (pp. 133-148). Dover Press. (Original work published 1844)

Emerson, R.W. (2009c). Spiritual laws. In *Nature and other essays* (pp. 81-96). Dover Press. (Original work published 1844)

Erikson, E.H. (1950). *Childhood and society*. Norton.

Erikson, E.H. & Erikson, J.M. (1997). *The life cycle completed (extended version)*. Norton.

Evans, F. B., III (2024). *Harry Stack Sullivan: Interpersonal theory and psychotherapy;* 2nd ed.). Routledge.

Farber, L.H. (1956). Martin Buber and psychiatry. *Psychiatry*, *19*(2), 109-120.

Farber, L.H. (2000). *The ways of the will* (R. Boyers & A. Farber Eds.). BasicBooks.

Feiner, A.H. (2005). Edgar A. Levenson, M.D.: An appreciation. *Contemporary Psychoanalysis*, *41*(4), 675-690.

Finkelman, I., Steinberg, D.L. & Liebert, E. (1938). The treatment of schizophrenia with Metrazol by the production of convulsions. *Journal of the American Medical Association, 110*(10), 706-709.

Foehl, J.C. (2008). Follow the fox: Edgar A. Levenson's pursuit of psychoanalytic process. *The Psychoanalytic Quarterly, 78*, 1231-1268.

Forbush, B. (1971). *The Sheppard & Enoch Pratt hospital 1853-1970: A History*. J. B. Lippincott & Co.

Frankl, V.E. (2000). *Recollections: An autobiography*. Basic Books.

Frederickson, J.L. (2001). Interview with Robert Cohen and Donald Burnham. *Psychiatry, 64*(1), 32-39.

Frederickson, J.L. (2002). An interview with Gloria and Morris Parloff. *Psychiatry, 65*(2), 103-109.

Frederickson, J.L. (2003). An interview with Marvin Adland and John Kafka. *Psychiatry, 66*(1), 1-8.

Fresh, D. (1985). Joy: two special memories of Dorothy Shaw. Square Dance History Project. https://squaredancehistory.org/items/show/943.

Freud, A. (1966). *The Ego and the mechanisms of defense (*Revised ed.*)*. International Universities Press.

Freud, S. (1933). *New Introductory lectures on psycho-analysis* (W.J.H. Sprott, Trans.), W.W. Norton.

Friedman, L.J. (1990). *Menninger: The family and the clinic*. Alfred A. Knopf.

Friedman, L.J. (1999). *Identity's architect: A biography of Erik H. Erikson*. Scribner.

Friedman, L.J. (2013). *The lives of Erich Fromm: Love's prophet*. Columbia University Press.

Friedman, M. (1991). *Encounter on the narrow ridge: A life of Martin Buber*. Paragon House.

Fromm, E. (1994). *The art of listening*. (Funk, R., Ed.). Continuum.

Fromm, M.G. (2004). Foreword. In F. Davoine & J. Gaudillière (S. Fairfield, Trans.), *History beyond trauma* (pp. xi-xv). Other Press.

Fromm, M.G. (2011). "We are all more human than otherwise:" psychoanalytic treatment of psychotic patients: a view from the Austen Riggs Center. *The American Psychoanalyst 45*(2), 17-19.

Fromm-Reichmann, F. (1950). *Principles of intensive psychotherapy*. University of Chicago Press.

Fromm-Reichmann, F. (1959). *Psychoanalysis and psychotherapy: Selected papers of Frieda Fromm-Reichmann*, (D.M. Bullard, Ed.). University of Chicago Press.

Fulbrook, M. (1991). *A concise history of Germany*; (2nd Ed.). Cambridge University Press.

Funeral Services for Stuard Zirkle. (1931, November 9). *Great Falls Tribune*, 9.

Gage, B. (2022). *G-Man: J. Edgar Hoover and the making of the American century*. Viking Press.

Gaarder, K.R. (2006). The life and legacy of Harry Stack Sullivan. *Psychiatry, 69*(2), 107-109.

Garff, J. (2005). *Søren Kierkegaard: A biography* (B.H. Kirmmse, Transl.). Princeton University Press.

Gay, V.P. (2001). *Joy and the objects of psychoanalysis: Literature, belief, and neurosis*. State University of New York Press.

Geddie, P.A. (2020). Trailblazing with cattle baron John Chisum, Sweet Jensie, and their descendants. *Country Life Magazine*. https://www.geddieconnections.com/2020/07/25/trailblazing-with-cattle-baron-john-chisum-sweet-jensie-and-their-descendants.

Gibson, R. W. (1989). The application of psychoanalytic principles to the hospitalized patient. In A-L. Silver (Ed.), *Psychoanalysis and psychosis* (pp. 183-205). International Universities Press.

Gill, M. M. (1987). The point of view of psychoanalysis: Energy discharge or person. In J. Sacksteder, D. Schwartz, & Y. Akabane (Eds.), *Attachment and the therapeutic process: Essays in honor of Otto Allen Will, Jr.* (pp. 17-41). International Universities Press.

Glück, L. (1994). *Proofs & theories: Essays on poetry*. Ecco Press.

Goldberger, L. (2021). A psychologist's encounters with Erik Erikson — in the Berkshires. Jewish Federation of the Berkshires. https://www.jewishberkshires.org/community-events/berkshire-jewish-voice/berkshire-jewish-voice-highlights/my-encounters-with-erik-eriksonin-the-berkshires.

Gordon, E.F. (2000). *Mockingbird years: A life in and out of therapy*. Basic Books.

Gordon, E.F. (2019, September 3). How I learned to talk. *The American Scholar*. https://theamericanscholar.org/how-i-learned-to-talk.

Gordon, M. (2018). *On Thomas Merton*. Shambhala.

Gorney, J.E. (2021). Otto Will and the artistry of relationship: more simply human than otherwise. *Contemporary Psychoanalysis*, *57*(1), 85-114.

Groth, M. (n.d.). Psychoanalytic leaders in Colorado: John D. Benjamin (1901-1965). https://www.denverinstituteforpsychoanalysis.org/page-18128.

Guerin, P.J. (1976). Family therapy: The first 25 years. In P.J. Guerin (Ed.), *Family therapy: theory and practice* (pp. 2-22). Gardner Press.

Guntrip, H. (1971). *Psychoanalytic theory, therapy, and the self.* BasicBooks.

Guntrip, H. (1975). My experience of analysis with Fairbairn and Winnicott — (how complete a result does psycho-analytic therapy achieve?). *International Review of Psycho-Analysis, 2,* 145-156.

Hale, N.G., Jr. (1995). *The rise and crisis of psychoanalysis in the United States: Freud and the Americans, 1917-1985*. Oxford University Press.

Hall, D. (2021). *Old poets: Reminiscences and opinions*. Godine Publishing.

Hall, E. T. (1992). *An anthropology of everyday life: An autobiography*. Doubleday.

Havens, L.L. (1976). *Participant observation.* Jason Aronson Press.

Havens, L.L. (1979). Harry Stack Sullivan's contribution to clinical method. *McLean Hospital Journal 4*, 20-32.

Havens, L.L. (1989). *A safe place: Laying the groundwork for psychotherapy*. Harvard University Press.

Havens, L.L. & Frank, J. (1971). Review of P. Mullahy, psychoanalysis and interpersonal psychiatry. *American Journal of Psychiatry, 127*, 1704-1705.

Haynal, A. E. (2002). *Disappearing and reviving: Sándor Ferenczi in the history of psychoanalysis*. Karnac.

Helm, W.H. (2002). Tuberculosis and the Brontë family. *The Journal of the Brontë Society*, *27*(2), 157-167.

Hinton, H.P. (2017). Chisum, John Simpson (1824-1884). *Texas State Historical Association*. https://www.tshaonline.org/handbook/entries/chisum-john-simpson.

Hirsch, I. (1998). Discussion of interview with Otto Will. *Contemporary Psychoanalysis*, *34*(2), 305-322.

Hirsch, I. (2015). *The Interpersonal Tradition*. Routledge.

Hobsbawm, E.J. (2001). *Revolutionaries*. The New Press.

Hoffman, J.T. (2002). *Chesty: The story of lieutenant general Lewis B. Puller, USMC*. Random House.

Høgland, P. (2014). Exploration of the patient-therapist relationship in psychotherapy. *American Journal of Psychiatry*, *171*(10), 1056-1066.

Holmes, J. (2014). *John Bowlby and attachment theory* (2nd Ed.). Routledge.

Hoopes, T., & Brinkley, D. (1992). *Driven patriot: The life and times of James Forrestal*. Alfred A. Knopf.

Horn, S. (2019). *Damnation island. Poor, sick, mad, and criminal in 19th-century New York*. Algonquin Books.

Horney, K. (1987). *Final lectures* (D.H. Ingram, Ed.). Norton.

Hornfischer, J.D. (2005). *The last stand of the tin can sailors: The extraordinary World War II story of the U.S. Navy's finest hour*. Bantam Books.

Hornfischer, J.D. (2011). *Neptune's inferno: The U.S. Navy at Guadalcanal*. Bantam Books.

Hornstein, G.A. (2000). *To redeem one person is to redeem the world: The life of Frieda Fromm-Reichmann*. The Free Press.

Hoyt, E.P. (1993). *Warlord: Tojo against the world*. Cooper Square Press.

Jacobson, E. (1955). Sullivan's interpersonal theory of psychiatry. *Journal of the American Psychoanalytic Association*, *3*(1), 149-156.

Jackson, L. P. (2002). *Ralph Ellison: Emergence of genius*. John Wiley & Sons.

Jones, A.H. (2005). The cautionary tale of psychiatrist Henry Aloysius Cotton. *The Lancet*, *366*(9483), 361-362.

Karpman, B. (1943). Mediate psychotherapy and the acute homosexual panic (Kempf's disease). *Journal of Nervous & Mental Disease*, *98*(5), 493-506.

Kastenberg, J.E. (2019). *The campaign to impeach Justice William O. Douglas: Nixon, Vietnam, and the conservative attack on judicial independence*. University Press of Kansas.

Katchadourian, H. (2012). *The way it turned out*. CRC Press.

Keeling-Barlow. (1883, October 25). *Caldwell Advance*, 3.

Keeling, H.C. (1925). My experience with the Cheyenne Indians. *Oklahoma Historical Society Chronicles of Oklahoma.* https://gateway.okhistory.org/ark:/67531/metadc2191539.

Keeling, William Henry 03/18/1835-3/6/1920. (n.d.). Nebraska State Historical Society. https://nebraska.lyrasistechnology.org/agents/people/21286.

Kimberly, C.H. (1936). The psychoneurotic depression. *Journal of the American Medical Association, 107*(14), 1112-1114.

King, F. (2006). Introduction. In du Maurier, D. *The winding stair: Francis Bacon, his rise and fall* (pp. ix-xiii). Virago Press.

Kohut, H. (1971). *The analysis of the self.* International Universities Press.

Kohut, H. (1977). *The restoration of the self.* International Universities Press.

Kohut, H. (1994). *The curve of life: Correspondence of Heinz Kohut 1923-1981* (G. Cocks, Ed.). University of Chicago Press.

Kramer, R. (2019). *The birth of relationship therapy: Carl Rogers meets Otto Rank.* Psychosozial-Verlag.

Krishnan, V. (2022). *Phantom plague: How tuberculosis shaped history*. PublicAffairs.

Kirschenbaum, H. (2007). *The life and work of Carl Rogers*. PCCS Books.

Kuklick, B. (1980). Harry Stack Sullivan and American intellectual life. *Contemporary Psychoanalysis, 16*(3), 307-319.

Kwawer, J.S. (2012). William Alanson White Institute: origins, theory, and practice, 1943-2012. https://wawhite.org/our-history.

Kwawer, J.S. (2019). The interpersonal legacy of Chestnut Lodge. *Contemporary Psychoanalysis, 55*(1-2), 86-98.

Laing, R.D. (1969). *The politics of the family (The CBC Massey Lectures)*. House of Anansi Press.

Laing, R.D. (1970). *Knots*. Pantheon Books.

Lamb, S.D. (2014). *Pathologist of the mind: Adolf Meyer and the origins of American psychiatry*. Johns Hopkins University Press.

Lamb, S.D. (2015). Social skills: Adolf Meyer's revision of clinical skill for the new psychiatry of the twentieth century, *Medical History, 59*(3), 443-464.

Langs, R. & Searles, H.F. (1980). *Intrapsychic and interpersonal dimensions of treatment.* Aronson Press.

Largent, M.A. (2011). *Breeding contempt: The history of coerced sterilization in the United States*. Rutgers University Press.

LaZebnik, J. (1957, April 1) The case of Ezra Pound. *The New Republic*. https://newrepublic.com/article/123283/case-ezra-pound.

Lessing, D. (1987). *Prisons we choose to live inside: Essays*. HarperCollins.

Levenson, E.A. (2017). *The purloined self* (A. Slomowitz, Ed.). Routledge.

Levenson, E.A. (2018). *Interpersonal psychoanalysis and the enigma of consciousness* (A. Slomowitz, Ed.). Routledge.

Lewin, B.D. (1966). John D. Benjamin 1901-1965. *The Psychoanalytic Quarterly*, *35*(1), 125-126.

Licenses to Wed in Iowa. (1945, October 5). Des Moines Tribune, 14.

Lieberman, E. J. (1985). *Acts of will: The life and work of Otto Rank*. University of Massachusetts Press.

Lifton, R.J. (2011). *Witness to an extreme century: A memoir*. The Free Press.

Lofgren, Lars Borje, M.D. (2010, July 7). Paid death notice. *New York Times*. https://archive.nytimes.com/query.nytimes.com/gst/fullpage-9D0CE1D7123AF934A35754C0A9669D8B63.html.

Lou W. Fink died Wednesday in Roswell. (1970, January 18). *Colorado Springs Gazette-Telegraph*, 53.

Loving, J. (1999). *Walt Whitman: The song of himself*. University of California Press.

Lurie, L. (2008). Theories are ideas. In G.M. Saiger, S. Rubenfeld, & M.D. Dluhy (Eds.). *Windows into today's group therapy* (pp. 173-176). Routledge.

Lynch, T. (2020). *The depositions: New and selected essays on being and ceasing to be*. W.W. Norton.

Maddox, B. (2007). *Freud's wizard: Ernest Jones and the transformation of psychoanalysis*. Da Capo Press.

Maisel, A.Q. (1946). Bedlam. *Parallels in time*. https://mn.gov/mnddc/parallels2/prologue/6a-bedlam/bedlam-life1946.pdf.

Marcus, J. (2024). *Glad to the brink of fear: A portrait of Ralph Waldo Emerson*. Princeton University Press.

Marold, R. (2012, April). Cheyenne Mountain School: A rich tradition. https://cmheritagecenter.org/wp-content/uploads/2012/04/history-of-cmsd-schools1.pdf.

Marriage licenses. (1908, December 2). *Monitor-Press,* 1.

Marriage license. (1930, November 28). Montana, U.S., Lake County, Marriage Index and Records, Vol 1-2: 1923-1959. https://www.ancestry.com/imageviewer/collections/61578/images/48279_555422-00489?pId=90546876.

Martin Cooperman Obituary. (2006, February 4). *Berkshire Eagle.*

Marx, O. (1993). Adolf Meyer and psychiatric training at the Phipps Clinic: an interview with Theodore Lidz. *History of Psychiatry*, *4,* 245-269.

May, J.D. (n.d.). Cantonment. *The Encyclopedia of Oklahoma History and Culture.* https://www.okhistory.org/publications/enc/entry?entry=CA049.

Mayberry, M. (2020). *On a cough and a prayer: the Modern Woodmen Sanitorium and the tuberculosis industry in the Pikes Peak region.* Colorado Springs Pioneers Museum. https://www.cspm.org/wp-content/uploads/2020/06/ON-A-COUGH-AND-A-PRAYER.pdf.

McQuown, N.A. (1955). Dr. Otto Will does three therapeutic interviews (1952): Interview microanalysis (audio recording). Online Language Archive, University of Chicago.

MeasuringWorth, (2025). Purchasing power today of a US dollar transaction in the past, URL: www.measuringworth.com/ppowerus/

Medicine: Guadalcanal neurosis. (1943, May 24). *Time.* https://time.com/archive/6866180/medicine-guadalcanal-neurosis.

Mendelson, E. (2017). *Early Auden, later Auden: A critical biography*. Princeton University Press.

Michels, R. (2019). In memoriam: Roy Schafer, Ph.D., 1922-2018. *The Psychoanalytic Quarterly*, *88*(1), 173-174.

Millet, J. A. (1969). Austen Fox Riggs: his significance to American psychiatry of today. *American Journal of Psychiatry*, *125*(7), 948-953.

Mitchell, S.A. (1988/2017). The intrapsychic and the interpersonal: different theories, different domains, or historical artifacts? In Stern, D.B. & Hirsch, I. (Eds.). *The interpersonal perspective in psychoanalysis, 1960s-1990s* (pp. 218-238). Routledge.

Minnesota Digital Library. (n,d.). Minnesota immigrants: People on the move. https://collection.mndigital.org/exhibits/minnesota-immigrants-people-on-the-move/feature/europeans.

Mooney, R.F. (1993, November 29). The strengths of Dr. Will. *Berkshire Eagle*, 10.

Moore, B. (1999). Gordon/Graham: Two recent accounts of psychotherapy with Leslie Farber. *Salmagundi, 122*, 256-267.

Moore, L. C. (1976). William Alanson White — a biography (1870-1937). In A. R. D'Amore (Ed.) *William Alanson White: The Washington years, 1903-1937* (pp. 13-17). DHEW Publication No. ADM 76-298, U.S. Government Printing Office.

Moore, M. (1938). The ingestion of iodine as a method of attempted suicide. *New England Journal of Medicine, 219*(11), pp. 383-388.

Moore, S. (1982, October 10). The view from a narrow window: Symposium honors life work of former Riggs director. *Berkshire Sampler*, P4-6.

Mondragon, S. (n.d.). Colorado Springs. *Colorado Encyclopedia.* https://coloradoencyclopedia.org/article/colorado-springs#id-field-additional-information-htm.

Much Truth in Old Saw. (1962, March 2). *Evening World-Herald*, 8.

Murphy, B.A. (2003). *Wild Bill: The legend and life of William O. Douglas*. Random House.

Mutsu, I. (1993). Tojo: how he was, an introduction. In E.P. Hoyt, *Warlord: Tojo against the world* (pp. xv-xix). Cooper Square Press.

Nathanson, D. (1987). Introduction to the sense of shame in psychosis: random comments on shame in the psychotic experience by O.A. Will, Jr. In D. Nathanson (Ed.). *The many faces of shame* (pp. 308-309). Guilford Press.

Nebraska State Historical Society. (n.d.). Keeling, William Henry (03/18/1835-03/06/1920). https://nebraska.lyrasistechnology.org/agents/people/21286.

Neill, J.R. (1982). Biographical introduction to the work of Carl Whitaker, MD. In J.R. Neill & D.P. Kniskern (Eds.) *From psyche to system: The evolving therapy of Carl Whitaker* (pp. 1-20). Guilford.

Noble, T. D. (1976). Discussion of paper by Dr. D'Amore. In A. R. D'Amore (Ed.) *William Alanson White: The Washington years, 1903-1937* (pp. 95-100). DHEW Publication No. ADM 76-298, U.S. Government Printing Office.

NPAP. (2021). *The training institute of NPAP: The National Psychological Association for Psychoanalysis*. NPAP.

Obituaries: Charles Oscar Giese. (1957). *American Review of Tuberculosis and Pulmonary Diseases, 75*(2), 352.

Ogden, E. (2022). *On not knowing how to love and other essays*. University of Chicago Press.

O'Neal, B. (1980). *Henry Brown: The outlaw-marshal.* Creative Publishing.

O'Neal, B. (2008). *Border Queen Caldwell: Toughest town on the Chisholm Trail.* Eakin Press.

Orcutt, C. (2018). The schizoid analysts who brought relationship to psychoanalysis. *Clio's Psyche, 24*(2), 135-153.

Orsborn, J. (n.d.) Lloyd "Pappy" Shaw - CSPM. *Colorado Springs Pioneers Museum.* https://www.cspm.org/cos-150-story/lloyd-shaw.

Orton, V. (1979). *Vermont afternoons with Robert Frost.* Alan C. Hood & Company.

Parini, J. (1999). *Robert Frost: A life*. Henry Holt & Co.

Parker, B. (1962). *My language is myself.* Basic Books.

Parker, B. (1978). *A mingled yarn*. Yale University Press.

Parker, B. (1987). *The evolution of a psychiatrist: Memoirs of a woman doctor*. Yale University Press.

Payne, S.G. (2008). *Franco and Hitler: Spain, Germany, and World War II.* Yale University Press.

Peattie, D.C. (1941). An Atlantic portrait: Dr. Austen Fox Riggs. *The Atlantic.* https://www.theatlantic.com/magazine/archive/1941/08/dr-austen-fox-riggs/653891.

Pepper, C. (2019). Damn the torpedos! A treatment memoir. *Contemporary Psychoanalysis, 55*(1-2), 99-115.

Percy, W. (1972, September 16). A doctor talks with the south and its young heroes. *The National Observer*, p. 14.

Perry, H.S. (1962). Introduction. In H.S. Sullivan *Schizophrenia as a human process*, xi-xxxv. Norton.

Perry, H.S. (1982). *Psychiatrist of America: The life of Harry Stack Sullivan*. Harvard University Press.

Phillips, A. (2021). *The cure for psychoanalysis*. Confer Books.

Phillips, C. (2022). *My trade is mystery*. Yale University Press.

Plakun, E.M. (2021). The man who could see with his heart. *Psychiatry*, *84,* 17-20.

Prabook: Otto Allen Will. (n.d.). https://prabook.com/web/otto_allen.will/787323.

Puig-Guri, J. (1942). General principles in the treatment of wounds and fractures in the Spanish war. *The Military Surgeon*, *91*(1), 39 —48.

Quotes. (1971, May 5). *Berkshire Eagle*, 25.

Ralph, R.A. (2004). Sheppard Pratt and a giant in psychiatry. *Maryland Medicine 5*(4), 19-20.

Rampersad, A. (2007). *Ralph Ellison: A biography*. Alfred A. Knopf.

Ranzato, G. (1999). *The Spanish Civil War*. Interlink Books.

Ratsabout, S. (2022). Immigrants and Refugees in Minnesota: Connecting Past and Present. https://www.mnopedia.org/immigrants-and-refugees-minnesota-connecting-past-and-present.

Rauchway, E. (2003). *Murdering McKinley: The making of Theodore Roosevelt's America*. Hill and Wang Books.

Read, C. (1940). Consequences of Metrazol shock therapy. *American Journal of Psychiatry*, *97*(3), 667.

Religion: I & Thou (1956, January 26). *Time*. https://time.com/archive/6799364/religion-i-thou.

Renik, O. (2006). *Practical psychoanalysis for therapists and patients*. Other Press.

Richards, A.D. & Mosher, P.W. (2006). Abraham Arden Brill, 1874-1948. *American Journal of Psychiatry*, *163*(3), 386.

Richardson, H.K. (1935). Psychopathy and the general practitioner. *The New England Journal of Medicine*, *213*(17), 787-795.

Richardson, R.D. (1995). *Emerson: The mind on fire*. University of California Press.

Ridenour, J.M. & Zimmerman, B.F. (2017). The evolution of psychological testing at the Austen Riggs Center: A theoretical analysis. *Journal of Personality Assessment*, *101*(1), 1-10.

Rilke, R.M. (2002). *Letters to a Young Poet*. Dover Press. (Original work published 1905)

Rioch, D. McK. (1984). Dexter Bullard, Sr., and Chestnut Lodge. *Psychiatry, 47*(1), 1-8.

Rioch, D. McK. (1985). Recollections of Harry Stack Sullivan and of the development of his interpersonal psychiatry. *Psychiatry, 48*, 141-158.

Rioch, M.J. (1960). The meaning of Martin Buber's 'elements of the interhuman' for the practice of psychotherapy. *Psychiatry, 23*(2): 133-140.

Rioch, M.J. (1986). Fifty years at the Washington School of Psychiatry. *Psychiatry, 49*(1), 33-44.

Roazen, P. (1999). Introduction. In J.B. Agassi (Ed.), *Martin Buber on psychology and psychotherapy: Essays, letters, and dialogues* (pp. xix-xxvi). Syracuse University Press.

Robert Bergman, MD. (n.d.). Northwest Alliance for Psychoanalytic Study. https://www.nwaps.org/about/robert-bergman-md.

Robert Knight of Riggs Center. (1966, May 1). *The New York Times*, 88. https://www.nytimes.com/1966/05/01/archives/dr-robert-knight-of-riggs-center-medical-director-of-mental-clinic.html.

Rodríguez, A.R. & Rodríguez, J. (2017). Oklahoma history: Fort Supply: The grocer of the west. https://www.hhhistory.com/2017/06/oklahoma-history-fort-supply-grocer-of.html.

Rose, A. C. (2005). Putting the south on the psychological map: The impact of region and race on the human sciences during the 1930s. *The Journal of Southern History 71*(2), 321-356.

Rosen, T. (2022). Bruch, Brunhilde [Hilde]. *Texas State Historical Association (TSHA)*. https://www.tshaonline.org/handbook/entries/bruch-brunhilde-hilde.

Rubin, J.B. (2014). Each individual is a surprise: A conversation with Marianne Horney Eckardt. *The American Journal of Psychoanalysis 74*(2), 115-122.

Rudnytsky, P.L. (2011). In praise of Nina Coltart. In Rudnytsky, P.L., & Preston, G. (Eds.). *Her hour come round at last: A garland for Nina Coltart* (pp. 163-186). Karnac Books.

Russell, B. (2002). *Yours faithfully, Bertrand Russell.* (R. Perkins, Ed.). Open Court.

Rytand, D.A. (1984). *Medicine and The Stanford University School of Medicine circa 1932: The way it was.* Stanford University School of Medicine.

Rytand, D.A., Cox, A.J., & Hilgard, E.R. (1962). *Memorial resolution: Arthur L. Bloomfield (1888-1962)*. https://purl.stanford.edu/bp205bd0950.

Samway, P.H. (1997). *Walker Percy: A life*. Farrar, Straus & Giroux.

Schoenberg, D. (2020). How the death of a child can impact a marriage. *Family Therapy Magazine, 19*(4). https://ftm.aamft.org/how-the-death-of-a-child-can-impact-a-marriage.

Schlein, S. (2016). *The clinical Erik Erikson: A psychoanalytic method of engagement and activation*. Routledge.

Schulz, C. (1987). Sullivan's influence on Sheppard Pratt. *Journal of the American Academy of Psychoanalysis, 15*(2), 247-259.

Schultz, D. (2025). Combat fatigue: how stress in battle was felt (and treated) in WWII. *Warfare History Network*. https://warfarehistorynetwork.com/combat-fatigue-how-stress-in-battle-was-felt-and-treated-in-wwii.

Schwartz, M.S. (1996). *Letting go*. Delta Books.

Schwartz, M.S. & Will, G.T. (1953). Low morale and mutual withdrawal on a mental hospital ward. *Psychiatry, 16*(4), 337-353.

Scott, J.P. (1987). The emotional basis of attachment and separation. In J. Sacksteder, D. Schwartz, & Y. Akabane (Eds.), *Attachment and the therapeutic process: Essays in honor of Otto Allen Will, Jr.* (pp. 43-62). International Universities Press.

Scull, A. (2005a). *Madhouse: A tragic tale of megalomania and modern medicine*. Yale University Press.

Scull, A. (2005b, April 24). A monster or a medical genius. *Los Angeles Times*. https://www.latimes.com/archives/la-xpm-2005-apr-24-bk-scull24-story.html.

Self, B.E. (2010). Dull Knife (ca. 1810-1883). The Encyclopedia of Oklahoma History and Culture. https://www.okhistory.org/publications/enc/entry?entry=DU004.

Shaw, D.S. (1973). *Christmas poems*. Independently published.

Sheriff's Sales. (1866, October 12). *Times-Picayune*, 6.

Shutter, M.D. (1923). G.A. Will. In *History of Minneapolis: Gateway to the northwest*; Vol.III (p.148). S.J. Clarke.

Silver, A-L. S. (1997). Chestnut Lodge, then and now. *Contemporary Psychoanalysis, 33*(2), 227-249.

Silver, A-L. S. (2000). The current relevance of Fromm-Reichmann's works. *Psychiatry*, *63*(4), 308-322.

Silverberg, W. V. (1952). *Childhood experience and personal destiny: A psychoanalytic theory of neurosis*. Springer Publishing Company.

Silverman, K. (1991). *Edgar A. Poe: Mournful and never-ending remembrance*. Harper Collins.

Singer, E. (2014). The patient aids the analyst: some clinical and theoretical observations. In Stern, D.B., Mann, C.H., Kantor, S. & G. Schlesinger (Eds.). *Pioneers of interpersonal psychoanalysis* (pp. 157-168). Routledge.

Skal, D.J. (2016). *Something in the blood: The untold story of Bram Stoker, the man who wrote* Dracula. Liveright Publishing.

Skårderud, F. (2009). Bruch revisited and revised. *European Eating Disorders Review*, *17*, 83-88.

Skårderud, F. (2013). Hilde Bruch (1904 —1984) — the constructive use of ignorance. *Advances in Eating Disorders: Theory, Research and Practice*, *1*(2), 174-181.

Slavinsky, A.T. & Krauss, J.B. (1980). Mutual withdrawal …or Gwen Tudor revisited. *Perspectives in Psychiatric Care*, *18*(5), 195-203.

Smith, J.E. (2007). *FDR*. Random House.

Snyder, T. (2024). *On freedom*. Crown Books.

Solem, B. (2024). Between decks on a sailing vessel. https://www.norwayheritage.com/steerage.asp.

Solomon, H.C. (1946). Karl Murdock Bowman, M.D., president 1944-1946: a biographical sketch. *American Journal of Psychiatry*, *103*(1), 18-19.

Steiner, E.A. (1906). *On the trail of the immigrant*. Fleming H. Revell Co.

Strupp, H.H. (1968). Psychoanalytic therapy of the individual. In Marmor, J. (Ed.). *Modern psychoanalysis* (pp. 293-342). BasicBooks.

Staatsarchiv Hamburg. (2008). Hamburg, Deutschland; Hamburger Passagierlisten; Volume: 373-7 I, VIII A 1 Band 028 A; Page: 25; Microfilm No.: K_1718.

Stanford Eating Clubs Records. (n.d.). https://oac.cdlib.org/findaid/ark:/13030/kt9199s51w.

Sullivan, H.S. (1942). Sullivan, Harry Stack. In *Current biography: Who's news and why, 1942*, 812-814. H.W. Wilson Company.

Sullivan, H.S. (1949). The theory of anxiety and the nature of psychotherapy. *Psychiatry*, *12* (1), 3-12.

Sullivan, H.S. (1950). The illusion of personal individuality. *Psychiatry*, *13,* 317-332.

Sullivan, H.S. (1953a). *Conceptions of modern psychiatry*. W. W. Norton.

Sullivan, H.S. (1953b). *The interpersonal theory of psychiatry* (H. S. Perry & M. L. Gawel, Eds.). W. W. Norton.

Sullivan, H.S. (1954). *The psychiatric interview* (H. S. Perry & M. L. Gawel, Eds.). W. W. Norton.

Sullivan, H.S. (1956). *Clinical studies in psychiatry* (H. S. Perry, M. L. Gawel, & M. Gibbon, Eds.). W. W. Norton.

Sullivan, H.S. (1962). *Schizophrenia as a human process* (H. S. Perry, Ed.). W. W. Norton.

Sullivan, P. (2007, June 22). Gwen Will, 89; NIH official advanced psychiatric nursing. *Washington Post.* https://www.washingtonpost.com/archive/local/2007/06/23/gwen-will-89-nih-official-advanced-psychiatric-nursing/9f2ad10d-659b-49c3-8d4c-72d60d0f0602.

Summers, D. (2019, June 19). From the sidelines: former heavyweight champ Jack Dempsey cut his teeth in gold camp. *Pikes Peak Courier*, https://gazette.com/pikespeakcourier/from-the-sidelines-former-heavyweight-champ-jack-dempsey-cut-his-teeth-in-gold-camp/article_4e1a9ed4-8e0f-11e9-a0be-cb0c0c17a3a4.html.

Sutherland, J.D. (1989). *Fairbairn's journey into the interior*. Free Association Books.

Swift, D. (2017). *The bughouse: The poetry, politics, and madness of Ezra Pound*. Farrar, Straus & Giroux.

Symington, N. (2006). *A healing conversation: How healing happens*. Karnac.

Szalita, A. (2015). Some thoughts on empathy: the eighteenth annual Frieda Fromm-Reichmann memorial lecture. *Psychiatry*, *78*(2), 103-113. (Original work published 1976)

Teicher, C.M. (2018). We begin in gladness: How poets progress, essays. Graywolf Press.

The Broadmoor. (n.d.). Colorado Encyclopedia. https://coloradoencyclopedia.org/article/broadmoor.

Thomas, A.J. (2020). *Cholera: The Victorian plague*. Pen & Sword.

Thomas, D. (2022). *A Child's Christmas in Wales*. New Directions. (Original work published 1952)

Thompson, M.G. & Thompson, S. (1998). Interview with Dr. Otto Allen Will, Jr. *Contemporary Psychoanalysis*, *34*(2), 289-394.

Thompson, M.G. (2025). *Existential psychoanalysis: A contemporary introduction*. Routledge.

Thoreau, H.D. (1993). Life without principle. In *Civil disobedience and other essays* (pp. 75-90). Dover Press. (Original work published 1863)

Toland, J. (1992). *Adolf Hitler: The definitive biography*. Anchor Books.

Tribute. (2007). Gwen Elizabeth Tudor Will, RN. *Journal of Psychosocial Nursing and Mental Health Services*, *45*(10), 14.

Trueta, J. (1943). *The principles and practice of war surgery. With reference to the biological method of the treatment of war wounds and fractures*. C. V. Mosby.

Tudor, G. (1952). A sociopsychiatric nursing approach to intervention in a problem of mutual withdrawal on a mental hospital ward. *Psychiatry*, *15*, 193-217.

Unger, H.G. (2018). *Dr. Benjamin Rush: The founding father who healed a wounded nation*. Da Capo Press.

U.S. Census Bureau. (1870a). Census of population and housing. https://www.census.gov/library/publications/1870/dec/garfield-report.html.

U.S. Census Bureau. (1870b). Schedule 1. https://www.ancestry.com/imageviewer/collections/7163/images/4263680_00078?pId=15508302

U.S. Census Bureau. (1880). Schedule 1. https://www.ancestry.com/imageviewer/collections/6742/images/4241839-00249?pId=48105929.

U.S. Census Bureau. (1900a). Schedule 1. https://www.ancestry.com/imageviewer/collections/7602/images/4120166_00871?pId=4917954

U.S. Census Bureau. (1900b). Schedule 1. https://www.ancestry.com/imageviewer/collections/7602/images/4120286_00641?pId=26532549.

U.S. Census Bureau. (1910). Census of population and housing. https://www2.census.gov/library/publications/decennial/1910/bulletins/demographics/122-estimates-of-population.pdf.

U.S. Census Bureau. (1920a). 1920-Population. https://www.ancestry.com/imageviewer/collections/6061/images/4300698_01143?pId=43814446.

U.S. Census Bureau. (1920b). Total Population for Iowa's Incorporated Places: 1850-2000. https://data.iowadatacenter.org/datatables/PlacesAll/plpopulation18502000.pdf.

U.S. Census Bureau. (1920). Schedule 1. https://www.ancestry.com/imageviewer/collections/6061/images/4313236-00269?pId=45696330.

U.S. Census Bureau. (1930a). Population Schedule. https://www.ancestry.com/search/collections/6224/records/114527421.

U.S. Census Bureau. (1930b). Population Schedule. https://www.ancestry.com/search/collections/6224/records/28114356.

U.S. Census Bureau. (1940). Population Schedule. https://www.ancestry.com/imageviewer/collections/2442/images/m-t0627-00319-00360?pId=71152006.

U.S. Census Bureau. (1970). 1970 Census of Population and Housing. https://www.census.gov/library/publications/1972/dec/phc-1.html.

U.S. National Park Service. (2024). Broadmoor Hotel. http://www.nps.gov/places/broadmoor-hotel.htm.

U.S. Navy and Marine Corps. (1944). *Register of commissioned and warrant officers of the United States Navy and Marine Corps*. U.S. Government Printing Office, p. 349.

USS *Stringham* DD-83 Ship History. (2016). *Dictionary of American Naval Fighting Ships*. https://www.history.navy.mil/research/histories/ship-histories/danfs/s/stringham-ii.html.

Vanier, J. (1998). *Becoming human*. Paulist Press.

Wabash Native dies in Southwest. (1925, October 28). *Daily Republican-Register*, 6.

Wallerstein, R.S. (1986). *Forty-Two lives in treatment: A study of psychoanalysis and psychotherapy*. Guilford Press.

Wallerstein, R.S. (1988). Psychoanalysis and psychotherapy: relative roles reconsidered. *Annual of Psychoanalysis*, *16*, 129-151.

Walls, L.D. (2017). *Henry David Thoreau: A life*. University of Chicago Press.

Wallis, M. (2007). *Billy the Kid: The endless ride*. W.W. Norton.

Waugaman, R.M. (2012). Sullivan and his polarizing legacy. *Psychiatry 75*(1), 26-31.

Waugaman, R.M. (2019). Chestnut Lodge: an unreal place. *Contemporary Psychoanalysis*, *55*(1), 1-21.

Weber, H. (1907). Climate as a factor in the treatment of tuberculosis. *The British Journal of Tuberculosis 1*(1), 46-52.

Weidner, D. (2024). Till death do us part: the political theology of "kulturkampf." *Journal of the Theoretical Humanities*, *29*(3), 109-118.

Weigert, E.V. (1959). Foreword. In D.M. Bullard (Ed.), *Psychoanalysis and psychotherapy: Selected papers of Frieda Fromm-Reichmann* (pp. v-x). University of Chicago Press.

Weininger, B. I. (1989). Chestnut Lodge — the early years: Krishnamurti and Buber. In A-L. Silver (Ed.), *Psychoanalysis and psychosis* (pp. 495-512). International Universities Press.

Wellington, A. (2022). Dr. Manfred J. Sakel: discoverer of insulin shock therapy — psychiatry in history. *British Journal of Psychiatry*, *221*(5), 682.

White, W.A. (1938). *The autobiography of a purpose*. Doubleday, Doran, & Co.

Whitehorn, J.C. (1950). Psychodynamic considerations in the treatment of psychotic patients. *Medical Journal of the University of Western Ontario*, *20*(2), 27-41.

Whitehorn, J.C. (1955). Understanding psychotherapy. *American Journal of Psychiatry*, *112*(5), 328-355.

Will, O.A. (1946). Remarks on the current problems of psychiatric therapy. *Quarterly Review of Psychiatry and Neurology*, *1*, 438-449.

Will, O.A. & Cohen, R.A. (1947). A report of a recorded interview in the course of psychotherapy. *Psychiatry*, *16*, 263-282.

Will, O.A. & Duval, A.M. (1947). The use of electro-shock therapy in psychiatric illnesses complicated by pulmonary tuberculosis. *Journal of Nervous and Mental Disorders*, *105*, 637-646.

Will, O.A., Rehfeldt, F.C, & Neumann, M.A. (1948). A fatality in electro-shock therapy: Report of a case and review of certain previously described cases. *Journal of Nervous and Mental Disorders, 107*, 105-126.

Will, O.A. (1949a, February 6). The career of Dr. Harry Stack Sullivan: D. C. doctor pitted psychiatry against war. *The Washington Post*, B5.

Will, O.A. (1949b). 'Data' and the psychiatric patient. *Journal of Clinical Pastoral Work, 2*, 91-107.

Will, O.A. (1954). Introduction. In H.S. Sullivan, *The psychiatric interview* (pp. ix-xxii). W.W. Norton.

Will, O.A. (1959a). Human relatedness and the schizophrenic reaction. *Psychiatry, 22*, 205-223.

Will, O.A. (1959b). Review of *Schizophrenia*, by M.A. Sakel. *Journal of Nervous and Mental Disorders, 128*, 374-378.

Will, O.A. (1960). The schizophrenic reaction and the interpersonal field. In L. Appleby, J.M. Scher, & J. Cumming (Eds.), *Chronic schizophrenia* (pp. 194-223). The Free Press.

Will, O.A. (1961a). Paranoid development and the concept of self: psychotherapeutic intervention. *Psychiatry, 24*, 74-86.

Will, O.A. (1961b). Process, psychotherapy, and schizophrenia. In A. Burton (Ed.), *Psychotherapy of the psychoses* (pp. 10-42). Basic Books.

Will, O.A. (1961c). Psychotherapy in reference to the schizophrenic reaction. In M. I. Stein (Ed.), *Contemporary psychotherapies* (pp. 128-140). The Free Press.

Will, O.A. (1962). Processes in psychoanalytic education. In J. Masserman (Ed.). *Psychoanalytic education* (pp. 84-100). Grune & Stratton.

Will, O.A. (1963a, March). The awareness of need and the schizophrenic reaction. Presented at the Fortieth Annual Meeting of the American Orthopsychiatric Association, Washington, DC.

Will, O.A. (1963b). Problems in the psychoanalytic treatment of depressions. *Bulletin of the Association for Psychoanalytic Medicine 2*(3), 35-40.

Will, O.A. (1964). Schizophrenia and the psychotherapeutic field. *Contemporary Psychoanalysis 1*, 1-29.

Will, O.A. (1965). The beginning of psychotherapeutic experience. In A. Burton (Ed.). *Modern psychotherapeutic practice* (pp. 3-35). Science & Behavior Books.

Will, O.A. (1966). Discussion: a case of depression in a homosexual young man. *Contemporary Psychoanalysis 3*(1), 14-20.

Will, O.A. (1968a). Proposal for a psychotherapeutic center. *International Journal of Psychiatry 6*(6), 442-448.

Will, O.A. (1968b). Schizophrenia and psychotherapy. In J. Marmor (Ed.), *Modern psychoanalysis: New directions and perspectives* (pp. 551-573). Basic Books.

Will, O.A. (1968/1987). The reluctant patient, the unwanted psychotherapist — and coercion. In J. Sacksteder, D. Schwartz, & Y. Akabane (Eds.), *Attachment and the therapeutic process: Essays in honor of Otto Allen Will, Jr.* (pp. 299-331). International Universities Press.

Will, O.A. (1970a). Psychotherapy, schizophrenia and the identity of the therapist. In A. Appelbaum (Reporter), Transactions of the Topeka Psychoanalytic Society, *Bulletin of the Menninger Clinic, 34,* 387-389.

Will, O.A. (1970b). The relationship of schizophrenia to psychotherapy. *Journal of the National Association of Private Psychiatric Hospitals, 2,* 18-24.

Will, O.A. (1970c). The therapeutic use of self. *Medical Arts and Sciences, 24,* 3-14.

Will, O.A. (1971a). Commentary on 'Paranoia or persecution: The case of Schreber' by Morton Schatzman, *Family Process, 10,* 207-210.

Will, O.A. (1971b). The patient and the psychotherapist: comments on the "uniqueness" of their relationship. In B. Landis & E. Tauber (Eds.). *In the name of life: Essays in honor of Erich Fromm* (pp. 15-43). Holt, Rinehart & Winston.

Will, O.A. (1972). Psychotherapy and schizophrenia: Implications for human living. In D. Rubinstein & Y.O. Alanen (Eds.), *Psychotherapy of schizophrenia: Proceedings of the fourth international symposium, Turku, Finland, August 4-7, 1971.* (pp. 25-37). Excerpta Medica.

Will, O.A. (1973). Changing styles in the treatment of schizophrenia. *American Journal of Psychiatry, 130,* 152-155.

Will, O.A. (1974). Individual psychotherapy of schizophrenia. In R. Cancro, N. Fox, & L. Shapiro (Eds.). *Strategic intervention in schizophrenia: Current developments in treatment* (pp. 17-33), Behavioral Publications.

Will, O.A. (1975). The conditions of being therapeutic. In J.G. Gunderson & L.R. Mosher (Eds.). *Psychotherapy of schizophrenia* (pp. 53-65). Jason Aronson.

Will, O.A. (1977a). The future of the therapeutic relationship as an agent of change. In O.L. McCabe (Ed.). *Changing human behavior: Current therapies and future directions* (pp. 5-19). Grune & Stratton.

Will, O.A. (1977b June 6). Halfway houses 'greatly needed.' *The Berkshire Eagle*, 20.

Will, O.A. (1977c). Psychiatry at the Austen Riggs Center. In C. Chiland (Ed.). *Long-term treatments of psychotic states* (pp. 361-374). Human Sciences Press.

Will, O.A. (1979). Comments on the professional life of the psychotherapist. *Contemporary Psychoanalysis, 15*, 560-576.

Will, O.A. (1980). Comments on the "elements" of schizophrenia, psychotherapy, and the schizophrenic person. In J.S. Strauss et al. (Eds.), *The psychotherapy of schizophrenia* (pp. 157-166). Plenum Publishing.

Will, O.A. (1981a, October). Memories of Harry Stack Sullivan. Unpublished paper presented at Chestnut Lodge Sanitarium, Rockville, MD.

Will, O.A. (1981b). Values and the Psychotherapist. *The American Journal of Psychoanalysis, 41,* 203-212.

Will, O.A. (1983). Foreword. In J. G. Gunderson, O. A. Will, & L. R. Mosher (Eds.). *Principles and practice of milieu therapy* (pp. vii-x). Jason Aronson.

Will, O.A. (1987a). Illuminations of the human condition. In J. Sacksteder, D. Schwartz, & Y. Akabane (Eds.), *Attachment and the therapeutic process: Essays in honor of Otto Allen Will, Jr.* (pp. 241-261). International Universities Press.

Will, O.A. (1987b). The sense of shame in psychosis: random comments on shame in the psychotic experience. In D.L. Nathanson (Ed.). *The many faces of shame* (pp. 308-317). Guilford Press.

Will, O.A. (1989a). Foreword. In Bonime, W. *Collaborative psychoanalysis: Anxiety, depression, dreams, and personality change*. Associated University Press.

Will, O.A. (1989b). In memory of Frieda. In A. Silver (Ed.), *Psychoanalysis and psychosis* (pp. 131-144). International Universities Press.

Will, O.A. (2021). On "caring" in psychotherapy. *Psychiatry, 84,* 2-15.

Wilson, J.L. (1999). *Stanford University School of Medicine and the predecessor schools: An historical perspective*. Lane Medical Library.

Wineapple, B. (2003). *Hawthorne: A life*. Alfred A. Knopf.

Woodward, E.R. (1987). The history of vagotomy. *The American Journal of Surgery, 153*(1), 9-17.

Yalom, I.D. (2002). *The gift of therapy*. HarperCollins.

Yalom, I.D. (2017). *Becoming myself: A psychiatrist's memoir*. BasicBooks.

Yanni, C. (2007). *The architecture of madness: Insane asylums in the United States.* University of Minnesota Press.

Young, B. (2012, August 23). Dr John C. Whitehorn: a wise and gentle man. *Psychiatric Times.* https://www.psychiatrictimes.com/view/dr-john-c-whitehorn-wise-and-gentle-man.

Young, J. (2020, May 19). The early years of Cheyenne Mountain School: the Cheyenne experience. https://gazette.com/cheyenneedition/the-early-years-of-cheyenne-mountain-school-the-cheyenne-experience/article_01e3238c-9468-11ea-b7c7-5f9d0389e255.html.

Yudofsky, S. (1987). Hilde, the teacher. *Journal of the American Medical Association, 257*(7), 975.

Yudofsky, S. (1996). Foreword. In J.H. Bruch, *Unlocking the Golden Cage: An Intimate Biography of Hilde Bruch, M.D.* (pp. vii-xiv). Gürze Books.

Ziff, K. (2012). *Asylum on the hill: History of a healing landscape.* Ohio University Press.

# Index


**A**

Albizzi, Marquis Nicoló Negli, 37–39, 46
American Psychiatric Association, 70, 91, 194, 217
American Psychoanalytic Association, 138, 151, 194, 195
Anémone, 36
Anxiety, 7, 27, 31, 46, 50, 70, 75, 87, 90, 98, 102, 104, 110, 111, 123, 140, 146, 156, 157, 169, 209, 210, 212, 213, 217, 230, 232, 247–248, 253, 254, 257
  defined, 241, 265
  hyper-anxiety, 77
  in personifications, 228
  in psychotherapy, 255–256
  symptoms. 238, 239, 242, 243
Attachment theory, 49, 163, 225
Austen Riggs Center (ARC), 3–4, 7, 106, 130, 142, 149, 188–190, 191ff, 209, 210, 215,
  founding of, 192–193
Automatism. 172
  defined, 265

**B**

Baylor University, 128–129
Behavior, defined, 265
Belief, defined, 265
Bellinger, Clarence, 95
Benét, Stephen Vincent, xxi
Benjamin, John D., 147–148
Bergman, Robert, 205
"Between decks" passage, 13
Bismarck, Otto von, 11–12
Blackburn, Isaac Wright, 78
Blackburn Laboratory, 78, 81
Bloch, Donald, 197
Bloland, Sue Erikson, 155, 277
Bloomfield, Arthur L., 56–57
Bourgeois, Wendy, 6, 248
Bourke-White, Margaret, 93
Bowlby, John, 163, 227, 228, 242, 243, 245, 267
Bowman, Karl Murdock, 217
Brehmer, Hermann, 26
Brenman-Gibson, Margaret, 197, 203
  early support for OAW at Austen Riggs, 195
  first American lay analyst, 195
  hostility toward OAW, 197
Brill, Abraham Arden, 115
Broadmoor Hotel, 45
Brown, Henry Newton, 28
Bruch, Hilde
  attempted suicide, 126
  death of, 131
  eating disorders, 131
  *The Golden Cage*, 129
  interest in schizophrenia, 128
  as inquisitive, 125, 129
  *Learning Psychotherapy*, 129–130
  as OAW's teacher, xix, 125
  resistance to lay analysts, 117
  view of Harry Stack Sullivan, 127–128
  view of Frieda Fromm-Reichmann, 127
Buber, Martin M., xv, 184, 224
  appearance of, 183
  contact with Freud, 181
  friendship with Frieda Fromm-Reichmann, 183
  *I and Thou*, 181-182
  lectures at the Washington School of Psychiatry, 179–180, 182
  meeting with patient at Chestnut Lodge, 183
Bullard, Anne (neé Wilson), 136
Bullard, Dexter Means, 116, 133, 134, 136, 138, 140, 141, 152, 173

education of, 135
fondness for bourbon, 138
OAW's teacher, as, 125
patient of Harry Stack Sullivan, 103
pragmatic approach to patients, 112, 139
training analysis with Ernest Hadley, 137, 153
Bullard, Ernest Luther
death of, 135–136
early psychiatric career of, 134
purchase of Chestnut Lodge, 134–135
Bullard, Roaslie (neé Means), 134, 135

**C**

Caldwell, Kansas, 15, 18–20, 24, 28–29
Campbell, Charles McFie, 135
Cantonment, 17–18, 19
Catatonia, 49
defined, 265
Chapman, Ross McClure, 90–91, 92
Chernin, Kim, xvii, 3, 4, 28, 48, 62, 66, 105, 109, 120, 123, 158–159, 160, 172, 175, 187, 189, 198, 209, 218, 246, 259, 277
Chestnut Lodge, 84, 93, 104, 116, 126, 130, 133, 136, 139, 145, 148, 158, 161, 183, 188–189, 198, 202, 203, 205
architecture of, 134
Frieda Fromm-Reichmann at, 152–155
open conflict among staff, 160–161
psychoanalytic hospital for schizophrenics, as, 137–138
Woodlawn Hotel, as, 134
Cheyenne Mountain School, 4ff, 47, 48, 56, 82
annual Christmas plays, 36–37
basketball team, 38
Chicago College of Medicine and Surgery, 89
Chisholm, Brock, 141
Chronic mental disorder, 50, 78, 140
defined, 265
Clinical study: "Anne,"164ff
Clinical study: "John," 109ff
Clinical study: "Kay," 211ff
Clinical study: "Miss A," 166ff
Clinical study: "Miss B," 169ff
Clinical study: "Miss C," 210ff
Clinical study: "Miss D," 212ff
Clinical study: "Miss M," 172ff
Clinical study: '"Professor M," 175ff
Coercion, defined, 266
Cohen, Robert, 116, 138, 154, 168, 169, 277
description of Frieda Fromm-Reichmann's technique, 154
recording of psychotherapy sessions, 167–168
Colorado gold rush, 33
Colorado Springs, Colorado, 33–34, 35, 38, 48, 50, 51, 53, 101, 147–148,
"city of sunshine," 34
pulmonary health center, 34
Columbia University Graduate School, 144
Columbia University College of Physicians and Surgeons, 117
Consensual validation, 168
Control, defined, 266
Cornell University, 89, 188, 264
Cotton, Henry, 57–58
focal sepsis, 57
personal mental illness, 58
relationship with Adolf Meyer, 57–58
search for physical basis of mental illness, 58
Superintendent of Trenton State Hospital, as, 57–58
Cooperman, Martin, 142, 199
Associate Medical Director at ARC, 198
naval service, 198
opinion of Harry Stack Sullivan, 142

as writer, 199
Countertransference, 40, 166–169, 248, 254, 256
defined, 266
Covert, defined, 266
Critical period, 225–226
defined, 266
Cure, 257
defined, 266

**D**

Dempsey, Jack, 45–46
sparring match with OAW, 45
Depression, 59, 75, 77, 159, 273
defined, 266
Desire, 92, 172, 214, 229, 234, 245, 256
defined, 266
Despair, 73, 75, 158, 183, 225, 237, 248
defined, 267
Dissociation, 168, 228, 242,
defined, 267
Dooley, Lucille, 115–116
Dull Knife's Raid (Northern Cheyenne Exodus), 17
Du Maurier, Daphne, 240
Dunham, Katharine, 93

**E**

Eckardt, Marianne Horney, 251
Education, defined, 267
Ego psychology, xx, 194, 195
Eiseley, Loren, 21
El Capitan Club, 49
Electroconvulsive Therapy (ECT), 79, 110, 164, 167, 170, 175, 210
Elgin, Will, 92
Ellison, Ralph Waldo, 93–94
Emerson, Ralph Waldo, xvi, xxi, 24, 35, 87, 88, 121, 232, 245, 252, 259, 260
Envy, 198–199
Erikson, Erik H., xx, 120, 155, 192, 195, 196, 197, 217, 218
conflict with OAW, 198–199, 202, 219
psychosocial developmental stages, 204, 225, 227
Erikson, Joan, 155
consulting Fromm-Reichmann, 155
distrust of psychoanalysis, 155
Erikson, Neil, 155
Evans, F. Barton, III, 196, 277

**F**

Fairbairn, W.R.D., 88, 113
Farber, Leslie H., 4, 101, 161, 175, 184, 209
boredom with Stockbridge, 199
conflicts with Harry Stack Sullivan, on, 179
existential psychoanalyst, as, 4
Martin Buber, on, 179–181
Ferenczi, Sandor, 151–152
Fink, Fred, 38, 39, 46
Fink, Lou, 38, 46
Focal sepsis, 57
Folk dancing, 37, 161
Foresight, 228
defined, 267
Forrestal, James, 77
Fort Leavenworth, 16
Franco-Prussian War, 10–11
Free Association Training Program, 219–220
Freeman, Walter Jackson II, 78–79
Freud, Anna, 194, 203
analyst to Erik Erikson, as, 195
views on psychosocial development, 195
Freud, Sigmund, xx, 54, 58, 59, 88, 116, 136, 142, 163, 181, 193, 203, 245
conception of mind, 224
figure of deification, as, xviii
*New Introductory Lectures on Psycho-Analysis*, 54
psychoanalytic assumptions, 250

psychosexual developmental stages, 224–225
relationship with Ferenczi, 152
repression, on, 241, 242
Fromm, Erich, 88, 116, 155, 182
relationship with Frieda Fromm-Reichmann, 152–153
views of clinical work, 88, 104
Fromm, Gerard M., 3–4, 5, 106, 138, 198, 209, 252, 277
Fromm-Reichmann, Frieda, 6, 115, 116, 117, 118, 126–127, 128, 147, 151, 155, 187
asexual, as, 152
characteristics as psychotherapist, 154
clinical supervisor, as, 133, 140
death of, 158
employment at Chestnut Lodge, 137, 139
fellow, Center for Advanced Study in the Behavioral Sciences, 176
godmother to Patrick Will, as, 157
hostility from classical analysts, 157
loss of hearing & loneliness, 158, 182–183
marriage to Erich Fromm, 152–153
OAW's analyst, as, 151, 157, 159, 167, 202
OAW's teacher, as, xix, 81, 111, 125
*Principles of Intensive Psychotherapy*, 156–157
Rumor of suicide, 158
stereotypes about men, 154
summer coverage at Chestnut Lodge, as, 154
vacations in New Mexico, 155
victim of rape, as, 152
Frost, Robert, xx, xxi, 26, 42, 83, 244–245

**G**

Gatchell, Horatio, 26
Gibson, Robert, 91, 138, 153–155, 277
Gibson, William, 197
Giese, Charles O., 34, 51–52
Gill, Merton, 195
Freudian metapsychology, on, 224
training analysis with Robert Knight, 203
Gleitsman, Joseph William, 26
Gordon, Emily Fox, 3–4, 7, 199
Gorney, James, xvii, 204, 209
Graham, Katharine, 199
Guadalcanal, 64ff
"Guadalcanal Neurosis," 69ff
"combat fatigue," 70, 78
Guiteau, Charles, 82
Guntrip, Harry, 88, 260

**H**

Hadley, Ernest, 115, 116, 137, 138, 153
Hall, Donald, 82, 260
Hall, Edward T., 3, 46, 116, 172, 199
Haney Family, 43
Havens, Leston, 102, 103, 254
Hawthorne, Nathanial, xxi, 87
Hill, Lewis, 115
Hirsch, Irwin, 5
Homosexuality, 90–91, 95, 217, 234
House Un-American Activities Committee (HUAC), 144
Horney, Karen, 140
Hotel Ritz, Paris, 141

**I**

Insulin Coma Therapy (ICT)/Insulin Shock Therapy (IST), 76–77, 164, 170, 210
Intensive Psychotherapy, xx, 84, 115, 129, 133, 146, 167
Internal Working Model, 228
defined, 267
International Congress on Mental Health, 141
*The Invisible Man*, 94
Iodine, 30

**J**
James, Henry, xvi
James, William, 192
Johns Hopkins University, 57, 115, 127, 136, 176, 187–188
  Phipps Clinic of, 127, 136
Johnson, Charles, 116
Jones, Ernest, 152

**K**
Kafka, John, 160, 277
Kaiser, Hellmuth, xx
Keeling, Caroline (Carrie), 16
Keeling, George, 16
Keeling, Henry Charles, 15–16
Keeling, Henry William, 15, 17, 18, 19
Keeling, Ida Barlow, 15, 20
Keeling, Jennett, 19
Keeling, Mary Ann, 16
Keeling, Nancy Hill, 16
Keeling, Sarah Johnston, 16
Keeling, William, 16, 17, 18
Kempf, Edward, 90
  "Kempf's Disease," 90
Kimberly, Charles H., 194
King, Francis, 240
Kirkbride, Thomas Story, 75–76
  Kirkbride hospitals, 75
Knight, Robert, 119, 189, 203
  clinician at Menninger Clinic, as, 194, 203
  death of, 189, 195
  as training analyst, 194
Knowledge, 88, 203, 206, 252
  defined, 267
Koch, Robert, 26
Kohut, Heinz, xx, 188, 250
*Kulturkampf*, 11–12

**L**
LaFollette, Robert, 134
Laing, R.D., 204–205, 219, 240
  *Knots*, 205
  meeting with OAW, 204
  mystification, on, 31, 42, 113
Lasswell, Harold, 92, 93
"Lavendar Scare," 234
Levenson, Edgar, 42, 100, 237, 241, 242
Liebenberg, Beatrice, 7, 117–118, 143, 277
Lifton, Robert Jay, 84, 120
Lofgren, Lars B., 195, 196
Loneliness, 43, 96, 98, 111, 158, 160, 183, 237, 246, 248
  defined, 267
Louisville Child Guidance Clinic, xx
Love, 7, 43, 87, 113, 171–172, 214, 234, 255, 260, 274, 275
  defined, 268
Lovecraft, H.P., 87, 194, 240
Lurie, Leon, 6, 277
Lynch, Thomas, 237

**M**
Maisel, Albert (Al), 74
Mare Island, 62, 70, 109
Maturity, 250
  defined, 268
Mayo Clinic, 83–84, 111
Mead, Margaret, 116, 155
Meduna, Ladislas von, 77
Melville, Henry, xvi, xxi
Menninger Clinic, 70, 93, 119, 137, 164, 165, 187, 189, 194, 203
Menninger, Florence, 239
Menninger Foundation Psychotherapy Research Project, 148
Menninger, Karl, 119, 189
Menninger, Roy, 189, 277
Menninger, William C., 77, 119, 189
Merton, Thomas, 4
Metrazol (pentylenetetrazol), 77
  emotional effects of, 77–78
Meyer, Adolf, 57–59, 115, 127
  Psychobiological approach to psychiatry, 57, 59, 127, 136
Mind, defined, 268
Minnesota, 13–14, 83, 84
Minneapolis, 14-15

Misattribution, 240, 243–244
Misattunement, 239–240
Mitchell, Steven, 244, 245
Modern Woodmen of America (MWA) Sanitorium, 34, 51
Moral treatment, 75, 135
Mount Zion Hospital, 206, 215, 218, 219, 235
Mussolini, Benito, 55, 82
Mystification, 31, 42, 128, 230, 243–245
  defined, 268

**N**

Naropa University, 188
Nathanson, Donald, 5
National Institute of Mental Health, 116, 145, 148
National Psychological Association for Psychoanalysis (NPAP), 116
Need, 226–227, 228, 234, 241, 243, 248
  defined, 268
Nellie Bly (Elizabeth Cochrane Seaman), 73, 75
Neutrality, 121, 210
  defined, 269
New England, xxi
New Hampshire, xxi
*The New York Herald*, 73
*The New York Tribune*, 73
*The New York World*, 73
Northern Cheyenne, 17-18

**O**

object constancy, 27
object relations theory, 88, 113, 154, 204, 218, 251
O'Connor, Flannery, 6
Ogden, Emily, 6, 251
One Genus Theorem, 90, 249
  defined, 269
"Operation Watchtower," 65
Orton, Vrest, 257

**P**

Panic, 90, 91, 259
  defined, 269
Paranoid solution to living, 231
  defined, 269
Parloff, Morris, 105, 277
Participant-Observation, xvi, 91, 145
Perry, Helen Swick, 96, 118
Personality, 59, 82, 93, 94, 99, 102, 117, 138, 169, 193, 196, 224, 226, 247, 255
  defined, 269
Phi Beta Kappa, 49, 53
Phillips, Adam, 257
Phillips, Carl, xvi, 260
Pittsfield, Massachusetts, 191, 205
Plakun, Eric, xvii, 5, 209
Poe, Edgar Allan, xvi, xxi, 24
Post-Traumatic Stress Disorder (PTSD), 78, 80
Pound, Ezra, 82–83
Problems in living, 6, 42, 88, 96, 113, 135, 214, 237, 238, 249, 269
  defined, 268
Professionalism, defined, 269
Prussia, 9, 10, 11, 12
*Psychiatry* (Journal), 99, 118, 142, 180, 184
*Psychoanalytic Review*, 139,
*Psychoanalytic Quarterly*, 5
Psychoanalysts, lay, 117, 151
Psychoneuroses, 192–193
Psychopathology
  *see* "problems in living"
Psychotherapy, defined, 269
Psychotic patients, 78, 90, 157
Puig-Guri, Jose, 144

**R**

Rank, Otto, xx, 135
Rapaport, David, 194, 202–203
Regression, 209, 238
  defined, 270
Reik, Theodor, 116
Relation, defined, 270

Renik, Owen, 5, 6, 235, 277
Resistance, 49, 129, 153, 156, 203
defined, 270
Richardson, Horace K., 194
Riggs, Austen Fox, 192–193
belief in care of the indigent, 193
strength of personality, 193
views on psychotherapy, 193
Rimpoche, Chögyam Trungpa, 183
tribute to OAW, 188
Rioch, David MacKenzie, 84–85, 97, 116, 136, 139, 229
Rioch, Margaret, 116, 179, 183, 196
Martin Buber, on, 183–184
Rilke, Rainier-Maria, 96
*Letters to a Young Poet*, 96
Rochester Child Guidance Clinic, xx
Rogers, Carl R., xx, 188,
Rockwell, Norman, 192, 199
Roswell, New Mexico, 27–29, 33, 34, 51
"cow town," as, 29
Wills' farm in, 29
Rowe, Adeline Emma, 59–60, 133
apartment shared with OAW, 60
death of first husband, 60
divorce from OAW, 80, 133
stress of losing a child, 80
Russell, Bertrand, 246

**S**

Saint Elizabeths Hospital, 70, 73, 74, 76, 78, 79, 82, 83, 84, 89, 90, 103–110, 115, 128, 133, 149
Architecture, 75
Blackburn Auditorium, 78
Kirkbride Hospital, 75
Sakel, Manfred J., 76–77
*San Francisco Examiner*, 60
Sapir, Edward, 92–93, 116, 217
Savo Island, Battle of, 66
Schafer, Roy, 195, 203
Schlein, Stephen, 3–4, 197–198, 277
"Schizoid analysts," 88, 128
Schizophrenia, 25, 50, 76, 77, 90, 91, 93, 128, 148, 152, 155, 159, 166, 198, 204, 214, 215, 217, 226, 229, 233, 238, 240, 246
defined, 270
treated as physical illness, 76–77
Schulz, Clarence, 101–103, 138, 154, 277
Schwartz, Daniel, 195
Schwartz, Morris (Morrie), 100, 145–146, 147
Scott, John, 163, 188
Searles, Harold, 138, 160
Security, 212, 227, 241
defined, 270
Security operations, 156, 242
Selective inattention, 145, 156, 228, 239, 241, 242, 243, 244, 266
defined, 270
The Self, 82, 90, 96, 99, 202, 227–228, 240, 242, 246, 250–251, 253, 256, 268, 271
defined, 270
Semrad, Elvin, 5
Sentiment, 113
defined, 270
Shame, 24, 50, 57, 94, 105, 214, 225, 237
defined, 271
Shaw, Dorothy Stott, 36, 37, 42, 43, 82
poet, as, 36, 42
Shaw, Lloyd "Pappy," 34, 35, 36, 37, 38, 39, 43
"Renaissance man," as, 35
source of identification, as, 39, 42, 46, 47
Sheppard and Enoch Pratt Hospital, 75, 87, 90–93, 102
Spanish Civil War, 55, 68, 144
S.S. *Hammonia*, 13, 14
Stanford University, 47–52, 53, 54, 55, 56, 57, 59, 83, 158, 179
Stanton, Alfred, 116
Steerage
*see* "between decks" passage

Stockbridge, Massachusetts, 149, 185, 190, 191–193, 199
Stoker, Bram, 245

stomach cancer, 24, 83
stomach resection, 83
Sullivan, Ella Stack, 89
Sullivan, Harry Stack, xx, 50, 59, 81–82, 83, 85, 87–94, 98–106, 109, 113, 115, 116, 117–118, 127, 128, 133, 137, 155, 156, 157, 175, 179, 180, 199, 217, 218, 223
avoidance of interpretation, 104–105, 121, 122, 140, 167
*Clinical Studies in Psychiatry*, 99
*Conceptions of Modern Psychiatry*, 99, 138
consultant to Chestnut Lodge, as, 138–139
death of, 141–142, 151, 158
definition of love, 171
developmental epochs, 224, 225, 226ff
eye color, 87
fee for psychotherapy, 97
heart disease, 99, 119
multiple selves, 95–96, 202, 250
OAW's teacher, as, xix, 6, 80, 111, 123, 125, 159, 160, 163, 195, 219
one-genus theorem, 90, 269
problems in living, 242, 246, 249, 270
*The Psychiatric Interview*, 99, 105, 168
Reassurance, on, 98, 105, 106
relationship with William Alanson White, 89–90
rumor of suicide, 142
sexuality of, 93, 95, 153
use of alcohol, 103
Sullivan, James Inscoe (Jimmie), 93, 95, 97, 103, 116, 142
Sullivan, Timothy, 89
System, xx, 103, 119, 146, 147, 187, 202, 203, 224, 233, 241, 242
defined, 271

**T**
Teacher, xv, xix, 6, 35, 121, 125, 126, 128, 188, 206
defined, 271
*Ten Days in a Mad-House*, 73
Termination, 159, 213, 257
Thoreau, Henry David, xxi, 24, 139, 243
Thomas, Dylan, 82
"A Child's Christmas in Wales," 82
Thompson, Clara, 116, 117, 118
Thompson, Michael Guy, xviii, 119, 204, 205, 219–220, 253, 277
Thoreau, Henry David, xxi, 24, 139, 243
*Times-Picayune* newspaper, 16
Transference, 105, 121, 122, 167, 168, 253-254, 255, 256
defined, 271
Trenton State Hospital, 57, 58, 75
Trueta, Josep, 68
Tuberculosis, 13, 24ff, 34, 41, 74, 77, 94, 148, 192, 242

**U**
United Nations International Tensions Project, 141
University of Chicago, 51, 92, 156, 169, 188, 205
*U.S.S. Stringham*, 62, 64-69
*U.S.S. Wasp*, 198

**V**
Vagotomy, 84
Values, defined, 271
Vinyard, Deirdre Will, xv, xvii, 4, 15, 62, 82, 105, 143, 161, 166, 184, 185, 186, 192, 203, 205, 206, 212, 234, 253, 260, 263, 277

**W**
Washington-Baltimore Psychoanalytic Institute, 116, 148, 187, 198
Washington-Baltimore Psychoanalytic Society, 127, 137, 138, 179

*The Washington Post*, 74, 118, 142, 246
Washington School of Psychiatry 6, 7, 115, 127, 133, 141, 142, 145, 148, 179, 180, 182, 187, 196, 197, 198, 264
Watts, James, 78
Weigert, Edith, 84, 85, 118, 139, 151
Weininger, Benjamin, 138, 140
Western New England Psychoanalytic Institute, 202
Western New England Psychoanalytic Society, 202
Whitaker, Carl, xx
White, William Alanson, 78–79, 89–90, 115, 242
Whitehorn, John C., 127
  psychodynamic psychotherapy, and, 127
  successor to Adolf Meyer, as, 127
Whitman, Walt, 193
Will, Beulah Parker, 62, 131, 215, 216, 218, 219, 220, 259
  *The Evolution of a Psychiatrist*, 216
  "Gordon," 217
  marriage to Leland "Punk" Vaughn, 218
  marriage to OAW, 206
  medical and psychiatric training, 216–217
  *A Mingled Yarn*, 215
  *My Language is Myself*, 215
  training analysis with Erik Erikson, 217
Will family trust, 15
Will, Florence Keeling, 15, 19, 21, 27, 29, 52, 147, 148
Will, Kathryn, 80
  death of, 80
Will, Gwen Tudor, 4, 5, 130, 143ff, 157, 158, 161, 165, 184, 185, 192, 205, 253, 260
  at the Berkshire Mental Health Center, 205
  clinical consultant to OAW, as, 149, 166
  Chief of Psychiatric Nursing, NIMH, 145
  divorce from OAW, 206, 214
  early life in Iowa, 143–144
  founding of Woodley House, 149
  homosexuality, acceptance of, 234
  Instructor & Assistant Professor at University of Iowa, 144
  marriage to Jose Puig-Guri1, 44
  marriage to OAW, 148, 205
  Master of Arts degree in Psychiatric Nursing, 144
  "mutual withdrawal," on, 75
  nursing morale ("burnout"), 146–147
  nursing pioneer, as, 148
  Registered Nurse, 144, 164
  research at Chestnut Lodge, 75, 145, 146
  sociopsychiatric nursing, 145
  testimony before HUAC, 144
Will, Otto Allen Jr. (OAW)
  abandonments of, 4, 216
  as analyst, descriptions of, xix, 5, 6, 120, 122, 171, 187, 218, 219, 220, 274
  and alcohol, 5
  on authenticity, 7, 113, 120, 121, 220
  birth of, 20, 24, 27
  caring in psychotherapy, on, 7, 172
  clinical consultant (supervisor), as, xix, 157, 159, 160, 218
  dating and sexuality, on, 46, 143
  death of, 206, 218, 220, 259
  Director of Psychotherapy at Chestnut Lodge, as, 158, 159–160
  father, as, 184-187
  divorce from Gwen Tudor Will, 206, 214
  dramatic storyteller, as, 3, 4, 188

enlistment in U.S. Navy, 62
extramarital affair of, 5, 205
friendship with Hilde Bruch, 125, 130, 172, 206
homosexuality, views on, 234
humanism of, xviii, 113
"illness" at Stanford, 48
lonely, as, 4, 43, 112, 157
love of music, xxi, 36, 38, 82, 161
marriage to Adeline Emma Rowe, 59, 60
marriage to Beulah Vaughn Parker, 206
marriage to Gwen Tudor, 148, 205
nanny of, 27, 28, 47
physical description of, 3, 4
poetry, interest in, 82
preoccupation with grades, 51
presence, importance of in psychotherapy, 111–113, 160, 197, 255
psychoanalytic education of, 119
psychoanalytic training, views on, 120, 121, 123, 219,
respect, on, xix, 6, 81, 90, 91, 112, 139, 140, 154, 164, 207, 253
schizoid qualities, 88, 128, 159
self-confidence, 69, 212
shame, on, 50, 57, 105, 214
spreading mother's ashes, 184
stomach cancer, and, 83–84
teacher, as, xv, 6, 121, 206
teachers of, xix, 125
on tipping, 53–54
uninterested in theory, 4, 48, 119, 159, 163, 248, 251
values, on, 120, 214, 256, 257
views on women, 5, 187

Will, Otto Allen/Augustus, 14
  bully, as, 29, 38, 42, 46, 47, 48, 105
  contempt for women, 5, 21, 48, 148
  daily routine, 30, 41
  death, 184
  diagnosis of tuberculosis, 13, 21, 24, 29, 33
  invalid, as, 30, 41, 52
  marriage to Florence Keeling, 15, 18
  "tyrannical," as, 15, 46, 159
Will, Patrick, xvii, 5, 15, 28, 30, 46, 51, 66, 80, 101, 119, 145, 148, 149, 157, 158, 161, 166, 183–187, 189, 196, 198, 202, 205, 206, 220, 253, 260, 261, 263, 277
Will, Reinholt, 9, 12, 14
  education of, 10
  family role, 14–15
  gardener, as, 10, 14
Will, Amalia Schumacher, 9
  family role, 10, 14–15
  marriage to Reinholt Will, 10
Will Brothers Florists, 14
William Alanson White Psychiatric Foundation, 115, 117
Winnicott, Donald, 88
Wisdom, 54, 128, 251
  defined, 271
Woodlawn Hotel, 134

**Y**

Yalom, Irvin, 160, 188
Young, Barbara, 127

**Z**

Zirkle, Stuard "Samuel," 59–60

For 40 years, Carlton Cornett was a clinical social worker practicing psychotherapy in a variety of settings. Between 2007 and 2021 he was an Assistant Clinical Professor of Psychiatry and Behavioral Sciences at the Vanderbilt University School of Medicine and between 2017 and 2021 he was a faculty member of the Nashville Center for Psychoanalysis and Dynamic Psychotherapy. He retired in 2022 and now lives in Keene, New Hampshire with his partner of over 30 years. He is a visiting faculty member at the Pine Psychoanalytic Society in Massachusetts, a founding member of the New Washington School of Psychiatry, and a member of the American Association for Psychoanalysis in Clinical Social Work. He is the author or coauthor of 30 journal articles and book chapters. This is his sixth book.

Contact him at
carlton@oawbook.com

www.ingramcontent.com/pod-product-compliance
Lightning Source LLC
Chambersburg PA
CBHW031139020426
42333CB00013B/447

* 9 7 8 1 6 2 8 8 0 3 1 3 6 *